FAMOUS VEGETARIANS

&

THEIR FAVORITE RECIPES

Books by Rynn Berry

The Vegetarians

The New Vegetarians

*Famous Vegetarians and
Their Favorite Recipes*

*Food for the Gods:
Vegetarianisn and the World's Religions*

"In short, Berry's book is scholarship at the end of a fork—and for writing it he deserves an 'A'."—*Vegetarian Times*

"Berry writes beautifully with a genuine gustatory relish for words and savory asides. The recipes are delightful—many researched and translated for the first time."—*The Boston Book Review*

"Anecdotal sketches give life to each of the 26 celebrities, from Tolstoy, Gandhi and George Bernard Shaw to 'contemporaries' like George Bernard Shaw and Isaac Bashevis Singer. The 70 recipes are not only fascinating, but have been kitchen-tested by the author for savoriness."—*Yoga Journal*

"Written with a scholarly tone, *Famous Vegetarians and Their Favorite Recipes* is an entertaining and educational way to get vegetarian recipes and philosophy into the hands of would-be vegetarians."—*Vegetarian Voice*

"Impeccably researched and written, Berry's book could inspire the already famous to adopt vegetarianism and the confirmed vegetarian to achieve fame."—*The Animals' Agenda*

FAMOUS VEGETARIANS

&

THEIR FAVORITE RECIPES

Lives & Lore from Buddha to Beatles

RYNN BERRY

*Inscribed for Ginni,
with cordial good wishes
& holiday greetings*

**PYTHAGOREAN
PUBLISHERS**

NEW YORK   LOS ANGELES

*by Rynn Berry
New York Christmas, 1997*

ACKNOWLEDGMENTS

Firstly, I would like to thank Jack Kroll, Senior Editor at *Newsweek*, for taking time from his busy writing schedule to contribute a preface for *Famous Vegetarians and Their Favorite Recipes*.

I owe a special debt of gratitude to Jon Wynne-Tyson, who is Henry Salt's literary executor, for providing me with a list of Salt's favorite dishes that he obtained from Salt's widow, Catherine.

Special thanks are also due to Bill Shurtleff for furnishing me with recipes and information on soyfoods, and for allowing me to see a portion of his manuscript on the history of soyfoods that pertained to Dr. John Harvey Kellogg.

Other particular thanks are due to the Louisa May Alcott Memorial Association; Nancy Kohl, editor of Abigail May Alcott's *Receipts and Simple Remedies;* and Jayne K. Gordon, Director of Orchard House "Home of the Alcotts" for permission to include Abigail May Alcott's recipes in this book.

My special appreciation goes to Mr. Leonard Beck, who is a collections specialist in the rare book division of the Library of Congress, for supplying me with hard-to-find material on Leonardo da Vinci's vegetarianism.

I am also grateful to the librarians in the rare book room at the New York Public Library, for allowing me to use the Library's 1498 edition of Bartolomeo Platina's *De Honesta Voluptate* in my translation of Platina's recipes for Leonardo da Vinci. I am also beholden to them for providing access to rare cookbooks of the 17th, 18th, 19th, and 20th centuries that I used in researching recipes for Percy Bysshe Shelley, Leo Tolstoy, Annie Besant, Sylvester Graham, and Dr. John Harvey Kellogg.

I am indebted to the Brooklyn Public Library and its staff for enabling me to research recipes for Pythagoras and Plutarch.

I would also like to thank Mr. Gerald Krimm of Taplinger Publishing Company Inc. for allowing me to reprint recipes from the *George Bernard Shaw Vegetarian Cookbook*.

To Armi Elizalde I would like to say a heart-felt thank-you for her pencil portrait of the author.

Space limitations prohibit me from paying adequate tribute to all the people who have helped me in the course of writing this book; so I must content myself with mentioning their names as follows: Hideko Abe, Jo-Nina Abron of the Institute for Food and Development Policy, Mark Braunstein, Rynn Berry, Sr., Kitty Muggeridge, Alma Singer, F. M. Esfandiary, Steve Shrimpton, Cedric Berry, Skip Heinecke, Rick and Glory

Brightfield, Brenda Jenkins, and Sir Michael Levey, Director of the National Gallery in London. Also to David Butler and Luanna Ewing for superb production and typesetting skills.

Finally, I would like to express my sincere thanks to each of the famous contemporary vegetarians for their participation in *FVTFR*.

CONTENTS

VISIONARIES

CONTEMPORARIES

ABOUT THE AUTHOR

TABLE OF RECIPES

SOUPS

GRAINS AND PASTA

SOYFOOD ENTREES

VEGETABLE ENTREES

SALADS AND SANDWICHES

BREADS

DESSERTS

PREFACE

Rynn Berry is the Boswell of vegetarianism. And in his new book he becomes its Julia Child as well, combining a diverting survey of notable vegetarians with a savory sampling of their favorite recipes. Vegetarians hardly seem eccentric these days, thanks to recent developments in nutrition, and Berry makes them seem like the most civilized people in history. Wearing his learning lightly, Berry cites the Dead Sea Scrolls to establish a strong case for Jesus Christ as a vegetarian who probably partook of the Essene Sprouted Bread whose ancient (and modern-sounding) recipe is included here. With ecumenical thoroughness Pythagoras and the Buddha are placed in the vegetarian ranks, and so is Leonardo da Vinci, whose favorite dishes (Chick-pea Soup, Almond Pudding, Fried Figs and Beans) Berry has tracked down with admirable enterprise. Ranging through history, Berry shows that veggie-addicts had many motivations, from Shelley's desire to be totally unlike his hated father to Tolstoy's belated reformation from debauchery to virtue. The book's cast of fascinating characters includes Sylvester Graham (father of the graham cracker) whose followers fought a pitched battle in Boston with the butchers and bakers whom he denounced; John Harvey Kellogg, who not only invented cornflakes but peanut butter; and Killer Kowalski, the legendary wrestler who thrived on such non-violent fare as peas and sauerkraut. From Gandhi's Chapatis to George Harrison's Dark Horse Lentil Soup, this is a book that stimulates your brain and your digestion.

Jack Kroll
Senior Editor
NEWSWEEK
New York, NY

Section I
IMMORTALS

PYTHAGORAS

Although Pythagoras is chiefly remembered for his discovery of the eponymous "Pythagorean theorem" (the square of the hypotenuse of a triangle equals the sum of the squares of the other two sides), he is also the father of vegetarianism. Indeed until the late 19th century, when the neologism "vegetarian" was coined, people who lived on a fleshless diet were usually referred to as "Pythagoreans."

Pythagoras was born on the Greek island of Samos in 580 B.C. or thereabouts. His father Mnesarchus was a Phonecian from the Levantine city of Tyre; his mother was a Samian Greek. The events of his early life are lost to us, but tradition has it that after studying with such great Ionian thinkers as Thales and Anaximander, he traveled to Egypt and Persia for a fifteen year postgraduate course in astronomy, number symbolism, comparative religion, and other arcane subjects.

However much wisdom he may have imbibed from the Egyptians and the Persians, his philosophy and personal conduct seem to owe more to the Jains and the *brāhmins* of ancient India than to anyone else. Of course much of India was under Persian rule at this time, and Indians traveled to Greek lands as recruits in the Persian king's army. As trade generally follows the flag, there was undoubtedly a lively commerce in ideas and goods between India and Greece. Certainly Pythagoras, the wandering sage who espoused vegetarianism and reincarnation, reminds one of nothing so much as a Hindu swami in the style of Krishnamurti, Prabhupada, or Rajneesh. He is the first in a line of "Hinduized" westerners, a guru for the Greeks.

Finding on his return to Samos that his native country was under the sway of the tyrant Polykrates, Pythagoras fled to southern Italy, where in 529 B.C., he settled in Croton.

As in most biographies of great men that have come down to us from antiquity, one must allow for the tendency of the writer (who is usually a disciple, or a gushing votary of his subject) to glorify these great men's deeds. But even discounting this, Pythagoras emerges as one of the most striking figures in the history of Western culture. Not only is he credited with having formulated the Pythagorean theorem, but he is also held to have been the author of many other mathematical and geometrical discoveries. It was Pythagoras who first perceived that musical harmony is determined by mathematical proportions, and it was Pythagoras who first conceived the idea of planetary motion. He anticipated, by two thousand years, Copernicus's speculation that the earth is a planetary sphere that moves about the sun.

3

He is also the first historically attested figure in Western culture to have founded a society that pursued wisdom for its own sweet sake— *philosophia* (a term that he is reported to have coined). Meat-eating and materialism were taboo in the Pythagorean brotherhood, not only because the Master considered them to be morally repugnant, but because he felt they interfered with the attainment of *theoria* (pure contemplation).

The fundamental tenet of the Pythagorean order was the doctrine of the transmigration of souls. Paralleling the Hindus, Pythagoras believed that the soul is condemned to pass through a seemingly endless cycle of rebirth during which it may be successively embodied in all the forms of life that exist on earth. After each incarnation the soul's conduct in its previous life is judged at a trial in Hades. Here the soul is punished or rewarded according to its deserts. The verdict determines whether the soul will be allowed to reincarnate as a snake, a deer, a bear, a prince, a slave, or a philosopher (which Pythagoras, not surprisingly, regarded as the highest incarnation). But the greatest reward that a soul can achieve is to be entirely liberated from the wheel of rebirth, and to return to the state of divine bliss from which it came.

Pythagoras taught that through the transmigration of souls, all the forms of animal life are interrelated. Precisely because the body of a deer may house the soul of a dear-departed relative, to eat of its flesh would be akin to an act of cannibalism. Similarly, Darwin's theory of evolution, which is a kind of biological transmigration, has shown us that by reason of their descent from a common ancestor (somewhere in the primordial ooze), all forms of life, from fish to philosopher, are kindred. Was it Shaw, paraphrasing Shakespeare, who said that "One touch of Darwin made the whole world kin"? Well, for the ancient Greeks, "One touch of Pythagoras made the whole world kin."[1]

Since Pythagoras' chief disciple Plato was being taught at Oxford as early as the 13th century, Englishmen were conversant with Pythagorean ideas long before they were being aired on the continent. Even Shakespeare who was no vegetarian was burlesquing the Pythagorean theory of reincarnation as this snatch of dialogue from Shakespeare's *Twelfth Night* illustrates:

> Clown: What is the opinion of Pythagoras concerning wild fowl?
> Malvolio: That the soul of our grandam might haply inhabit a bird.
> Clown: What think'st thou of his opinion?
> Malvolio: I think nobly of the soul, and no way approve of his opinion.
> Clown: Fare thee well. Remain thou still in darkness: thou shalt hold th'opinion of Pythagoras ere I will allow of thy wits; and fear to kill a woodcock, lest thou dispossess the soul of thy grandam.

Closer to Pythagoras' own time, the poet-philosopher Xenophanes satirized his theory of reincarnation as this mocking verse makes plain:

> They say that once when a puppy was being whipped, Pythagoras, who was passing by, took pity on it, saying, "Stop! Do not beat it! It is the soul of a friend; I recognize his voice!"

With its emphasis on privacy, meditation, and splendid isolation, there is much about the Pythagorean brotherhood that is redolent of the monastery. But the similarities are merely superficial: from the very start, women were admitted to the society on an equal footing with men, and were allowed to rise through its ranks according to their abilities. This was at variance with the prevailing attitude towards women throughout Greece. Even in democratic Athens, women were kept in a kind of oriental seclusion. Owing, however, in large part to the example set by Pythagoras, it became customary for women to be taken into scientific and philosophical societies as the intellectual peers of men. Moreover, there was nothing monkish about the Pythagoreans' views on sex. They took a dim view of celibacy. Male and female members were urged to marry and to raise little Pythagoreans.

Pythagoras himself stood exemplar, for he married the mathematical genius Theano, who held a high position in the Order.

Not only did the Pythagorean society serve as a model for Plato's Academy and more orthodox philosophical groups, but it also stimulated the formation of such esoteric and mystical philosophical societies as the Essenes (a Jewish, mystical brotherhood that flourished in the 2nd and 1st centuries B.C.). Like the Pythagoreans, the Essenes held their goods in common, gave themselves up to a life of contemplation, practiced a form of numerology, and were vegetarians.

Since Pythagoras's utterances were shrouded in secrecy, with the Master actually holding forth to his followers from behind a veil, much of his teaching had to be reconstructed from the writings of his followers. Among his disciples are numbered some of the greatest thinkers in antiquity. They include his protégés, Empedocles of Akragas, Porphyry, Plotinus, and of course Plato (whose philosophy is deeply indebted to Pythagoras). As professor Moses Hadas observes, "The largest precipitate of Pythagoreanism is to be found in Plato."[2] Some of Plato's most "Platonic" theories actually have their origin in Pythagoras. For example, Plato's belief in reincarnation and the tripartition of the soul is Pythagorean. Also Pythagorean is his theory of the forms; the "Platonic ideals": the notion that the world is a badly smudged copy of an ideal world, and the idea that mathematical reasoning can give us access to this ideal world.

Many latter-day admirers of Pythagoras have been bemused by his taboo on the eating of beans. Could Pythagoras really have prohibited such a versatile and nutritious food? Some of his meatatarian critics have seized upon this fatuous-seeming taboo to laugh out of court his injunction against the slaughter of animals for food (which Pythagoras believed led to warfare). However, classical scholarship suggests a rational motive for his ban on beans: In antiquity the Greeks elected their political candidates to office by casting a bean rather than a ballot (a modern ballot is a ticket or a strip of paper, and paper was a precious commodity in the ancient world). So what Pythagoras was really saying to his followers was "Stay out of politics!"—perhaps the sagest advice of all.

Asked by a Hellenic king what sort of man was a philosopher (a term that Pythagoras first minted and applied to himself), Pythagoras answered with a parable. He said that there were three types of men who attend the Olympic games—the athletes who compete for glory; the merchants who hawk their wares to the crowd for money; and the spectators who take an unabashed delight in contemplation. A philosopher is like the spectator at the games.

Although Pythagoras was fond of punning on the two Greek words *soma* (body), and *sema* (tomb), this does not suggest that he felt the body should be allowed to deteriorate before its death. On the contrary, he had a yogi-like conviction that the body should be developed and made flexible so that it could become a more efficient instrument of the spirit. A rundown body, he felt, interferes with philosophizing.

So he urged all the Pythagoreans, men and women alike, to undergo a daily program of vigorous exercise that included running, shadow boxing, wrestling, and gymnastics. Consequently, along with brilliant mathematicians and philosophers, the society turned out a disproportionate number of athletic champions (like the famous Milo of Croton, who credited his Olympic victories to Pythagorean dietetics). In sum, the Pythagorean society was a combination health spa and think tank. With its emphasis on contemplation, physical fitness, and dietetics, it would not be out of place in the hills of Southern California.

Why Pythagoras Ate Unfired Fruits and Vegetables

Two of the following three recipes are for unfired dishes. In antiquity, many Greeks ate their vegetable and fruit dishes unfired. Cooking, while feasible certainly, was not so widely practiced as it is today. We have it on the authority of Diogenes Laertius that it was not uncommon for Pythagoras and the Pythagoreans to eat their fruits and vegetables *apura* (unfired): "For this is the Pythagoras who forbade the killing much less the eating of animals who share with us the right of having a soul. This was their pretext for eating vegetarian fare, but the real reason that he prohibited the eating of our fellow ensouled beings was that he wanted to accustom people to a contented life so that they should eat unfired (*apura*) food and drink plain water. Hence, they would have sharp minds and healthy bodies." (Diogenes Laertius, VIII, 13, translation mine).

Another reason why Pythagoras may have encouraged his disciples (among whom Plato and Socrates would have been among the most prominent) to eat unfired fruits and vegetables is that he may have wanted further to dramatize the difference between *iera* or the barbecued flesh of animals that was sacrificed to the gods on a fiery altar and shared out among the worshippers, and the raw, uncooked *apura* foods that formed the sustenance of ethical vegetarians.

"Pythagoras was concerned to sacrifice only cakes, meal and flour at the temple of Apollo the Lifegiver, which is behind the temple of Horns, because he could make these offerings *without fire* and *without an animal victim*, as Aristotle tells us in his *Politics of Delos*." (Diogenes Laertius, VIII, 13, italics mine, translation mine).

Nut-Stuffed Cabbage Rolls

12 large cabbage leaves
1 loaf barley bread or Essene bread
    made from sprouted whole grains
    (see recipes for Essene and barley breads)
2 tablespoons grated onion
1 cup hazelnuts or pecans
½ cup diced celery
2 teaspoons mixed herbs
Salt and pepper to taste

Crumble the Essene bread into a mixing bowl. (NB: Essene bread is moist and friable and crumbles easily.) Then add the grated onion, the chopped nuts, the diced celery, the mixed herbs and the spices.

With a sharp knife, cut out the hard stem from each cabbage leaf. Lay the leaf flat on a working surface, and spoon the filling onto the edge of the leaf. Coat the edge evenly, then roll it up tightly. If the cabbage leaves are small in size, take two leaves and arrange them so that one edge overlaps the other; line the leading edge with the filling and roll it up.

Serve garnished with sprigs of parsley or mint.

Serves four.

Note: This is an unfired (*apura*) recipe.

This recipe should really be called "Acorn-Stuffed Cabbage Rolls," because the Golden-Age inhabitants of Greece, who were strict vegetarians (according to Hesiod, Empedokles, Ovid, et al.) were reputed to have fed on acorns. This at any rate is the legend attested to by Ovid (*Metam.* XV, 96f.); Lucretius (V, 692; 1414); Horace (*Sat.*, I, 3, 100); Vergil (Georg., I, 148); et al. These *balanaphagoi* (acorn-eaters) and their tradition would certainly have been known to Pythagoras, who was trying to restore Greece to the pristine diet of the Golden Age, when all men were vegetarians. In *The Republic*, when Plato proposed that the citizens of his ideal city should eat among other vegetarian foods "acorns to roast at the fire," (*Republic*, II, 372, d); doubtless he had this tradition in mind. Since acorns were a deeply symbolic vegetarian food, bound up with the symbolism of the Golden Age, there is no doubt that Pythagoras and the Pythagoreans partook of them. It is quite possible that Plato, who was a Pythagorean, was making an allusion to Pythagoreanism when he recommended that the citizens of his ideal society should sit by the fire and eat roasted acorns. In prehistoric Greece, acorns were a popular food and remained so down to classical times. According to Galen (VI, 620), the Arcadians continued to eat acorns long after the other Greeks had turned to the gifts of Demeter. Some strains of acorn are highly edible, and in times of famine are still resorted to when people grind them into flour in place of grain or use them as a coffee substitute. However, they are now chiefly harvested as fodder for pigs, who are particularly partial to them. In fact Plato, through his dragoman Socrates in *The Republic* (II, 372, d), was accused of trying to found a "city of pigs," when he urged that the citizens of his ideal city adopt a vegetarian diet that included roasted acorns. Since edible strains of acorns are not readily available, one may substitute pecans or hazelnuts, which are botanically closer to acorns than any other nut.

According to Pliny (24–79 A.D.), Pythagoras was so fond of cabbage that he extolled its virtues in a book. Therefore, I have combined cabbage with hazelnuts or pecans (as acorn substitute) to furnish this recipe. Here is my translation of the passage from Pliny's *Natural History* (XX, xxxii) in which he mentions that Pythagoras and other great sages wrote books in praise of the cabbage:

> It would take a long time to recount the praises of cabbage, since Chrysippus the physician devoted a special volume to it, arranged according to its effect on each part of the body, and Dieuches also wrote a book about it; however, before all of them Pythagoras wrote a book about it, and Cato in his writings glorified it no less than they.

Sautéed Cabbage with Mustard Seed

1 medium head cabbage cored
3 tablespoons olive oil

1 teaspoon mustard seed
Salt and pepper to taste

Finely chop the cabbage. In a large skillet heat the olive oil and add the mustard seed, salt and pepper. As soon as the mustard seed starts to sputter, add the chopped cabbage. Cook over a high flame for three minutes, while stirring briskly to prevent scorching. Serve with whole barley grain bread.

Serves four.

In his *Natural History* (XX, lxxxvii), Pliny tells us that mustard, like cabbage, was highly esteemed by Pythagoras. Here is my rendering of the pertinent passage:

> Mustard of which we have discussed three varieties among the cultivated plants was considered by Pythagoras to be the chief among those herbs that have the power to mount upwards, seeing that no other penetrates deeper into the nostrils and the brain.

Barley Bread

2 cups sprouted barley
½ cup ground, dried figs

Grind all together, and knead. Shape into a loaf, and set aside for 12 hours before serving. No heating or baking is necessary, as this is an unfired (*apura*) bread. Slice for serving.

Porphyry in his life of Pythagoras tells us that Pythagoras customarily dined on bread of millet or barley, and vegetables. "Of his diet, the breakfast was honeycomb or honey, the dinner, bread of millet or barley and vegetables, whether boiled or raw." Moses Hadas and Morton Smith, *Heroes and Gods* (New York: Harper and Row, 1965), p. 118. This bread was a staple of Greek diet in Pythagoras's lifetime and is a reasonable facsimile of the bread to which Porphyry refers. It should be remembered that in antiquity einkorn and emmer wheats were almost twice as rich in protein as the breadwheats of today. Eaten daily in conjunction with vegetables, boiled or fresh, it was truly the staff of life.

GAUTAMA THE BUDDHA

The story of Buddhism really begins in the latter part of the 2nd millenium B.C., when tribes of marauding nomads burst forth from the steppes of southern Russia, and descended upon the peaceful agricultural settlements in Iran and northwestern India. With their swift chariots, drawn by pairs of horses, and their fierce weapons they rode roughshod over the farms and villages in their path. These were a desperate, warlike people who lived by stealing cattle and waging war. Their very word for warfare, *gavishti,* in Sanskrit, originally meant "to search for cows." They called themselves Aryans, "the people"—the implication being that non-Aryans were non-people. That the Aryans held themselves superior to the peoples whom they conquered is suggested by the word "Aryan" itself, which is the root for our word "aristocracy" (rule of the best people).

The invading Aryans treated the dark-skinned natives of northern India as non-people, or as little lower than cattle. Those natives who could make good their escape were forced to flee to central or southern India: those who stayed behind were enslaved and consigned to the lowliest caste, called the *śūdras* (laborers). It is the Aryans who are credited with having imposed the caste system on India.

Originally the caste system was designed to preserve the racial purity of the Aryans, who had a horror of mingling with the dark-skinned peoples of India. The word for caste in Sanskrit was *varna* (color). It was the duty of the dark-skinned peoples, the native Dravidians of India, to serve the three higher castes, which were made up of the fair-skinned, Sanskrit-speaking Aryan conquerors.

At the top of the caste system were the *brāhmans* (*brāhmana*), or priests. Just below them in the pecking order were the *ksatriyas* (warriors). And below them were the *vaiśyas* (tradesmen). At the very bottom of course were the *śūdras,* whose duty it was to attend to the upper castes.

Each Aryan tribe had a king, or chieftain who was furnished by a dynastic family in the warrior caste. The king was specially selected for the purpose of breeding *rajahs* (princes). As might be expected, Aryan families were patrilineal and patriarchal.

Now it might seem strange that Aryan society should be dominated by priests, when it was the warriors who wielded the weapons. However, we have only to reflect on the career of a man like Cardinal Richelieu in 17th century France, or on the temporal power of the Pope to realize that the altar is mightier than the sword.

The India of the Aryan invasions, like Medieval Europe, was pervaded with superstition. The livelihood of the Aryan chiefs, depending as it did

11

upon plundering villages, and making war on other tribes, left a great deal
to chance. Every battle, every foray into unknown lands to loot and pil-
lage was a gamble, a leap into the dark. Therefore, to turn the odds in
their favor, they relied on the brāhmans to propitiate their gods with
animal sacrifices. Especially dear to the Aryan gods were sacrifices of
cattle. Indra, the warrior god of the Aryans, is reported in the *Rg Veda* to
have devoured hundreds of cows at a single sitting.

As battles grew riskier and the natives became more skilled at defend-
ing themselves, the Aryans came more and more to depend on the brāhman's sacrificial magic. This dependancy caused the Aryans to put their
lives and kingdoms in the hands of the brāhmans.

By the 6th century B.C., the century of the Buddha's birth, the Aryan
tribes had extended their sway over all of India. Those dark-skinned
Dravidians who had not been pressed into slavery, had literally been
driven into the sea. They had been forced to seek shelter in Ceylon, and
the lands of Southeast Asia, traveling by boat.

The caste system had spread to the farthest reaches of the continent,
and had become so entrenched and rigidified that it ruled out all social
mobility. A boy or girl who was born into the *śūdra* caste, no matter how
intelligent he or she might be, was forbidden to learn Sanskrit (the language of educated, upper-caste Indians), or receive anything beyond the
most rudimentary education.

It was into this social and religious milieu that Siddhartha Gautama was
born in 563 B.C. He was the son of a *rajah* who ruled a small but thriving kingdom in northeastern India. It might seem odd that a man who
gave his life to spreading the doctrine of *ahimsā,* or non-violence, should
have been born a *ksatriya* prince. But this is an irony that he shares with
Mahavira (also a member of the *ksatriya* caste), founder of the Jain sect,
who preached an almost impossibly rigorous form of vegetarianism in
which one is not permitted to kill insects.

However, the *ksatriya* virtues of courage, stamina, and self-reliance may
have helped to fit Siddhartha for the strenuous life of a wandering teacher.
He traveled by foot to the remotest parts of the continent to bring his
message to the people. Perhaps too, in his willingness to relinquish three
palaces, a voluptuous wife, and superfluous riches in order to seek enlightenment, there was something of the professional warrior's scorn for
creature comforts and luxury.

Shorn of splendid clothes, wealth, family ties, and all claim to his
father's throne, he undertook what is called by the Buddhists, "The Great
Departure." Taking on the appearance of a homeless vagabond, at twenty-
nine he started on the journey that would last for the remaining fifty years
of his life. He lived principally by begging alms—a hallowed tradition in
India for those on a genuine spritual quest.

But the life of a holy beggar, living in the cities and villages, soon palled on him. He retired from society to dwell in the forest as a solitary contemplative. For six years he sought spiritual uplift through self-mortification and fasting. By the end of six years, he had grown so emaciated through constant fasting, that he was little more than a living skeleton. He looked as though he could be carried into the next world by a stiff breeze. Finally, he realized the futility of this course. Self-torture was bringing him no closer to the wisdom that tantalizingly eluded him.

As soon as he decided to take solid food again, as if by magic, Sujata, the daughter of a nearby farmer, appeared. She took pity on his feeble appearance and offered him a dish that she had made of curds and rice. After eating the dish, he felt so invigorated, so revitalized that he began to think that it had been wrong to inflict such hardship on his body. The body, he perceived, was the instrument through which one can gain enlightenment. To deny the body is to blunt the instrument.

Thus fortified with Sujata's dish, he sat down beneath a fig tree, and resolved to keep sitting there until he found the answer to the riddle of human suffering. It looked as if he might be in for a long sit, one that could take a lifetime, or more. At length, after forty-nine days of deep meditation—Eureka!!!—his mind was suddenly filled with insight, and the answer to the riddle of human suffering flashed upon him. Siddhartha Gautama had become "The Buddha," which in Sanskrit means "one who has gained enlightenment."

Not one for flitting about aimlessly, Gautama sat cross-legged under the sacred fig tree for another seven weeks pondering on his Buddhahood. While meditating, he took the time to work out his religious system. Assailed by doubts, he deliberated as to whether he should keep his system to himself or not. Finally, he fought back his fears and decided to go forth and share his spiritual insights with others. It was a decision that Arnold Toynbee said was more momentous for mankind than the founding of the Platonic Academy.

Essentially, the Buddha's religious system is best understood or appreciated as a sort of anti-Brāhmanism. It articulated the common people's opposition to the costly animal sacrifices that formed the chief ritual of the brāhman's religion. Not only did these sacrifices entail needless cruelty to animals, but they also strained the finances of the common people who were taxed to pay for them. One of the few "thou shalt not's" in Buddhism is the law that forbids doing harm to any living creature. By making this a fundamental precept of his religious system, the Buddha was giving the back of his hand to the bloody sacrificial rites of the brāhmans.

Also in defiance of the brāhmans, who taught that self-realization was the supreme object of existence, the Buddha taught that the self was illusory. He explained that the only way to achieve contentment (*nirvana*) was to accept the transitory and fugitive nature of life, and follow the middle road between craving and self-denial.

Buddhism also differed from Brāhmanism by being democratic. Any Indian, from the most despised outcaste to the most privileged brāhman, was eligible to join the order. Women, who were barred from participating in the brāhman priesthood—save as breeders of male baby brāhmans —were admitted to the Buddhist order on an equal footing with men. It is not hard to see why Buddhism held a great deal of charm for talented Indians, who had the bad luck to be born in the wrong caste.

It is instructive to compare the life of the Buddha with the life of Christ, for there are some striking similarities. As with Christ, there is a legendary account of the Buddha's having been the offspring of an immaculate conception—though in the Buddha's case the divine impregnator is not a white-bearded patriarch, but a sacred white elephant. Like Christianity, Buddhism was founded on the teachings of a man of flesh and blood who was later deified by his followers. Just as Christ was critical of the prosperous temple priests in Palestine (the pharisees), so too was the Buddha critical of the overfed brāhmans. Like Christianity, Buddhism died out in the land of its origin, but took root and flourished elsewhere. Buddhism spread through the great nations of the East, and is now the dominant religion of Asia. Christianity perished on the vine in Palestine, but when transplanted to Europe, it struck root and grew into the predominant religion of the West. Finally, even as Christianity found a champion in the Roman emperor Constantine, so Buddhism enjoyed the support of the Indian emperor Ashoka, who elevated Buddhism from a fledgling sect into the state religion of India.

Ashoka was the grandson of Chandragupta Maurya, one of the mightiest conquerors in Indian history, who had piled up more territory than any ruler before him. Ashoka came to power in 272 B.C. Every bit as capable as his grandfather, Ashoka not only maintained his grandfather's empire, but with the conquest of Kalinga (the gateway to the South), he enlarged it even further. However, the Kalingan conquest took one hundred thousand lives.

Filled with remorse at the suffering and carnage his victories had caused, he turned away from the brāhman strategists who had been the architects of his grandfather's victories, and sought the advice of the Buddhist sages. Not conquest, but a policy of peace and non-violence (*ahimsā*) should be his destiny, they told him. Intrigued by this unusual advice, he began to apply himself to the study of the Buddhist scriptures. Within a short time he was a changed person. He gave up military campaigning and became a strict vegetarian. Ashoka's empire crumbled in the hands of his successors, but his campaigns to promote Buddhism, vegetarianism, and the doctrine of *ahimsā,* exerted an empire over the minds of men that will endure forever.

Curds and Rice (À la Sujata)

After subjecting his body to the severest austerities, and limiting his food intake to only a few grains of rice and *sesamum* (sesame) per day, Siddhartha Gautama was getting no closer to the enlightenment that he longed for. So he tried a new tack. No longer would he deny himself nourishment as a form of self-discipline. Lack of food seemed to make him more rather than less mindful of his appetites, and hunger interfered with his concentration. From now on he would meditate on a full stomach.

Not long after he had come to his senses, as previously described, Sujata, the daughter of a nearby farmer, came by. She was carrying a golden bowl filled with the most delicious curds and rice, and catching sight of Gautama's shrunken figure, she offered him the dish. After eating a bit of it with relish, he divided the remainder into forty-nine portions so that there would be enough to sustain him through the seven weeks of meditation that led up to his enlightenment.

This dish is as popular in India today as it was in the Buddha's time. Here with a few added flourishes is my version of it.

For the Curds

1 lb. firm tofu
1 cup vegetable oil (for deep frying)

For the Rice Pulao

2 cups long grain rice (Indian *basmati* rice preferred)
1 medium Spanish onion, chopped
3 tablespoons vegetable oil
2 cloves garlic, chopped fine
1 teaspoon tumeric
½ teaspoon cayenne pepper
4 cloves
½ cup fresh, shelled peas
½ inch stick cinnamon
½ ounce fresh ginger, grated fine
2 ground cardamom pods (optional)
2 green chilies, chopped (optional)
1 teaspoon *garam masala,* or chili powder
1 teaspoon coriander powder
Salt to taste

Instead of deep-fried curds (or paneer), I have substituted deep-fried tofu cubes (to keep recipes as dairyless as possible). Take a pound of firm tofu. Cut it into ½ inch cubes. Heat one cup of vegetable oil in a sauce pan, and deep-fry the tofu cubes in the oil until brown. Remove from the oil with a slotted spoon, and drain the cubes on paper towels. Set aside.

Pick over the rice and rinse thoroughly. Then soak the rice in four cups of water for one-half hour.

While the rice is soaking, sauté the chopped onion in oil in a heavy skillet. When it has cooked for a few minutes, add the salt, tumeric, cumin seeds, cayenne, and cloves. Stir for a minute or two, then add the peas, chopped green chilies, stick cinnamon, garlic, cardamom seeds, grated ginger, and *garam masala.* Cook for a few minutes, then reserve the water in which the rice has been soaking (there should be about three cups), and add the rice to the skillet. Continue cooking until rice is heated through. Then add the water in which the rice was soaking. Bring the liquid to a boil, then reduce heat to low flame, and simmer until liquids are absorbed and rice is fluffy (about ten minutes).
   When the deep-fried tofu cubes have drained sufficiently, add them to the rice pulao along with a teaspoon of coriander powder. Mix thoroughly and let stand for five minutes. Remove the Curds and Rice Pulao from the heat, and serve topped with a garnish of chopped cucumber and tomatoes.

Serves six.

Curried Spinach
(Sak)

2 lb. fresh spinach
⅔ cup golden raisins
2 tablespoons sesame oil
⅓ teaspoon fennel seed
⅓ teaspoon black mustard seed
⅓ teaspoon cumin seed
2 cloves
1 tablespoon chopped, fresh ginger
¼ teaspoon cayenne pepper
½ teaspoon garam masala
½ cup pine nuts
½ teaspoon salt

Wash and pick over the spinach. Dry in a salad spinner or on paper towels, and set aside. Place the raisins in a cup of filtered water, and let soak for two hours. When the raisins have plumped, drain them in a colander or strainer and set aside.

Heat the sesame oil in a heavy skillet. Grind the fennel, mustard seeds, cumin and cloves and add to the skillet. Cook for one minute; then add the ginger, the cayenne pepper, the raisins and the garam masala. Sauté for two minutes. Turn off the stove. Then add the spinach leaves and mix them vigorously with the raisins and spices. Within two minutes the uncooked spinach leaves will have wilted. As soon as they have wilted, add the pine nuts and the salt, and stir vigorously. Serve immediately.

Serves four.

Note: the spinach is wilted, not cooked, to preserve its flavor and enzymes. It will have the appearance of a wilted salad, but it tastes like a curry.

According to Om Prakash, in his book, *Food and Drinks in Ancient India* [(New Delhi: 1961), p. 73], spinach was one of the vegetables that the Buddha urged his followers to eat. Cooking at this time was highly sophisticated in India, and spinach curries, as well as other vegetable curries were as popular then as they are today. Although the dish is an imaginative recreation, all the spices were in use during the Buddha's period (see pages 69, 70). In his discussion of the fine points of Buddhist etiquette, he says (p. 83), "An ideal monk, according to the Buddha, does not kill any animal for food, accepts only one course, does not take food at improper times. He does not accept uncooked foodgrains or meat."

Mango, Coconut and Mung Bean Salad
(Aam, Nariyal, Moong Kachamber)

½ cup split mung beans
1½ cups filtered water
½ cup grated or finely shredded fresh coconut
½ cup diced mango
1 hot green chili pepper
1 teaspoon salt
1 teaspoon sesame oil
1 teaspoon black mustard seeds
1 teaspoon cumin seed
1 teaspoon powdered coriander
1 tablespoon fresh lemon juice

Soak the split mung beans in water overnight, or for six hours. Rinse and drain in a strainer. In a salad bowl, mix together the mung beans, coconut, mango, green chili and lime juice.

In a skillet, heat the sesame oil and add the black mustard seeds, the cumin seeds, and the coriander. Cook for two minutes. Turn off the stove and add the mung beans, mangoes, coconut and chili. Stir vigorously until they are coated with the spices. Then serve immediately.

Note: The mung beans are soaked, not cooked. Soaking renders them soft and edible, and full of enzymes.

This is a dish that combines three foods that were highly esteemed among Buddhist monks during the Buddha's lifetime. According to Om Prakash, *Food and Drink in Ancient India*, p. 71, mangoes and other fruits were so popular among the monks that the Buddha had to appoint "a distributor of fruits."

MAHAVIRA

No survey of vegetarians in history would be complete without paying homage to Mahavira, the historical founder of Jainism. The term "historical" founder is used advisedly, because the Jains have always claimed that their religion is far older than the birth of its putative founder Mahavira. In fact they stoutly maintain that Jainism is the ur-religion of India—the parent religion from which Buddhism and Brahmanic Hinduism have stemmed—and that such concepts as *ahimsa*, reincarnation and ethical vegetarianism originated with the Jains. Recently scholarship has lent color to these claims by demonstrating that Mahavira was in fact the 24th Jain Tirthankara—that is to say he was the 24th in a line of inspired religious teachers who have guided and promulgated Jainism from its neolithic beginnings, which may stretch back some 8,000 years. For most Jain *sadhus*, however, 8,000 years would be too abbreviated a time-span; they say that Jainism has been the religious conscience of India from time immemorial. It has no beginning point and no end point, but is perpetual and eternal.

Like the Pythagoreans, the Jains were great mathematicians and astronomers. (They are credited with having invented the concept of infinity.) It's conceivable that the exaltation of mathematics among the members of the Pythagorean Order as well as their *ahimsa*-like philosophy of compassion may have been the result of Jain influences transmitted to Greece via trade or commerce with Persia. The first verifiable direct link between Jainism and Ancient Greece occurred in 326 B.C. when Alexander the Great during his invasion of Northeastern India encountered men who fit the description of Jain *sadhus*. They were sky-clad ascetics—the Greeks called them *gymnosophists* "naked philosophers"—and they were seemingly indifferent to Alexander's splendor; as practitioners of *ahimsa*, they would not consent to talk to him until he had removed his armor.

Mahavira's name was really a sobriquet like Plato—"the broad-browed, or broad-shouldered one"; Christ—"the anointed one"; the Buddha—"the enlightened one"; or Pythagoras—which some scholars have interpreted to be a corruption of the Sanskrit term "Pitta Goru," meaning "the Wise Man," (and which suggests the Indian sources of Pythagorean doctrine). It is curious how so many of the great vegetarian religious teachers had names of this sort.

Literally translated, the title or honorific Mahavira means "the great man" or "the hero." After he attained complete knowledge *(kevala jnana)* at the age of 42, he was called *jina* "conqueror" (whence the name Jain

19

is derived), which refers to the conquest of self and soul-purification that he achieved through his devotion to asceticism and *ahimsa* (non-injury to any living creature).

Mahavira's real name was Prince Vardhamana Nataputta. Like the Buddha, he was born into a princely family who governed the kingdom that contained the once flourishing city of Vaishali (modern Bihar) in Northeastern India. In fact, Mahavira and the Buddha were contemporaries, and in the course of their itinerant preachings they became friendly rivals. It is really quite remarkable that two of the greatest world teachers in the annals of humanity should have been members of the same caste (the *kshatriya* or warrior caste), should have spoken the same local dialect *Magadhi*, should have been born in the same century in the same part of India. But the parallels do not end there: Both renounced their princely comforts and prerogatives to become mendicant monks; both founded religious orders that endure to this day; both became religious teachers in order to protest against the excesses of Brahmanic Hinduism (which included animal sacrifice, subjection of women, and caste discrimination); both made ethical vegetarianism and animal rights the first precept of their religious systems. There is even compelling evidence to suggest that the Buddha himself had become a Jain monk before he formulated his own version of Jainism that he stamped with the impress of his personality. And indeed there is something to the notion that Buddhism might almost be called a Jainism for the export market. It is less demanding than Jainism—(it doesn't have overstringent rules against the killing of insects, or the eating of root vegetables, or the eating of left-over food)—and its greater flexibility in these matters may account for Buddhism's wider appeal.

Something of the rigor of Jainism can be appreciated when we examine the life of Mahavira, which exemplifies many of the basic doctrines of Jainism.

The region of Northeastern India where the Buddha and Mahavira were born, preserved much of the ethical vegetarianism and *ahimsa* of pre-Aryan India. In the middle of the second millenium B.C. (circa 1500 B.C.), the horse-borne tribes of Aryan nomads had made themselves masters of Northwestern India by plundering the prosperous but gentle vegetarian peoples of Harrapa and Mohenjo-Daro. To propitiate their gods of war, the Aryans sacrificed bulls, cows, and horses on their fiery altars, then devoured their flesh. Now the Aryan fire-priests were spreading the cult of ritual sacrifice among the remote Jain kingdoms of Northeastern India. It was to check the spread of this cruel religion that Mahavira and the Buddha rose up to protest and reform it. So powerful and persuasive were their teachings, that the Aryan war gods such as Indra and

Rudra were discredited, the doctrine of transmigration or reincarnation was incorporated into Hinduism (it is nowhere mentioned in the *Vedas*) and the Aryan fire-priests turned vegetarian (which is why most *brahmins* today are devout vegetarians).

Mahavira was born into a family of practicing Jains circa 540 B.C. His parents were followers of the 23rd Tirthankara, Parshwa, who had preached *ahimsa* in the 9th century B.C. Like all Jains, they held life sacred and revered the lowliest insect. In the Jain scheme, animal souls and human souls are accorded equal weight. The term for soul in Jainism is *jiva*, which actually means "sentient essence." The highest number of senses, five senses, are assigned to humans and other animals such as monkeys, parrots, fish, cattle, horses, elephants, dogs, lizards, et al. Insects fall into two classifications—those that have 4 and 3 senses respectively. The higher insects are considered to have only four senses: smell, taste, touch and hearing; they include the larger insects such as bees, flies and grasshoppers; insects with 3 senses are thought to lack the sense of sight; they include moths, ants, mosquitoes and bed bugs. Creatures with only two senses are held to have only the senses of taste and touch; they include mollusks, crustaceans, worms, leeches, slugs, et al. One sense is assigned to trees and plants and to such seemingly inanimate objects as stones, the earth itself, water-bodies, fire-bodies and wind-bodies. For the Jains the material world is charged with vitality. The ethical and ecological implications of the Jain worldview are stunningly clear. If one is cruel and unfeeling towards other life-forms, be they even so footling as a stone, water, a tree, or a worm—one runs the risk of attracting to one's own *jiva* the gluey, greasy, gummy residue of bad karma that sticks like tar to the spirit and can turn one's next incarnation into an unhappy one—one's *jiva* might be imprisoned in a stone, or it might live for an instant in the flare of a fire-body, or the splash of a water-body. On the other hand, if one is compassionate towards other life forms; one's soul becomes *satvic* (light, spiritual), one may escape the wheel of rebirth and dwell in blissful omniscience.

Of course the very act of eating involves the destruction of other life forms; but Jainism urges that one eat as far down on the scale of pain as possible—which means eating one-sensed life-forms instead of eating—as is done in Western countries—five-sensed life forms (which to the Jain smacks of cannibalism!). So eating low on the food chain for ethical as well as ecological reasons is nothing new: The Jains have been doing it for millenia!

Like many orthodox Jains today, when Mahavira was growing up, his parents did not permit him to eat root vegetables such as carrots, turnips, parsnips and radishes. For Jains root vegetables are prohibited foods because insects and other organisms take up residence in their root systems: Uprooting them causes the acute discomfort and the annihilation of millions of these little creatures. Having said this, it is only fair to point out that a great many younger Jains living in such cosmopolitan cities as Delhi, Calcutta, and Bombay, while remaining devout vegetarians, have nonetheless taken to flouting the ban on root vegetables and guiltlessly feed on forbidden potatoes, carrots and turnips. On the contrary, Jain *sadhus* or monks will refuse to accept root vegetables in their almsbowls. For unlike most Buddhist monks, who will accept with alacrity even non-veg. foods in their almsbowls, Jain *sadhus* will take only *satvic* (spiritual) food: It must be vegetarian; it must contain no root vegetables; it must be mildly seasoned; and it must be prepared the same day. On no account will *sadhus* and orthodox Jains eat leftover food—as it would invariably contain more bacteria and more micro-organisms that it would be bad form and bad *karma* to ingest.

As with most Jain families today, Mahavira and his family used a special cloth to strain their water before drinking it so as to filter out swimming insects and other aquatic small fry. He, his parents, his sister and his older brother were also scrupulous about taking their evening meal before sundown—(a rite that is still observed by modern Jains)—lest the flickering torchlight attract winged insects who might alight on the food or fly into the unwary mouth.

Although Mahavira's parents were very ascetic in their dietary practices, and spent many of their waking hours in meditation, they were a royal couple and lived in opulent surroundings. Since even the poorest Indian families tend to spoil their children—especially their sons, as the scion of a royal family Mahavira was raised with every mark of favor. There were servants to dress him in the most splendid finery; there were servants to undress and bathe him; there were servants to play with him and indulge his princely whims. At meal times he was plied with the tastiest vegetarian dishes—(Jain vegetarian cooking is still prized as one of India's most delectable cuisines)—from the hands of the most highly skilled cooks in the royal kitchen.

It may seem incongruous that the 24th Jain Tirthankara (cosmic spiritual teacher) and the historical founder of such an abstemious religion should have been raised amid such luxury, but this is one of the juicier paradoxes of Jainism: Despite their adherence to the most austere dietary laws of any religion extant, the Jains have always been the most prosperous religious group in India. Their prodigious wealth is reflected in their extravagant urban temples and their vast mountain-top temple complexes such as those at Mount Abu and Palitina that are famous for their magnificient colonnades and porticoes, soaring domes and pillars so delicately carved as to make the works of Donatello and Brunelleschi look clumsy.

Since the Jains constitute only one percent of the Indian population, what accounts for their disproportionate financial success? Perhaps it is a result of the good *karma* that accrues to them for their practicing *ahimsa*. Since long before Mahavira, the Jains have been forbidden to enter such trades as food preparation, silk-making and agriculture—because they entail the descruction of numberless life forms. On the other hand, they've been encouraged to enter harmless professions that put a premium on brain power, thrift, and a willingness to live in urban as opposed to rural areas (which is why the preponderance of Jains live in cities). Happily for the Jains these professions have traditionally been among India's most high-paying; they include law, commerce, finance, banking, science, and the professorate. So by turning this seeming disadvantage to their account, the Jains have achieved enviable financial success in a land where for the past half-century it has been all too rare.

Incredible as it may seem, Mahavira grew up without that *sine qua non* of Western domestic life—the household pet. There were no poodles frisking about the palace grounds; nor were there horses champing in the royal stables; nor parrots gossiping in the royal aviary; nor elephants gallumphing in the royal menagerie—because Jains are not supposed to keep pets. This is as true today as it was in Mahavira's time. Let him visit any bustling Jain household, which is apt to be bursting at the seams with children , friends, and relatives, and the Western visitor will be struck by a conspicuous absence of bow-wows, miaows, and chirp-chirps. It's not that the Jains don't love animals; on the contrary, their sympathy for animals runs so deep that the impulse to possess them and turn them into domestic playthings is kept firmly in check.

Dr. Albert Schweitzer was a great admirer of Jainism. In fact he was inspired by the Jain concept of *ahimsa* to coin his deathless phrase "reverence for life." Nonetheless, he criticized the Jains for being more concerned with purification than with compassion. It was his contention that the Jains were vegetarians and practised *ahimsa* not from any great empathy for their fellow creatures, but from their wish to avoid defiling themselves with the bad karma and spiritual pollution that they would incur if they disobeyed the dictates of their religion.

Unfortunately, the sainted Dr. Schweitzer (who contrary to popular belief, was not a vegetarian)—had never visited India, and had no direct experience of Jainism. Had he but met a Jain *sadhu*, or lived for a time with a Jain family, he would have realized that they have a horror of injuring the smallest creatures—a horror that springs from compassion —not from a fetish for purification. By watching a typical Jain housewife pick through the rice and the vegetables that she will be preparing for the family dinner, he would have seen that she carefully removes the insects and sets them gently in the garden. Nor apparently had he read the life of Mahavira that is preserved in the Jain scriptural canon; had he done so, he would have read of Mahavira's exploit as a young ascetic when he risked his life to rescue an elephant that had run amok. He would also have noted that Mahavira's "reverence for life" was such that he allowed insects, reptiles, and small animals to bite and sting him while he was in meditation without his turning a hair.

Furthermore, there is a venerable Jain institution called the *pinjarpol*, which dates from before Mahavira's time and also contradicts Dr. Schwietzer's thesis. There is scarcely a city or a town in the Jain states of Gujerat and Rajasthan that doesn't boast a *pinjarpol*. *Pinjarpols* take care of homeless and decrepit animals. The larger *pinjarpols* have rooms reserved for birds and insects. Every Jain *sadhu* takes a personal interest in the *pinjarpols*. In fact many *sadhus* and *sadhuis* carry photos of the *pinjarpols* with which they are associated. Had Dr. Schweitzer but visited one of these *pinjarpols*, he would have formed a much higher estimate of the Jains' compassion for animals.

Although Mahavira felt the call to become a monk begin to stir in him when he was in his early twenties, his parents made him promise to postpone taking his vows until after their death. This sort of filial piety is not uncommon among Jains even today. As a dutiful son, Mahavira did not want to cause his parents any anxiety or distress; for he realized that if he were to become a *sadhu*, he would have to sever his ties with them.

When Mahavira was thirty, his parents went into a serious decline; they sensed that their life was nearing its end; so they performed upon themselves the only act of violence that Jainism condones: They took their own lives by fasting to death. Called *sallakhana*—the rite of voluntary self-starvation, it is countenanced only if one is in the final throes of one's existence and then only if it is undertaken with the purest of intentions.

After his parents' death, Mahavira asked his older brother Nandivardhana's permission to enter upon the life of a *sadhu*. His brother who was now the titular head of the clan, and *rajah* of Vaishali, gave his consent with the stipulation that Mahavira wait one more year. Having mourned his parents for a year, he stripped off all his clothes and became a *digambara* or sky-clad monk. He then plucked out his facial and scalp hair in clumps—a ritual that is still performed by Jain *sadhus* once every six months. Finally, he slipped off his sandals—for then as now, the Jain *sadhu* is forbidden to wear sandals or shoes; they regularly walk vast distances barefooted. (They are forbidden to ride in vehicles.) The foot of the *sadhus* and the *sadhuis* is heavily calloused; through constant wear, the bottoms of their feet become as tough as shoe leather. Do they resent this archaic custom? Not at all. They would rather walk on their hands than wear the hide of an animal on their feet. Mahavira completed the transformation from prince into *sadhu* by removing his ear-rings and his chunky gold ornaments, and exchanged them for two other appurtenances of the Jain *sadhu*—the alsmbowl and the *pincha*—which is a soft broom that Jains use to sweep the path whenever it might be covered with insects.

At length, after having joined the order of the sky-clad followers of Parshwa, of which his parents had been lay members, Mahavira struck out on his own. He entered the forests and wandered for twelve years, practising prolonged meditation and subjecting himself to the severest austerities. More often than not, when he would approach a village to ask for food in his cupped hands, he would be set upon by rustics who pelted him with fruit, potsherds and mud, for having the audacity to go about sky-clad. But he bore it all stoically. Finally, the ultimate experience that he had been seeking was not denied him. In the thirteenth year of his wanderings, during the fourth fortnight of summer, seated in a squatting position under a sal tree in the field of the householder Samaga, he achieved nirvana, and became a Jina (the Conqueror). He then went forth to share his knowledge with the world. In his sermons, he launched a vigorous attack against flesh-eating, animal sacrifice, the caste system and the subjection of women. Those who wished to follow him were required to adopt *ahimsa* as a cardinal principle, to practice honesty and sexual continence. He also made his followers promise that they would try to attain nirvana without the aid of mediatory priests. (In Jainism, the *sadhus* or monks are not treated as a race apart as are the *brahmins* in Brahmanic Hinduism—but rather as advanced laymen who lead a more stringent life. In the Jain temples the lay members perform their own *puja* and *arati*, effectively serving as their own priests.) By his seventy-second year, Mahavira had attracted a following of over 200,000 adherents. In this same year, the final year of his life, Mahavira committed *sallakhana* at the village of Pavam, which was not far from his birthplace. It has since become one of the most sacred places of pilgrimage and annually is visited by thousands of barefooted processions of Jains who have walked hundreds of kilometers to pay their respects to the twenty-fourth Tirthankara.

Dal Bhaat
(Rice with Lentils)

1 cup moong dal
¾ cups water
1 teaspoon powdered ginger (*sadhus* eat only dry
    or powdered ginger)
1 teaspoon white pepper
1½ teaspoons coriander powder
1 teaspoon salt (or to taste)
2 tablespoons oil
1 teaspoon turmeric powder
1 teaspoon garam masala (or curry powder)
1 tomato (optional—anachronistic)
1 teaspoon cumin seeds
A pinch of *hing* (asafoetida)
Fresh, chopped coriander leaves

For the Rice

1 cup *basmati* rice
2 cups water

Clean and pick over the dal by hand. Then rinse it in a pot. Add 4 cups of water and cook over a medium flame until the dal begins to disintegrate. Use a fork or spatula to mash the dal and give it the consistency of a thick soup. Now add the white pepper, powdered ginger, turmeric, garam masala, coriander powder, and tomato. Cook for approximately five more minutes.

In a small pan, heat the oil. Add the cumin seeds. When the seeds begin to splutter, remove from heat and add the garam masala. Quickly pour this over the cooked dal. Garnish with chopped coriander leaves. Serve over hot *basmati* rice.

Soak the rice in 2 cups of water for ½ hour. Bring the water to a boil then lower to medium flame and let simmer until the rice starts to crackle. Cover the pot with a lid and remove from flame. Allow it to sit covered for ten minutes more. Then serve.

This recipe was supplied by Shakuntala Jain. For the biographical evidence, see footnote on page 29.

Spiced Green Beans
(Fali)

1½ lbs. green beans
6 tablespoons oil
1 teaspoon cumin seeds
4 teaspoons coriander powder
⅓ teaspoon turmeric powder
½ teaspoon *garam masala*
1 teaspoon salt (or to taste)
1 tomato, chopped (optional)*

Wash and pick over the beans. Nip off the ends and cut the beans into one-half inch pieces. Heat the oil in a (heavy base) pot. Add the cumin seeds. When the cumin seeds start to splutter, add the beans and the remaining spices. Toss the beans and spices either with a spoon or by shaking the pot. Cover the pot and cook over a low flame. When the beans turn bright green, add the tomato and toss again. Cook for two more minutes with the lid half-covering the pot. Remove from the burner when the beans are as cooked as you like them.

Serves 4.

According to Kailash Chand Jain in his book *Lord Mahavira and His Times* (Delhi: Motilal Banarsidass, 1991), p. 42, Mahavira sustained himself on rice, beans and pounded jujube. The recipe for this dish was furnished by Shakuntala Jain, a Jain housewife and mother from Bombay. Her parents are orthodox Jains, who like Mahavira abstained from eating root vegetables. Missing from this recipe are such familiar Indian spices as garlic and onions because orthodox Jains are forbidden to eat them.

*Tomatoes were not introduced into India until after the Columbian exchange; therefore Mahavira couldn't have eaten them; they're classified as a New World fruit.

LAO TZU
AND THE TAOISTS

Taoism is one of the three main religions of China, and is the most ancient of the three. (The other two are Confucianism and Buddhism). It has survived—with characteristic resiliency—the Chinese Communist Party's attempts to tear it out of the Chinese cultural soil, root and branch—perhaps the greatest challenge that Taoism has had to face since Kublai Khan ordered the burning of all Taoist books (save the *Tao Te Ching*) in 1281 A.D. There are some who hold that Religious Taoism in Maoist China was strengthened through persecution and adversity, much as bamboo is said to draw its strength from the winds that buffet it.

Furthermore, the orthodox Taoist monasteries in keeping with the Taoist affinity to nature, are sited on remote mountain fastnesses. These beautiful mountain temples are designed to merge with their craggy surroundings. Consequently, they are not easy to get to. Some of these hermitages are so out of the way that doubtless they were spared the worst depredations of the Maoist Cultural Revolution because of their very aloofness.

Like Buddhism, its archrival among Chinese religions for almost 2000 years, Taoism has always required a vegetarian diet of its closest followers. The Taoist lay vegetarian societies, which since the Maoist takeover in the early 1950's have had to operate secretly, have long promoted vegetarianism among the Chinese peasantry and middle class. Writing in his history of Chinese Religious, D. H. Smith says: "Yet Taoism still maintained some hold through its lay vegetarian societies, promoted for mutual encouragement in the religious life; meditation; study and good works in its secret societies among the peasants giving a sanction to revolutionary activity in times of trouble."[1]

Like many other Eastern religions such as Buddhism, Zen, Hinduism and Yoga, Taoism is becoming increasingly popular in the West. Since Taoism is a religion with a strong vegetarian imperative, this augurs well for the future of vegetarianism (to say nothing of Taoism itself) in the West.

As a measure of Taoism's growing popularity in the West, there are over twenty-five titles in print that begin with the three magic words "The Tao of . . ." *The Tao of Health, The Tao of Peace, The Tao of Longevity, The Tao of Power, The Tao of Pooh*—these are just a few of the books that feature the word "Tao" in their title, as though the word itself had talismanic powers. Certainly the word "Tao" seems to have a magical effect on sales. Any book with the word Tao in its title seems destined to become a best-

seller; so perhaps the word Tao does have talismanic powers after all.

The extraordinary thing about the first "Tao of . . ." book—the *Tao Te Ching*—is that shorn of its mystery, and its cryptic language, it is essentially a manual of yoga. It was written in the third century B.C. by a Chinese sage named Lao Tzu (which means literally "the old boy").

Scholars consider the *Tao Te Ching* by the Chinese sage Lao Tzu to be a "Warring States" work, because it was composed during the time of the "Fighting States" from 700–300 B.C. It is called the time of the Fighting States because China, which had hitherto been a fairly placid place, had degenerated into a collection of petty kingdoms that were constantly at war with each other. It had become a time of unimaginable brutality and cruelty. The warrior princes who had always conducted warfare in a chivalrous manner, had been replaced by upstarts and usurpers who would stop at nothing to gain their ends. They were not above poisoning rivers; invading without warning; breaking treaties or betraying friendships and alliances at a whim. Whole cities were sacked and all their male inhabitants were put to the sword. To enhance their prestige, they would boil their foes in a caldron and gulp down the broth.[2]

Despite the tendency among the upstart princes of this period to make a wonton soup of their fallen enemies and toss it off with gusto, the princes were not without cultural pretensions; they read widely, and they wrote and commissioned poetry; many of them plumed themselves on being patrons of the arts. World-weary and often bored to extinction, the Chinese nobles used warfare and hunting as an antidote to boredom. It is worth quoting Professor Jacques Gernet on this point: "Apart from its religious activities, the noble class devoted its time to hunting and warfare. In the archaic period no distinction was made between the two. The weapons used were the same, and the great hunting parties were useful for training troops. Even the assembly places were the same. Captives and game were treated identically and consecrated to the ancestors and the gods. Some of the prisoners were in fact executed at the moment of triumph, or else kept in reserve as sacrificial offerings."[3]

Of course the Fighting States period occurs some time after this; but the attitudes of the nobility towards animals and peasants hadn't changed; only the weapons had gotten better: the invention of the composite bow and iron slashing swords made both hunting and the game of warfare at once deadlier and more intoxicating. Gernet calls the noble classes of this period "carnivorous by preference."[4]

How to persuade the warrior princes to stop waging war and rending the country—that was the task that Lao Tzu had set himself. He decided to do the same thing that another great political thinker would do some 2,000 years hence—Nicolo Machiavelli in Renaissance Florence—and that was to write a treatise on statecraft. Machiavelli called his little how-to-do-it book, *The Prince*; Lao Tzu called his, the *Tao Te Ching*. Whereas

Machiavelli urges the prince to be a combination of the lion and the fox—a tellingly carnivorous pair—Lao Tzu urges the prince to be like water whose strength paradoxically resides in its passivity, plasticity and downward pull. Water embodies Lao Tzu's concept of how an enlightened ruler should govern—through *wu wei* or effortless action. "Water is of all things most yielding and can overcome rock, which is of all things most hard." Instead of instructing the prince on how to make another conquest or commit a fresh chicane a la Machiavelli, Lao Tzu urges the prince to look inward, adopt a contemplative manner, meditate on his ingoing and outgoing breaths—in a word to study yoga. And the first precept of any classic system of yoga is the same as that of Buddhism and Jainism—to do no harm to any other life form—in essence to become an ethical vegetarian. Having become a vegetarian and learned to practice breath control, the prince could look forward to achieving yogic trance, ecstasy and longevity. By thus cultivating his interior life, and ruling over his people with effortless action or *wu wei*, he could become the ideal ruler, the yogic sage king.

Scholars are divided on the question of whether the trance state that these Taoist yogins achieved was ecstatic. But Henri Maspero, the great Taoist scholar, asserts that ecstasy was routinely achieved by the Taoist adepts. Moreover, he also says that Lao Tzu and Chuang Tzu were quite energetic in promoting a yoga of ecstasy.[5] Indeed a psychotropic payoff was one of the enticements for a young Chinese prince to take up yoga in the first place. How else could Lao Tzu and his disciple Chuang Tzu have turned the heads of the young warlords for whom their works were written other than by offering them an ecstatic experience and the promise of a long life? For increased longevity was the other prospect that the practice of Taoist yoga held out for the young prince.

Little is known about the life of Lao Tzu (born in 500 B.C. in Ch'en). As nearly as it can be pieced together, the evidence suggests that he was a librarian in the royal library of the kingdom of Hu. Apparently, he was of a retiring nature and was rather solitary in his habits. Legend has it that at the age of 160,[6] he was on the point of embarking on a permanent retreat to some remote and secluded hermitage when he was persuaded by a minor government functionary (some reports say that it was a customs official), who prevailed upon him to set down his message to the world before withdrawing from it. It may be an apocryphal story; yet it is interesting in and of itself because it throws light on the nature of Taoism.

First of all, there is Lao Tzu's predilection for anonymity—which is rather fitting because Taoists tend to be reclusive, and they don't give a fig for celebrity or fame; in fact they have a horror of it. There is also something quintessentially Taoistic about Lao Tzu's honoring the request of a humble customs official to interrupt his journey and dash off one of the world's great literary masterpieces in impromptu fashion. For Taoism teaches that one must seek knowledge and contentment in the lowliest places—like water that flows downward and seeks the lowest level. Taoism sets its face against the social climbing and mindless striving after high office of the Confucians.

Taoist too, is the quickness and spontaneity with which he dashes off the great work. It illustrates the Taoist concept of creation through spontaneity (*tzu-jan*) that one can see exemplified today in the lightning brush strokes of the great Chinese calligraphers and *sumie* painters. That the "Old Boy" could produce one of the greatest masterworks of world literature "off the cuff" is the ultimate act of *tzu-jan*.

Significant as well is Lao Tzu's age at the time he is supposed to have written the *Tao Te Ching*. Legend has it that he was from 160 to 200 years old. Since long life is one of the chief aims of Taoism, the fact that its historical founder was mentally adroit enough to compose the *Tao Te Ching* at such an over-ripe age is a good advertisement for the Taoist way of life—and for the diet that propelled the "Old Boy" through the vagaries of life for 200 years and more. Undoubtedly his diet was a vegetarian one, as Taoists have eaten vegetarian food since the inception. Even today, the food eaten by Taoist monks and nuns in Taoist monasteries and by reclusive lay Taoists is exclusively vegetarian as the eminent sinologist, Dr. Michael Saso points out in his book *A Taoist Cookbook*: "Taoist monks, nuns, and recluses, who follow the strictest rules of Taoist cooking, observe an almost pure vegetarian diet."[7]

Although it has been some 2400 years since Lao Tzu composed it, the *Tao Te Ching* is still the fundamental text used by the conservative Taoist monasteries in China. Taoist monks study it, invoke it, debate it and endlessly reinterpret it, much as Christian monks do scripture. Despite its brevity—it's a very slender volume of only 4000 Chinese characters, it is so profound, multilayered and mystical that the commentary on the Tao is voluminous. Indeed, there are commentaries on commentaries. However, beginning with Arthur Waley's key work *The Way and Its Power*, scholars have finally cracked the code of the *Tao Te Ching*. The most recent confirmation that Waley's theory was correct: that the *Tao Te Ching* is a covert manual of yoga comes from Professor Victor Mair, who in his new translation of the *Tao Te Ching*, has lent color to Waley's findings.

With Arthur Waley, whose insight it first was, Mair believes that the *Tao Te Ching*, in addition to being a guide to statecraft that anticipates Machiavelli's *The Prince*, is also a manual of yoga that gives specific instructions on how to induce a yogic trance: "There are so many correspondences between yoga and Taoism even in the smallest and oddest details—throughout the history of their development that we might almost think of them as two variants of a single religious and philosophical system."[8]

Among some of the more striking parallels that Mair points out are that both the yoga of the *Upanishads* and the yoga of early Taoism lay stress upon the vital breath, and both conceive of it as flowing through channels in the body. He points out that yoga and Taoism "share a close association with external and internal alchemy. Both resort to the use of charms, sacred syllables and talismans as aids in meditation and for conveying secret knowledge. He also mentions that both yoga and Taoism claim that those who become adepts can easily achieve supernatural powers such as clairvoyance, clauraudience, and of course longevity. He concludes his lengthy list of correspondences between Indic yoga and Taoism with the following summation: "By now it is hoped that even the most hardened skeptic and the most ardent Chinese isolationist will admit that Yoga and Taoism bear such striking affinities to each other that they must be related in some fashion."

"In most instances, however, what the founders of Taoism absorbed from Yoga were radically new ideas concerning man and his place in the universe and a complementary physiological regimen (meditational discipline, dietary practices, flexing exercises and so forth.) Considering the immense linguistic, social and philosophical differences between China and India, it is astounding that the kindredness of the *Bhagavad Gita* and the *Tao Te Ching* shines through so conspicuously."[9]

It is important to note that among the "radically new ideas" that the founders of Taoism absorbed from yoga were "dietary practices." Although Mair doesn't spell it out for us, the new dietary practices associated with Yoga could only have meant one thing—vegetarianism. For it is obligatory on the serious student of Yoga that he be a strict vegetarian. In his book *Light on Yoga*, B. K. S. Iyengar one of the world's foremost experts on yoga observes: "A vegetarian diet is essential to the practice of yoga." Let's face it, yoga without a vegetarian component would be merely a system of stretching exercises. It is the meditation and the vegetarian regimen that make of yoga something more than just a set of preposterous postures, and help raise it to a metaphysical plane.

Not only does a flesh diet interfere with meditation, but some yogins have even gone so far as to say that a flesh-eating yogin runs the risk of being accosted on the psychic plane by the disembodied spirits of the animals that he or she may have dined on the night before. Meeting on the astral plane the disembodied soul of the animal from whose carcass one's dinner was plucked could seriously disrupt *samadhi*! [Apropos of this, one is reminded of Theosophist Annie Besant's vivid account of her train trip to Chicago, when Chicago was "Hog butcher to the world." As her train chugged towards the city looming in the distance "a profound sense of desolation oppressed her spirit," because from the South Chicago stockyards, she received astral messages of reproach from thousands of slaughtered beasts, suspended between the physical world and the thought world.]

Although Taoist yoga derived from India, its goal, according to Taoist scholar J. C. Cooper, was very different from that of Indian yoga. Whereas the Indian yogin tried to reach a state of *samadhi* (ecstatic trance), the Taoist yogin's objective was to achieve *samadhi* as well as immortality. As Cooper writes in *Chinese Alchemy, The Taoist Quest for Immortality*: "This goal of immortality marks a difference between Indian and Chinese yoga; the former is concerned with the control of the body as a preparation for meditation and other religious exercises for the sake of the spirit, while the Chinese cult of immortality in some cases made the achievement of immortality a goal in itself."[10]

Thus one of the most irresistible features of Taoism was its promise of—if not immortality—then the prolonging of life beyond the normal compass. The implication was that this could be done by practicing yoga and eating *sattvic*, or spiritual, vegetarian food.

Although most Western scholars disparage the mystical quest for immortality in Taoism (they regard it as a corruption that crept in during the Three Dynasties Period), Henri Maspero, the French Taoist scholar who made the study of Taoism his life's work, believed that the concern for prolonging one's life and increasing vitality were present in Taoism from the very start. He writes as follows: "From the fourth and third centuries B.C., the Taoists were seekers of immortality; from its origin, Taoism has been a doctrine of individual salvation which claimed to conduct the adept to immortality. The methods must have varied: each master had his own, which he kept secret and transmitted only to certain chosen disciples; from this time on we see most of these which were to be current at the time of the Six Dynasties and Tang."[11]

What part did vegetarianism have to play in the Taoist quest for immortality? Here is what Professor Maspero has to say:

"The prohibition of eating meat had nothing to do with the similar Buddhist prohibition. In Buddhism, it is the consequence of the interdict upon killing living beings; for the Taoists, it is because the spirits of the interior of the body have a horror of blood, the Breath of which wounds them, causes them to flee, and thus shortens life."[12]

In sum, although the Taoists were compassionate towards animals and forbade scientific experiments on them (indeed, the Taoist doctrine of *wu wei*, or "non-interference" has much in common with the Jain concept of not interfering in the lives of other beings), Taoists have always been vegetarians for reasons that were unabashedly health-conscious; the main purpose of the Taoist religion is to increase vital energy and prolong life; they believed that a meatless diet would help them attain physical immortality, and the quest for the *elixir vitae* has been the consuming passion of religious Taoists from time out of mind. Many useful byproducts have emerged from the Taoist quest for immortality. To list but a few: the discovery of the pulse; the science of acupuncture; herbology; the martial arts; alchemy as the precursor of chemistry; and the discovery of gunpowder and metallurgy. Their sampling of almost everything edible in their attempt to find the *elixir vitae* led them to collect the wide range of spices and herbs used in Chinese cookery; it also, in all likelihood, led them to the discovery of tofu and other soy foods, whose anti-carcinogenic and anti-angina properties have recently been confirmed scientifically in the West.[13] To the indefatigable Taoist quest for eternal life, the Chinese also owe their vast *materia medica* which boasts the world's earliest and most sophisticated pharmacopoeia. The history of Taoism shows there are moral as well as utilitarian benefits to being a vegetarian for health reasons.

Dried Fruits and Nuts

1 bowl of dried dates
1 bowl mixed nuts (filberts, pine nuts, cashews, almonds)
1 bowl of raisins
1 bowl mixed dried fruits (figs, dates, apricots,
    dried pears and dried apples)

"Dried and candied fruit has a special meaning in the Taoist temple and monastic tradition. Since dried fruit keeps almost indefinitely, it is used as a symbol of longevity, good health and life after death."

From Dr. Michael Saso, *A Taoist Cookbook*, op. cit. p. 83.

Taoist Carrot Stew

The following is an adaptation of a dish that I was served in the Ching Chung Koon Temple in Hong Kong. The meals prepared in the temple kitchen followed Taoist cooking rules, which mandate a dairyless vegetarian diet. One of the chief aims of Taoism is to increase vital energy and to promote longevity; Taoists eat vegetarian food and undercook their vegetables (or uncook them), to that end.

12 carrots
1 4-oz. container water chestnuts
2 16-oz. containers tofu
2 bunches spring onions
ginger
soy sauce
1 teaspoon chili bean paste with black bean sauce
oil for shallow frying

Cut the tofu into bite-size chunks and shallow fry them in vegetable oil until they are golden. Drain and set aside. Cut the carrots into 2-inch wafer-thin slices with a vegetable slicer, and set aside. Chop the water chestnuts into small chunks and set aside. Chop half the spring onions and sauté them in oil for one minute; add soy sauce, ginger and chili bean paste. Cook for two more minutes. Remove from flame and stir in the tofu until the tofu is permeated with the sauce. Stir in the uncooked carrot slices, the water chestnut pieces and the chopped uncooked spring onions. Stir vigorously and serve.

Serves two.

Note: This dish is partially cooked—to preserve flavor and enzymes—in the Taoist style.

PLATO (AND SOCRATES)

"The European philosophical tradition," said the great twentieth century British philosopher Alfred North Whitehead, "consists in a series of footnotes to Plato." By this he meant that Plato, who was born in Athens on May 27, 427 B.C., posed so many of the basic philosophical, ethical and theological problems that he laid the groundwork for all those who came after him. However, it's important to note that Plato's influence wasn't limited only to philosophers; he also had an enormous impact on European literature, education, theology, science and mathematics. Had he done nothing more than found the Academy—which was modeled on the Pythagorean school at Croton and was the forerunner of the modern University—his reputation would have been secure. When Leibnitz and Newton invented the calculus, they expanded on the mathematical ideas that had been developed in the first generation of Plato's Academy. In a reversal of the usual trend in which Europe set the cultural and artistic tone for England, the study of Plato's works was being ardently promoted by Franciscan scholars at Oxford University in the 13th century—fully two hundred years before Plato was admitted into the curricula of universities on the continent. That Platonic ideas were so much in the air in Medieval and Renaissance England undoubtedly explains why Shakespeare and Marlowe were so conversant with Pythagorean-Platonic mythology. Transmitted through the works of the neoplatonists, Porphyry and Plotinus, Plato influenced such great Christian thinkers as Augustine, St. Francis, and Boethius—who helped liberate medieval theology and science from the dead hand of Thomist-Aristotelianism (which held that animals were soulless machines). Furthermore because of the Pythagorean-Platonic belief in *metempsychosis*—that animal bodies might incorporate human souls—the spread of the Augustinian-Franciscan tradition throughout Europe prepared the ground for the growing awareness that animals may not only have souls, but that they may also have rights.

Unlike Hegel or Kant, Plato was not a philosophical system builder; there is no guidebook or skeleton-key to his work because he didn't have an all-embracing theory of everything. For Plato, philosophy like life itself was pure process—an open-ended pursuit of truth and beauty. If his work seems free of the intellectual aridity and mustiness that dwell in the works of the great system-makers, it's because his dialogues have the effervescence of salon or drawing room conversation raised to a high art. Perhaps because he was a dramatist manqué (he burned all his plays before they could be produced on the Athenian stage), he invented a quasi-dramatic literary form that he called "dialectic"—from the Greek *dia-legein-techne*, meaning the art of conversation or debate. Dialectic is really just a fancy word for conversation in which the participants actually listen to what each other has to say, and who try to learn from each other's ideas—a rare enough event in this age of the remorseless monologue.

"Plato" was actually a sobriquet that was derived from the Greek adjective *platus*, which means "wide or broad," and is said by various accounts to have referred to his wide forehead (a feature that connoted high intelligence), and to his broad, well-proportioned shoulders.[1] For Plato in the best Pythagorean tradition kept himself physically as well as mentally fit. Like his friend and teacher Socrates who frequented the gymnasium, Plato was an habitué of the local gym, where he put his ample pectorals and deltoids through their paces.

Admittedly, it is hard to picture Plato, who epitomizes the Western intellectual tradition, as the broad-shouldered, prizewinning gymnast that his biographers tell us that he was—but it heightens our sense of incongruity even further when we learn from Alcibiades, who was Athens' most brilliant (and perfidious) general—(in Plato's *Symposium*, 219–223) —that Socrates, the archetypal wise man of Western Civ., was an absolute Achilles on the battlefield! With typical contempt for his own safety and with the enemy pressing down on him, Socrates saved Alcibiades' life. As Alcibiades lay wounded, his arms scattered about him on the ground, Socrates scooped up Alcibiades in his arms and carried him to safety. One look at Socrates—even a retreating Socrates—with his cool, contemplative stare, and his impregnable air, and the enemy, Alcibiades assures us, would be thrown into consternation. What's more: Socrates used to amaze his fellow *hoplites* (heavily armed infantrymen) with his powers of endurance: he could go for days without food, and even though he was a conscript in his late thirties, he could outmarch and outlast men in their early twenties. Once during a winter campaign in Macedonia, when the earth was frozen and covered with ice, Alcibiades watched Socrates outmarching his fellow *hoplites;* whereas they had bundled themselves up in heavy woolen cloaks, and were wearing furs and fleeces on their feet, Socrates was clad in a light cotton tunic and *himation*, and was racing over the frozen earth in bare feet! Socrates' unwillingness to wear animal skins on his feet may have proceeded from Pythagorean scruples; for like the Jains and *brahmins* of India—(and Leonardo da Vinci's friend Zoroastro, *qv*)—Pythagoras would wear no article of clothing made from an animal's skin.

Plato's sinewy athleticism, and Socrates' feats of strength on the battlefield fly in the face of the convention that Western philosophers are supposed to be sedentary types with flaccid muscles and overdeveloped brains. On the contrary, if we were suddenly to behold them descending the limestone staircase of a Greek revival building in one of our modern European or American capitals, we would be astonished at how muscular they were. With their granitic faces, taurean necks, arms that looked like legs, massive chests, and legs that looked like tree trunks, they could easily be mistaken for professional wrestlers oddly dressed in flowing *chitons* and *himations*. The Renaissance painter Raphael's imaginative portrait of the Platonic Academy—"The School of Athens"—probably comes closest to presenting an accurate picture of how Plato and other philosophers of the Academy must have looked—(like professional wrestlers tricked out in *chitons* and *himations*). If Raphael was able to paint them almost to the life, it's doubtless because the artists and intellectuals of his own era (15th century Italy) whom he took as models—such as the quintessential Renaissance man (and vegetarian) Leonardo da Vinci—were also heroically built. Could it be that our bodies and minds have become so atrophied by virtue of our having eaten depraved food for so many generations that we are incapable of imagining a society in which even its intellectuals are robust physical specimens?

Plato's real name was "Aristocles," which sounds like the name of an Athenian aristocrat, and that is precisely what he was. His pedigree-conscious parents claimed to be able to trace their descent from such demigods and gods as Solon, the great Athenian reformer and law-giver, and Poseidon (Zeus's brother), who ruled over horses, earthquakes and the navigable waters. Not only was Plato well-born and well-connected, but he was also well-fixed financially. His ample funds enabled him to educate himself in the desultory fashion of a "professional student," who doesn't have to worry overmuch about money. With utmost lassitude he was gradually preparing himself for the only career that was suitable for a man of his rank. Like so many of his aristocratic relatives, Plato had been groomed almost from birth for a career in politics. But then in the year 399 B.C., an event occurred in Plato's life that put iron in his soul and made him despair of entering politics—his dear friend and mentor Socrates, who was perhaps the greatest teacher and Pythagorean philosopher of his time, was put to death on trumped up charges by of all things the recently restored democratic government.

The authorities allowed friends and relatives to be admitted to Socrates' prison cell on his final day, but Plato felt so dejected by the injustice of the verdict that he could not bring himself to be present at Socrates' death bed. Nonetheless, in one of his most beautiful dialogues, the *Phaedo*, Plato captures every verbal nuance that Socrates uttered; and he provides a picture of Socrates' courage and equanimity in his last hours that cannot fail to move the reader to tears. Since Plato had absented himself from the death scene, how did he manage to describe it so faithfully? Fortunately for Plato, there were several witnesses who had attended Socrates in his final hours and watched him drink the poison. His wife Xanthippe was there, carrying the baby that Socrates had fathered on her at the age of 70 (however, to spare her feelings, he insisted that she not stay for the climax). The remaining spectators were Pythagorean philosophers such as Phaedo of Elis, Simmias and Cebes of Thebes (who had studied with the noted Pythagorean Philolaus), Euclides and Terpsion of Megara. As their native cities were still at war with Athens, they were putting their lives at risk to pay their final respects to the teacher whom they held in such veneration. Chief among them was Phaedo of Elis, who doubtless reported to Plato all that had happened, and whom Plato cast in the role of narrator of the dialogue. In the conversation that these philosophers had with Socrates leading up to the death scene, they discuss, appropriately enough, Pythagorean subjects such as the imperishability of the soul; *anamnesis*—the theory that learning is the recalling to mind of knowledge gained in previous lives (which was also treated at length in the *Meno*); and the doctrine of reincarnation *(metemsomatosis)*—of which the corollary as every Jain and Hindu knows is a strict vegetarian diet; for one cannot believe in reincarnation, or soul transmigration and not be a vegetarian.

Death held no terror for Socrates because—as one who practiced the Pythagorean concept of *katharsis*—he saw death as the culmination of a lifelong struggle to purify the soul and liberate it from the tomblike body. (Plato undoubtedly means for us to interpret Socrates' prison cell in which the *Phaedo* is set as a metaphor for the body; and Socrates' winged thoughts, which Phaedo and the others have traveled so far to catch, must represent the soul.) Despite Socrates' philosophical bravado in the face of death, when he actually drinks the poison—which owing to his tremendous bodily vigor takes an unconscionable time to kill him—Phaedo and the other Pythagoreans can barely fight back their tears.

Embittered at the judicial murder of the man who had been like a father to him, Plato quit Athens in disgust, and spent the next twelve years in self-imposed exile. German scholars refer to these "lost years" as the *Wanderjahre*[2]—in which he wandered from Megara (where he studied geometry with the Pythagorean Euclid); to Cairo and Heliopolis in Egypt (where he studied the arcana of the Egyptians); to Persia (where he may have learned the secrets of the Magi and the esoteric teachings of Zoroaster); and thence possibly to India, where he may have tried to trace the roots of such Pythagorean doctrines as reincarnation, ethical vegetarianism, and compassion for animals; *anamnesis* (the evoking of memories from past-lives); and the yoga-like cultivation of the body as a preparation for *theoria* (pure contemplation). A cynic might say that Socrates' death at the hands of the Athenian *dikastes* had furnished Plato with an excuse to indulge his propensity for being a perpetual (and highly parapatetic) student, but in the end the *Dialogues*, many of which reflect the esoteric knowledge that he gained during these travels, vindicate him. The so-called "lost years" turned out to be highly productive ones.

Towards the end of his twelve-year odyssey, he made his way to Tarentum in Southern Italy, which was the new home of the scientific and religious community, noted throughout Greece for its ethical vegetarianism—the Pythagorean Order. An inveterate student, even at the ripe age of 40, Plato became the pupil of Archytas—Pythagoras's successor (at several removes)—as head of the Order. Archytas was a many-sided genius. He was such an able ruler—(of the Pythagorean Order as well as of the city-state of Tarentum itself)—that he may have served as the prototype for the ideal ruler, the philosopher-king in Plato's *Republic*. In addition to being a gifted mathematician who solved the problem of duplicating the cube; he also established mechanics as a branch of Physics, and is credited with having invented the first automaton—a wooden pigeon that flapped its wooden wings and sustained itself aloft by an ingenious system of pulleys and a jet of compressed air.[3]

Finally, after completing his studies with Archytas in statecraft, mathematics, and Pythagorean metaphysics, Plato was ready to put his days as a wandering student behind him and take ship for Athens. However, on his homeward voyage, he decided to make a side-trip to Sicily, where he toured the volcano Mt. Aetna, into whose fiery crater the vegetarian philosopher Empedocles is reported to have made a suicide leap. Plato might well have been the second eminent vegetarian philosopher to have perished by misadventure in Sicily had not Fate played her hand. While he was visiting the court of the local tyrant, Dionysos I, Plato deeply angered the touchy tyrant, who was given to fits of homicidal rage. Sicily at this time was the most prosperous of the Greek colonies. It had long since outstripped the mother country as a commercial power (the comparison of the United States with England is often invoked). Sicily had even crushed Athens in a decisive battle that had turned the tide of the Peloponnesian War (in 412 B.C.). With a tendency toward conspicuous consumption to which the *nouveau riche* are prone, the Sicilians were flaunting their wealth by eating animal flesh at dinner parties. Repelled by the sight and smells of this impenitent gorging, Plato was so incautious as to give a speech before Dionysos, his family, and the court in which he urged them to adopt a Pythagorean diet and to try to live more simply.[4] Quivering with outrage at what he considered to be a breach of decorum and a gross insult to his wife Queen Aristomache, and his two daughters Arete (virtue) and Sophrosyne (moderation)—(would that he possessed these qualities himself!), Dionysos snapped his fingers to summon the palace guard. Had his son-in-law Dion not pleaded for Plato's life, the *fons et origo* of Western philosophy might have been strangled in a tin-pot tyrant's palace.

Although Dionysos allowed Plato to leave Sicily, he had prepared for him a subtle revenge. On Plato's homeward voyage, the ship made an unscheduled stop at Aegina (a city hostile to Athens). It was the policy of Aegina to put to death any citizen of Athens who strayed into its territory. Luckily, Plato was recognized as a philosopher; so his life was spared, and he was auctioned off as a slave. It looked as if he might have to spend the rest of his life as a slave-tutor to rich Aeginian brats—a fate that even Plato might have considered worse than death. Fate, however, allied herself with Philosophy; for just as the auctioneer was touting Plato's broad shoulders and obvious mental gifts, Anniceris, a Cyreanic philosopher, stepped up and purchased Plato's freedom for the considerable sum of 30 *minae*.[5] Plato's family fortunes had grown threadbare during his *Wanderjahre;* so his friends took up a collection among themselves to repay Anniceris for the ransom. But Anniceris refused to take any money; instead the funds that they had raised were used to buy Plato a house with a garden hard by the Academy gymnasium, or playing field. Amid the groves of Academe, Plato founded his school which he modeled after the Pythagorean Order. It quickly acquired an international reputation and scholars and students flocked to it from all over Greece. It became the archetype for the modern university, which alas has abandoned the Pythagorean principles on which it was founded.

Ironically, because Plato was so self-effacing in his written works (he appears only on several brief occasions in all 27 of his dialogues, whereas Socrates is the protagonist in most of them) we know more about Socrates' life than we do about Plato's. Many critics say that the Socrates character in Plato's dialogues is just a persona or mask that Plato put on to dramatize his own ideas. While it's undoubtedly true that Plato used Socrates as a mouthpiece for his own ideas, by comparing Plato's account of Socrates' life with the ones in Aristophanes' *The Clouds* and Xenophon's *Memorabilia* (Xenophon had been for a brief space Socrates' pupil before he set off on his *anabasis* throughout Persia), we find that they largely agree—especially with regard to Socrates' most salient features—his ascetic life, his scanty clothes, his shoeless feet, and his Pythagorean diet.

Although *The Clouds* is a savage caricature of Socrates' school, which Aristophanes has dubbed "the Thinkery," the play, like all satire, enshrines a great deal of truth. *The Clouds* as with Aristophanes' other comedies is a rich source of historical information about life in 5th century Athens. In this instance it throws a revealing light on the diet observed by Socrates and his school, which not suprisingly, is a Pythagorean or vegetarian one. In the play Strepsiades, a bumptious Athenian rustic with a spendthrift son, is trying to gain admission to Socrates' school in order to learn a rhetorical sophistry called the Unjust Argument. He calculates that if he learns this rhetorical trick, he'll so bedazzle his creditors with his forensic skill that he'll be able to escape all his debts. But before he can be admitted to Socrates' school, he must first convince him that he can endure the school's mental and physical rigors—not the least of which is its vegetarian fare. In *Clouds* (lines 420–422), Stepsiades reassures Socrates on this score and says: "Don't worry, I have a toughness of spirit that can endure brainracking ideas and a vegetarian diet: I offer myself up on an anvil that you may use it to shape me into a student of your society."[6]

As we've seen, it was a cardinal principle of the Pythagorean Order that its members had to avoid causing injury to animals and to abstain from eating their flesh. By Plato's time, the word "Pythagorean" had become so closely identified with the eating habits of the Pythagorean Order that the term "Pythagorean" became synonymous with *phytophagy* (plant-eating) and *anti-kreophagy* (against flesh-eating). In a word, "Pythagorean" had acquired the force of our term "ethical-vegetarian," and it gained currency throughout Europe that lasted until the mid-nineteenth century when the term "vegetarian" was coined. (In 1812, Percy Shelley's first wife, Harriet Westbrooke wrote: "You do not know that we have forsworn meat and adopted the *Pythagorean* system . . . we are delighted with it and think it the best thing in the world.")

Thus, by peopling so many of his dialogues with Pythagoreans such as Phaedo of Elis, Crito of Athens, Socrates of Athens, and Timaeus of Locris (whose eponymous dialogue *The Timaeus* presents a picture of Pythagorean cosmology)—the question poses itself: Was Plato subtly promoting ethical vegetarianism?

For like Plutarch, who sedulously imitated Plato in his own dialogues, Plato was too fine an artist to browbeat his readers with his vegetarian views; rather, he weaves them into his dialogues with a silken finesse. Nevertheless, there are times when he openly states his vegetarian views, as when he says in *Timaeus* (77a–c, 80d) that a vegetarian diet is divinely sanctioned; or in *Statesman* (271e–272a) when like Hesiod and Empedocles he casts back to a mythical golden age when humans lived in peace and harmony, and subsisted on a plant-based diet.

There is also a touch of golden-age nostalgia in Plato's construction of the ideal city in the *Republic*. In *Republic* II, 372b–e, he makes it plain (through the personna of Socrates) that the ideal city would be an exclusively vegetarian one; in reply Glaucon says, "Socrates, if you were going to provide for a *city of pigs*, what other food than this would you fatten your citizens on?"

Glaucon's phrase for Plato's vegetarian city "a city of pigs" has been taken by Platonic scholars to be an abusive epithet; but there are reasons for doubting that it may be the insult that it at first seems to be. Our society having reduced the pig to pork, bacon and leather (as one meat-packer recently bragged: "We use very part of the pig except the scream!"), tends to hold the pig in low esteem—so much so, that the word "pig" in our culture has become a term of disparagement. On the contrary, in Classical Greece, the pig was associated with the goddess Demeter, who ruled over the fruits of the earth. Moreover, the Greek word for pig "us" was thought to be related to the Greek word for womb "ustera." At the Eleusinian Mysteries, which were performed in honor of Demeter in the town of Eleusis in Attica in early autumn, pigs made of dough were dedicated to Demeter as votive offerings. The Eleusinian Mysteries were the most famous mystery rites in the Greek and Roman world and persisted well into the Christian era. The three Eleusinian laws were: "Honor your parents, sacrifice fruits to the gods, don't harm any animal." The Mysteries celebrated the cycle of agricultural rebirth (from seed to fruit to seed to fruit) via the earth-womb of Demeter as Earth Mother (possibly derived from the two Greek words ge—earth and meter —mother); the Mysteries also celebrated the cycle of human and animal rebirth (from soul to body to soul to body) via the human and animal uterus. So the pig was seen as a symbol of reincarnation, fertility, and spiritual renewal. This links the pig not only with the reincarnative myth of Er at the end of The Republic, but also with the Pythagorean doctrine of metemsomatosis (reincarnation). So when Glaucon calls Plato's ideal city "a city of pigs," he was invoking Demeter as the Great Goddess, as well as the ethical vegetarianism of Pythagoras—hardly an insult!

Did Plato Eat Unfired Foods?

Although Plato recommends some cooked dishes for the ideal state, kallipolis, in Republic II, it would appear that he himself ate a great many unfired foods. We have it on the authority of Diogenes Laertius that it was not uncommon for Pythagoras and the Pythagoreans to eat their fruits and vegetables apura (unfired): "For this is the Pythagoras who forbade the killing much less the eating of animals who share with us the right of having a soul. This was his pretext for eating vegetarian fare, but the real reason that he prohibited the eating of our fellow ensouled beings was that he wanted to accustom people to a contented life so that they should eat unfired (apura) food and drink plain water. Hence, they would have sharp minds and healthy bodies." (Diogenes Laertius, VIII, 12-14, italics mine, translation mine).

Another reason why Pythagoras may have encouraged his disciples (among whom Plato and Socrates would have been the most prominent) to eat unfired fruits and vegetables is that he may have wanted further to dramatize the difference between ieara or the barbecued flesh of animals that was sacrificed to the gods on a fiery altar and shared out among the worshippers, and the raw, uncooked apura foods that formed the sustenance of ethical vegetarians.

Furthermore, it's likely that Plato's fellow Athenians ate much of their fruits and vegetables in their raw state anyway. Cooking in antiquity was an arduous process, it would have been much more expedient to munch on some fresh apples, some dried figs, and some fresh olives and call it *deipnon* (dinner), or *ariston* (lunch)—which is evidently what Plato often did. As it happens, we have an eyewitness to Plato's dining habits, namely Diogenes the cynic who once wished that Demeter (goddess of foodstuffs and hunger), could be as easily appeased as Aphrodite (goddess of love and lust)—merely by rubbing one's tummy.

Olives and Figs

According to Diogenes Laertius' Life of Diogenes the Cynic—a passage from which I've translated below—Plato sustained himself largely on a diet of fresh olives and figs:

"And when Diogenes observed Plato at a sumptuous banquet, grasping olives and stuffing them into his mouth, he said to Plato, 'Why did you the philosopher who sailed to Sicily for the sake of the rich dishes there (at the court of Dionysos I)—why are you not now enjoying these same splendid dishes when they have been laid before you?' And Plato said, 'By the gods Diogenes, when I was there, I lived on olives and such like (simple) fare.' Said Diogenes, 'Why then was it necessary for you to travel to Syracuse? Didn't Attica then bear delicious olives?'"

At another time Diogenes was eating dried figs, when he met up with Plato and said, "It's possible to share the figs." After Plato took the figs and devoured them, Diogenes said, "I said to share them not to eat them all up." (Diogenes Laertius, VI, 25).

Serves two

    1 lb. fresh Greek olives
    1 lb. dried figs, prefer Black Mission
    1 loaf Barley Bread (see Pythagoras's Barley Bread)

Serve the olives as a first course, then follow them with a course of dried figs. Slice the bread and serve it on the side.

Humus

1 cup chickpeas (soaked for 48 hours)
2 tablespoons finely chopped garlic
2 tablespoons chopped parsley
Juice of one lemon
½ cup tahini mixed with ⅓ cup water
2 tablespoons chopped dill
2 scallions, chopped
1 tablespoon toasted sesame seeds
Salt and pepper to taste
12 lettuce leaves

Let the chickpeas soak for 48 hours. Drain the chickpeas and mash them with a fork. (The peas will be soft—no cooking is required). Add the remaining ingredients, except the lettuce, and mix them together thoroughly. Line edge of each lettuce leaf with humus and roll it into a scroll.

Serves four.

Note: This is an unfired (*apura*) recipe.

Every town and city throughout Greece has its own version of this recipe, as it did in Plato's time, which is why I believe that he was referring to humus in *Republic* (372d) when through his dragoman Socrates, he discusses the sort of vegetarian dishes that would be served in the ideal state: "And we shall provide choice morsels for them—figs, chickpeas and beans. . . ."

Stewed Onions in Chick-Pea Sauce

2 tablespoons olive oil
2 cups peeled baby onions
4 large white onions, chopped
2 tablespoons whole wheat flour
½ cup chick-pea sauce
A dash of mustard

For the Chick-Pea Sauce

3 spring onions, chopped
1 tablespoon olive oil
2 tablespoons whole wheat flour
2 tablespoons fermented chick-pea paste, or chick-pea miso
1 cup water or vegetable broth

In a heavy skillet, sauté the onions in the olive oil until they turn golden. Next add two tablespoons of flour, the salt and pepper. When the whole baby onions, and the chopped onions are done, add a dash of mustard. Mix thoroughly and add the chick-pea sauce. Mix again and serve with coarse-grained barley bread.

While the onions are stewing, sauté the three spring onions in a saucepan. When they turn transparent, add two tablespoons of whole wheat flour. Add two tablespoons of chick-pea paste and the vegetable stock. Let simmer until the chick-pea paste has dissolved in the broth. As soon as it thickens into a gravy, remove from flame and mix with the stewed onions.   Serves 4.

This highly aromatic dish can be found in every hamlet and city in the former *Magna Graecia*—Southern Italy, Sicily and Greece. When Plato mentions stewed onions as a dish that will be served in the ideal state, is there any doubt that he was referring to this classic Mediterranean dish? Here is my translation of the relevant passage from *Republic* (372d): "Clearly they will have salt and olives and cheese—not to mention onions and vegetables of the sort that are stewed in the country, which they would stew up together." The Greek word for onion *bolbos* is cognate with the Latin *bulbus*.

JESUS CHRIST

On a crisp spring day in 1947, a Bedouin boy, named Muhammed the Wolf, was tending some goats in the Quamran Valley, hard by the western shore of the Dead Sea. The boy was a member of a party of smugglers, who were conveying the goats and contraband goods to sell on the black market in Bethlehem. One of the goats went astray, and the boy followed it to the mouth of a cave. His curiosity piqued, the boy took a fair-sized rock and shied it into the depths of the cave. When the rock landed, it produced the unexpected sound of pottery breaking into shards. Frightened, the boy ran off to summon a friend. The two of them returned to explore the cave, and found a number of tall, clay jars, with tightly sealed lids. The jars yielded up what appeared at first to be fetid lumps of linen coated with wax. But the linen wrappings concealed priceless treasure—a series of ancient scrolls, any one of which could have made these smugglers rich beyond their dreams. These scrolls, the Dead Sea Scrolls, as they came to be known, would send shock waves through the fusty world of Biblical scholarship, and present to Christian dogma, as one writer put it, "the greatest challenge since Darwin's theory of evolution."[1]

Inscribed on these leather, copper, and parchment scrolls were sacred texts written in a Hebrew script so ancient that at first even eminent Hebraists had trouble identifying it. After a good deal of squabbling, the scrolls found their way to the American School of Oriental Research in Jerusalem, where they were photographed, dated (to the 1st century B.C.), and at length translated by an international team of scholars.

The scholars were astonished to find that although the scrolls antedated the birth of Christ by as much as one hundred years, they contained passages that occur almost verbatim in the New Testament. And many of the utterances attributed to Jesus in the Gospels, appear in the Dead Sea Scrolls as the sayings of the Essene, "Teacher of Righteousness."[2]

Although Biblical scholars have been unable to identify the Teacher of Righteousness, the mention of his "purgations by sprinklings"[3] in the scroll called "The Manual of Discipline," immediately reminded scholars of John the Baptist, who ritually cleansed his followers by bathing them in the River Jordan. John was born and raised in Hebron, which is not far from Quamran. In addition, he is said to have baptized Jesus personally, and to have prepared the way for Jesus' ministry, much as the Teacher of Righteousness is thought to have been the precursor of Jesus.

The scrolls found by the Bedouin smugglers formed part of a vast collection of scrolls in a library at Quamran. The library was established by

51

a Jewish religious sect, who were known as the *Essenes*—a word that derives from the Greek word *osios*, "holy." Scholars have long held that Jesus himself was a member of an Essene sect called the *Nazoreans*. The discovery of the Dead Sea Scrolls has done much to encourage this view. In fact, scholars have suggested that a likely explanation for the New Testament's similarity to the Essene writings, is that Jesus was probably educated as an Essene, and was steeped in their mysteries and doctrines. Thus, it is perfectly natural that the sayings of the Teacher of Righteousness, and other Essene sages should be constantly on his lips.

Based on the foregoing explanation, the story of Jesus' confounding the religious teachers in the Temple with his searching questions—at the age of twelve—does not seem so far-fetched. He may well have been a prodigy. The crude, folksy image of Jesus as an untutored hillbilly preacher from Galilee is no longer valid.

Jesus' image began to change in the mid-19th century, when Ernest Renan, professor of religion at the University of Paris, published his *Life of Jesus*—one of the first biographies of Jesus to treat him as a man rather than an idol. It was Renan who popularized the idea that Jesus might have been an Essene. Other scholars such as Dr. Thomas Walker, in *What Jesus Read* (1925), have theorized that he was a well-read young man, who could probably read, in the original Greek, the words of his contemporary—the great Jewish philosopher, Philo of Alexandria.

Galilee, where Jesus grew to manhood, was by no means the cultural backwater that is commonly described. In fact, during Jesus' lifetime, there was a great deal of intellectual ferment in this region. Galilee was culturally broadened and stimulated by the commercial traffic that flowed from Athens and Alexandria in the west, to Damascus and the other cities of the Decapolis, in the east. The Decapolis consisted of ten Hellenistic cities in Syria, which served as commerical entrepôts between East and West. Alexandria, in particular, that most cosmopolitan of Near Eastern cities, which boasted the largest library in antiquity (with some 500,000 papyrus rolls), produced exotic sects, and luxuriant cross-pollinations of eastern and western religions, like the cults of Isis, Adonis, Serapis, Osiris, and Christianity itself.

The great historian of ideas, Eduard Zeller, held that Essenism had its origin among the Jews in Alexandria during the middle of the 2nd century B.C., and from there it spread throughout Palestine. Incredibly enough, there were actually more Jews living in Alexandria at that time, than there were in Jerusalem. In addition, Greek, not Hebrew, was their first language. Even the Jewish philosopher, Philo of Alexandria, was more at home using Greek than Hebrew. In Alexandria, the Jews came into touch with the neo-Pythagorean philosophy of the Greeks. In imitation of the Pythagorean societies, Jewish societies such as the Essenes and

the Therapeutae were formed. These societies combined Pythagorean customs such as abstinence from animal food, the wearing of white linen
garments, ritual bathing, the sharing of personal property, interest in
numerology, the eating of a sacred meal, and belief in the imperishability
of the soul, with such Jewish practices as circumcision, and the observance of the Jewish Sabbath.

According to the Jewish historian and military commander, Josephus
(he was to the Jews of antiquity what Thucydides was to the Greeks), the
Essenes had a great deal in common with the Pythagoreans. Josephus,
having lived for serveral years as a member of the Essene sect either at
Quamran, or nearby, certainly knew whereof he spoke. He said: "The
Essenes, also, as we call a group of ours, lived the same kind of life as that
which Pythagoras introduced among the Greeks."[4]

Although the evidence for Jesus' vegetarianism is largely circumstan-
tial, it is nonetheless compelling. Even Dr. Hugh Schonfield, writing in
The Passover Plot—probably the most rigorous and demythologized life of
Jesus ever written—asserts that Jesus belonged to a strict vegetarian
branch of the Essenes in northern Judea—the Nazoreans. Schonfield
writes: "The name borne by the earliest followers of Jesus was not Christians, they were called 'Nazoreans' (Nazarenes), and Jesus himself was
known as the 'Nazorean'."[5]

It is important to emphasize that the term "Nazorean" is not the name
of a place. New Testament scholars have searched in vain for evidence
that any such town existed in Galilee during Jesus' lifetime. Josephus,
who was military commander of the Jewish forces in Galilee during the
Jewish uprising against the Romans, makes no mention of a town called
"Nazorean" in his history of that region.

That the Nazoreans were vegetarians is well-attested. Dr. Schonfield
writes:

> Epiphanius, himself of Jewish origin, is a very important authority on
> the early Jewish sects. Some of them were still extant in Northern
> Palestine in his own time, late fourth century. The old Nazoreans, like
> the Samaritans, were opposed to the Judean traditions, holding that the
> southerners had falsified the Law of Moses. They were vegetarians, and
> rejected animal sacrifices, but practised circumcision and observed the
> Jewish Sabbath and festivals.[6]

According to the ancient sources, Jesus' Nazorean-vegetarian way of life
may have been a family legacy. Tradition has it that his brother James was
raised by their mother Miriam (Mary) as a Nazorean-vegetarian:
"Moreover, we learn from the Church Father Eusebius, quoting Neges-
sipus (circa 160 A.D.), that James was 'holy from his mother's womb,
drank no wine, or strong drink, nor ate animal food'."[7]

Another of Jesus' relatives who appears to have been a vegetarian was

John the Baptist. According to Luke, the Baptist was a kinsman of Jesus on Jesus' mother's side. Professor Robert Eisler, in his fascinating book *The Messiah Jesus* (1931), maintains that the Gospel account of John the Baptist's eating locusts was a deliberate distortion. He argues that there was a good deal of rivalry within the Nazorean sect between the follow-ers of Jesus and the followers of the Baptist; each faction was keen to dis-credit the other. Eisler believed that the characterization of the Baptist as an insect-eater was a smear from the pen of a partisan of Jesus, who was anxious lest the Baptist steal his thunder. If so, Jesus' fears were not entirely groundless: to this day there is still a sect of Nazoreans who live on the lower Euphrates and regard Jesus as an inspired teacher, but con-tinue to venerate John the Baptist as the true Messiah. Eisler writes:

> The express statement of Josephus that the Baptist abhorred all animal food, flatly contradicts the Gospel tradition of his feeding on locusts, but agrees perfectly with an almost unanimous tradition of the Greek Church, according to which John restricted himself on principle to a vegetable diet, the *akrides* of the Gospels being explained as "points," or "shoots" of some plants.
> I am myself much more inclined to believe that the word *akrodura* = "tree fruits" was maliciously distorted into *akridas* ("locusts") by the hand of an enemy of the Baptist's sect, desirous of making the Baptist appear as one feeding on vermin, naturally loathsome to Gentile Christians of the educated class.[8]

Similarly, there is a tradition in the New Testament of Jesus' having eaten fish, and performed the miracle of the fishes and the loaves. How is one to square this with the contention that, like his kinsman John the Baptist, or his brother James the Just, Jesus was a Nazorean vegetarian? It has to be remembered that the Gospels were written down more than a century after Jesus' death, and were copied, recopied, and edited, count-less times. The same fallible or malicious scribal hand that could make an insect-eater out of John the Baptist, could just as easily have made a fish-eater or meat-eater out of the Nazorean-vegetarian, Jesus. It was the intention of the writers and editors of the Gospels to make Jesus as widely appealing as possible. Thus, many of his personal tics and eccentricities were toned down. It was probably thought that a vegetarian messiah would be less glamorous, or less palatable to the multitudes in Rome, who were worshippers of Mithras. Indeed, it was touch and go as to whether Christianity or Mithraism would capture the imagination of the Roman people.

Barley and Lentils

1 cup barley
1 cup green lentils
6 cups water
1 teaspoon sea salt
1 tablespoon olive oil
1 teaspoon cumin seed
1 handful fresh dill
1 handful fresh parsley

Wash and pick over the barley and lentils. Then combine them in a heavy pot. Add six cups of water, a teaspoon of sea salt, and the olive oil. Bring the water to a boil. Lower heat, and simmer for an hour to an hour-and-a-half, or until liquid is absorbed. Ten minutes before it is done, add the fresh dill, cumin seed, and parsley. A few dashes of soy sauce are also welcome.

Serves four.

According to the *Encyclopedia Judaica* barley and lentils were staples in Palestine during Jesus' lifetime.

Wheat, Mint and Parsley Salad

Wheat salad was popular in the Palestine of Jesus' time, as it was throughout the ancient Near East. It is no less popular in the Middle East today. As with Barley and Lentils, it is a dish that, as a vegetarian, Jesus would customarily have eaten.

> 1 cup large grain bulgur (cracked wheat)
> 1 qt. water
> 1 cup finely chopped scallions
> 1 cup chopped parsley
> ½ cup finely chopped mint
> ½ cup lemon juice
> ¾ cup olive oil
> Black olives
> Salt and pepper to taste
> Lettuce

Soak the bulgur in a bowl of water for at least half-an-hour. As soon as the grains have softened, remove them from the water: drain them and press them with a towel to expel all the water. Combine the bulgur with all the remaining ingredients, save the olives and lettuce, and toss. Serve on a bed of crisp, dry lettuce. Top with olives. To partake of this salad in true Near Eastern fashion, scoop up dollops of the salad with lettuce leaves.

Serves four.

Essene Sprouted Bread

> 1½ cups wheat berries
> 2 cups water

Soak the wheatberries overnight in a bowl with enough water to cover the berries. Then drain in a colander. Wrap the berries in a tea towel made of cheese cloth or muslin. Store them in a cool, dark place to facilitate germination. After three days, hundreds of whiskery shoots will be poking through the holes in the cheesecloth. The berries have started to sprout! Remove the sprouted berries from the cloth and rinse them thoroughly. Don't bother to dry them, but place them into a blender with the water still clinging to the sprouts. Purée them for about two minutes. This should yield a mushy dough. Add just a bit more water to give the dough a pasty consistency. Remove from the blender and knead by hand for about ten minutes until the ball of dough gets softer. (Before kneading it is a good idea to coat one's hands with oil to keep them from getting gummed up with dough). Hand-shape the dough into a round loaf and place on an oiled baking sheet. Preheat the oven to 350°, and bake for about an hour or until the loaf is baked through and browned on top.

Serves 4.

According to Biblical scholars such as Schonfield and Renan *inter alia,* it is likely that Jesus Christ was an Essene. It is well-attested that the Essenes were devout vegetarians. Their chief article of diet was a loaf of bread made from sprouted wheat. In fact there is a bakery in Canada called "Lifestream" that does a thriving business in Essene breads, whose recipe, they proclaim on the back of the package, is taken from *The Essene Gospel of Peace*—which purports to be a 3rd century A.D. Aramaic manuscript from secret Vatican archives. In this "gospel," which portrays Christ as an Essene and a strict vegetarian, Christ instructs his followers thus: " 'But eat nothing to which only the fire of death gives savor, for such is of Satan.' "

" 'How should we cook our daily bread without fire, Master?' asked some with great astonishment."

" 'Let the angels of God prepare your bread. Moisten your wheat that the angel of water may enter it. Then set it in the air, that the angel of air also may embrace it. And leave it from morning to evening beneath the sun, that the angel of sunshine may descend upon it. And the blessing of the three angels will soon make the germ of life to sprout in your wheat. Then crush your grain, and make thin wafers, as did your forefathers when they departed out of Egypt, the house of bondage.' " (*The Essene Gospel of Peace,* trans. Edmond Bordeaux Szekely (San Diego Academy Books, 1976), p. 50)

PLUTARCH

It would be hard to think of a literary genre that Plutarch's writings have not touched. His influence on Western literature has probably been greater than that of any other writer in antiquity. Plutarch's *Lives* provided Shakespeare with the characters and incidents for some of his most stirring plays—*Coriolanus, Julius Caesar,* and *Antony and Cleopatra;* and the tragic grandeur of Plutarch's noble Greeks and Romans inspired Shakespeare's conception of the tragic hero.

On the continent, Plutarch's works created a literary sensation when they were first translated from Greek into French by Jacques Aymot in the middle of the 16th century. That Rabelais knew Plutarch intimately is evidenced by the countless quotations from the *Lives* and *Moralia* that are scattered through his works like raisins in a fruitcake. But it was through the *Essays* of Montaigne that Plutarch's ideas entered the mainstream of European culture. Through Montaigne, Plutarch's notion of the heroically moral man gave rise to the humanist ideal of the European Renaissance.

In France right up to the time of the French Revolution, Plutarch's works enjoyed a tremendous vogue. All of Paris, it seemed, on the eve of the Revolution, were perusing their Plutarch. It was thought that his thrilling accounts of the bloody overthrow of Greek and Roman tyrants had enflamed the Parisian Revolutionary Mob. For this reason he fell out of favor with the European Aristocracy after the Revolution. To be fair, these recriminations were not without foundation in fact. Charlotte Corday, the assassin of Jean Marat, was brought up on Plutarch, and she is known to have read the *Lives* on the night before she stabbed Marat as he lay reading (Plutarch no doubt) in his bathtub.

Another Frenchman and another case in point was J. J. Rousseau, that firebrand of the Revolution, who had devoured the *Lives* and memorized them entire by the time he reached the age of eight. Plutarch's *Lives,* Rousseau claimed, had fired him with the ambition to introduce into France the republican reforms of the great Hellenic lawgiver, Lycurgus, and the great Roman lawgiver, Numa (who by the way was a Pythagorean vegetarian). Doubtless Rousseau's vegetarian proclivities—in his book *Emile* he urged the raising of all children as vegetarians—derive from Plutarch.

In America, Ralph Waldo Emerson, whose best friends were the devout vegetarian Bronson Alcott, and the inconstant vegetarian, Henry David Thoreau (Emerson was also a vegetarian manqué), was a perfervid admirer of Plutarch. For the American edition of Plutarch's *Moralia,* Emerson wrote a lengthy introduction that showed he was one of Plutarch's deepest students.

In England during the 19th century, Percy Shelley translated Plutarch's essays on vegetarianism into exquisite English prose. It has been conjectured that Plutarch's vegetarian writings may have been a factor in Shelley's converting to vegetarianism in 1811 right after he was sent down from Oxford.

Tolstoy, who taught himself to read ancient Greek as an intellectual exercise after he had written Anna Karenina, was able to read Plutarch in the original Greek. There is no doubt that Plutarch's vegetarian essays made an impact on Tolstoy's thinking. There are reverberations of Plutarch's essay "On the Eating of Animal Flesh" in Tolstoy's own savage invective against flesh-eating, "The First Step."

Plutarch's works fall into two distinct categories—the *Moralia* and the *Lives*. The *Lives*, of which some sixty-three survive, are biographical portraits of the great historical figures of antiquity, beginning with the legendary figure of Theseus, and ending with the Roman consul, Marc Antony. On the other hand, the *Moralia* (*Ethika* in Greek) are a collection of essays, dialogues, and miscellaneous writings. As Plutarch translator, Ian Scott-Kilvert succinctly put it: "The *Moralia* celebrate the thought of the past, as the *Lives* celebrate its action."[1]

Plutarch was born in the year 46 A.D. into an ancient Theban family. His father, Aristobolus, was himself a biographer and philosopher of some note. Plutarch's birthplace, from which he seldom strayed as an adult, was Chaeronea—a small town in the vast Boeotian Plain of Greece, which the Greeks called "the War-God Ares' dancing place."[2] The Boeotian Plain is a region not unlike Rajasthan in northwestern India, where military traditions were strong, where fierce warriors like the Sacred Band were bred, and where battlefields seem to have been as commonly harvested as cornfields. Plutarch's admiration for the martial spirit of the personalities whom he writes about in the *Lives*, reminds one of a rather juicy paradox—it is very often the men who are born into military castes such as Buddha, Mahavira, Tolstoy, and Henry Salt who make the fiercest vegetarians and pacifists.

The son of a wealthy landowner and gentleman farmer, Plutarch received an education befitting his rank (which by Greek standards was upper-class). When Nero visited Greece in 66 A.D., to preside over the festivals, Plutarch was studying mathematics and philosophy under Ammonius at the Academy in Athens. The Academy, which was the forerunner of the modern university, had been founded by Plato almost five hundred years earlier, and was modeled on the school that Pythagoras had started at Croton in the 5th century B.C. So infused is Plato's philosophy with that of Pythagoras that it's a little hard to tell where one leaves off and the other begins. Ammonius, Plutarch's teacher, was both a Platonist and a Pythagorean. As might be expected, he was also a thoroughgoing vegetarian. Whether Plutarch inherited his vegetarianism from his parents, or whether he absorbed it along with other Pythagorean teachings from Ammonius, is difficult to say. It is known, however, that after studying with Ammonius, Plutarch went on to become one of the first sparks in the revival of Pythagorean philosophy that culminated in the writings of such late Empire neoplatonists as Plotinus, Porphyry, Iamblichus and the emperor Julian.

For all his sophistication and urbanity, Plutarch was at heart a country-man who chose to remain in the small town of Chaeronea rather than join the "brain drain" of talented young Greeks who were drawn by the lure of opportunity and high salaries to fill administrative posts in the Roman government. Before settling down to manage his estates, Plutarch took the equivalent of the 18th century European Grand Tour without which no young aristocrat's education was complete. He visited Rome, Alexandria, and parts of Asia Minor, where he may have come into touch with prominent Pythagoreans or their vegetarian counterparts in Alexandria and the East—the Essenes and the Therapeutae.

Rather than live amid the social and intellectual sophisticates at Athens or Rome, Plutarch chose to live in the rural community of Chaeronea. In doing so, he calls to mind another vegetarian immortal—Leo Tolstoy—who turned his back on the glittering society of Tsarist Moscow to run his estate, and write his epic historical novels. Like Tolstoy, who set up an experimental school on his estate to teach the local children, Plutarch started a small academy at Chaeronea, which he ran along the lines of the Platonic Academy in Athens. When he was not teaching, farming his estates, or looking after his wife and five children (also like Tolstoy), he would shut himself up in his study to do the writing and research for his essays and biographies. An indefatigable collector—of curious facts, gossipy tidbits, antiquarian lore, and above all, books—Plutarch is known to have amassed one of the largest private libraries in antiquity—which is no mean feat considering that Chaeronea was something of a cultural backwater.

Despite its small size and its bucolic setting, Chaeronea was admirably situated for such an incurable antiquarian as Plutarch. The area surrounding Chaeronea was dotted with historical sites. Sparse though the human population of this area might have been, it was teeming with the heroic figures of myth, legend and history. Legend has it that at Chaeronea a party of Amazons lay buried (after having fought to the death with a band of local male chauvinists). Twenty miles to the east of the town proper stood the temple of Apollo at Delphi, which was famous throughout the ancient world for the prophetic powers of its Pythian priestess (and where, from the nineties A.D., Plutarch held a lifelong position in the priesthood.) A few miles to the west there rose the towering crags of Mount Parnassus, which was sacred to Apollo and his muses. To the north (about twenty-five miles) was the famous pass at Thermopylae, where in 480 B.C. a handful of Spartans held off the entire Persian army for about three-quarters of an hour before dying to a man. Thebes, not far to the south, was the birthplace of Oedipus—he of the swollen foot, the strange bedfellows, and the Freudian complex. South of Thebes lay Athens, where Plutarch had been educated at the Academy, and which was still in Roman times the cultural center of the ancient world. It isn't hard to see how Plutarch, having grown up in a place that was so redolent of the great men and events of the past should have been inspired to take up his pen and write about them.

In addition to being regarded as the first biographer worthy of the name, Plutarch had another literary first to his credit that deserves to be better known. He was the first author to write an essay that denounced the eating of animal flesh, and urged the adoption of a vegetarian diet. Here is an excerpt from his essay "On the Eating of Flesh," which I have translated from the Greek.

> But how can you ask for what reason Pythagoras abstained from eating animal flesh? I wonder by what misfortune and by what state of mind, and by what rationale the first man touched gore to his mouth, and pressed to his lips the flesh of dead creatures, and dished up at his table the stale corpses of dead animals, and called 'food' and 'nourishment' the parts that only a short time before had bellowed, uttered sounds, moved, and looked? How could his eyes bear the slaughter when the throats of animals were being slit, their skins flayed, and their legs torn from their bodies? How did his sense of smell bear the stench? How did the defilement not turn away his taste, which touched the sores of others and sucked the juices and the putrefying blood from mortal wounds?[3]

To be sure, Pythagoras and Buddha had preached vegetarianism back in the 6th century B.C., as had Pythagoras's pupil, Empedokles of Akragas (who even wrote a poem about vegetarianism called "The Purifications"). But both the Buddha's and Pythagoras's teachings were transmitted orally, from master to pupil; and were never written down. Empedokles's poem "The Purifications" was just that—a poem, and not a diatribe against meat-eating such as we find in Plutarch.

Some people have accused Plutarch of being a lukewarm vegetarian. But anyone who doubts the intensity of his feeling for animals or the strength of his devotion to Pythagorean principles, has only to read such essays as "On the Eating of Animal Flesh," "Whether Land or Sea Animals Are Cleverer," and "Beasts Are Rational," to realize that these writings are far too deeply felt for vegetarianism to have been anything but central to Plutarch's vision as a thinker.

Although Plutarch does not foist his vegetarian views upon the reader, it is clear that the topic was never far from his mind. Even in essays that are concerned with other subjects, he contrives to sneak in references to vegetarianism. Sometimes these references are so subtle as almost to escape notice. Often they may consist in nothing more than his identifying the character in a dialogue as a Pythagorean. For instance, the mysterious stranger in Plutarch's essay "Socrates's Sign" turns out to be a Pythagorean "holy man." In Plutarch's scientific essay on the moon, which he cast in the form of a dialogue, one of the principle speakers is Lucius, a Pythagorean, about whose vegetarian scruples he writes in another dialogue. Here is my translation from Plutarch's Greek of the passage from one of his *Table Talk* dialogues in which he introduces Lucius, the Pythagorean:

> Sulla the Carthaginian, on my arrival in Rome after a long absence, announced a 'welcome dinner,' as the Romans call it, and invited a few other companions of mine among whom was a certain pupil of Moderatus, the Pythagorean, named Lucius, who was originally from Etruria. When he saw that my friend Philinus was abstaining from animal flesh, he was naturally led into a discussion about the teachings of Pythagoras.[4]

Plutarch's collection of dialogues called *The Symposiacs*, or *Table Talk* are modeled after Plato's *Symposium*, which Plato wrote in 385 B.C. Widely imitated by Xenephon, Athenaeus, and countless other classical writers, including Plutarch, *The Symposium* was Plato's most popular and entertaining dialogue. In a typical Platonic or Plutarchian symposium, which means literally "a drinking party," a group made up of statesmen, artists and philosophers would gather to discuss knotty issues over dinner and wine. In the relaxed atmosphere of the dining room, with their tongues loosened by wine and fine food, the symposium's speakers talked more freely than did the characters in a conventional Platonic dialogue.

Unlike Plato, who kept himself out of his dialogues, Plutarch is a little like certain Hollywood movie directors of the 1940s, who could not resist appearing in their own films, if only in a bit part. Plutarch, however, cast himself as a full-blown character in so many of his own dialogues that it provokes the moviegoer's eternal question—how much of the real-life Plutarch is there in the Plutarch of the dialogues?

While Plutarch played a leading role in the *Table Talk* dialogues, he usually kept silent during discussions about vegetarianism, or the mistreatment of animals, although these were matters of obvious concern to him. Instead, he used the device of trotting out his Pythagorean friend, Philinus, who pops up from time to time to express the Pythagorean (i.e. the vegetarian) view of things. It is not hard to see why Plutarch might wish to have Philinus speak for him: Philinus has some pretty harsh things to say about meat-eating and the "sport" of hunting. Were Plutarch himself to have indulged in such special pleading, instead of his dragoman Philinus, it would have been bad form, socially as well as rhetorically.

There are times, however, when he cannot contain himself, and he gives way to an outburst of indignation against flesh-eating. Here is an excerpt from one of his *Table Talk* tirades against fishing and fish-eating, which I have translated from Plutarch's Greek:

> But the angling and the casting of nets for all kinds of fish is clearly an act of gluttony and greediness for fish; it is also a roiling of the sea waters and a plumbing of their depths for no good reason. Whence Homer portrayed not only the Hellenes as abstaining from eating fish, although their camp was on the shore of the Hellespont, but he also never set a sea-fish meal before the pleasure-loving Phaecians, or the debauched suitors even though both groups were island dwellers. The companions of Odysseus, while sailing on such a long sea-voyage, never let down a hook into the waters, nor a fish trap, nor a fishing net, so long as they had barley bread.
>
> Whence not only among the Egyptians and the Syrians, but also among the Hellenes there was an element of sanctity in their abstinence for the eating of fish. With the aid of justice, I think we should reject with abhorrence the wasteful luxury of fish-eating.[5]

Asparagus with Tahini

2½ pounds asparagus (large bunch)
3 tablespoons olive oil
3 cloves garlic, minced
1 medium onion, chopped
½ cup sesame tahini
1 cup filtered water
Sea salt
2 tablespoons *shoyu* (opt.)
3 tablespoons *miso* paste (opt.)

Cut off the tough, woody ends of the asparagus and discard. Scrub the stalks and tips. Divide the stalks into three small bundles and fasten each tightly with a string. Stand the bundles upright in a tall pot filled with an inch of water. Cover and steam gently for about four minutes or until the spears are tender. Remove from flame and set aside.

In a large skillet, heat three tablespoons of olive oil and add the minced garlic and onions. Cook until the onions turn golden. Turn off flame, then add the sesame tahini and one cup of water. Do not cook. Stir briskly until the tahini and water are well blended. To give the sauce more authority, you might wish at this point to add three tablespoons of *miso* paste. This of course is optional, as (like *shoyu*) it would not have been available to Plutarch.

Place the asparagus spears into a serving dish. Pour the sesame sauce over the spears and serve immediately.

Serves four.

Note: This is a high-enzyme, live food recipe.

Plutarch refers to asparagus in several places in his writings. For instance, in his "Table Talk," IV, 1, 663, in the *Moralia,* Plutarch considers whether he should have asparagus or some other dish for his supper. And in his life of Julius Caesar, Plutarch mentions that Caesar once dined on asparagus dressed with myrrh. I have translated this passage from Plutarch's Greek "Of Caesar's compliancy concerning his diet, the following incident is offered as proof, when the host who was treating him to dinner in Mediolanum (Milan), Valerius Leo, dished up asparagus dressed with myrrh instead of with olive oil, Caesar ate it without a fuss, but he lashed out at his friends who could not hide their dislike: 'Surely,' said he, 'it is enough for them not to eat; but for them to disparage the host's lack of urbanity, is itself rude and boorish.' " (Plutarch, *Caesar,* 17).

According to my Liddel and Scott (unabridged), the Greek word "muron" means perfumed oil, or oil scented with myrrh. In other words Valerius Leo may have used olive oil to dress the asparagus, but he committed the unpardonable *faux pas* of tarting it up with myrrh or some such perfume. Had he rather used the oil from another plant from the same provenance as myrrh (North Africa and the Near East)—sesame oil—Caesar's friends might well have preferred its nutty flavor to olive oil. On the other hand, had Valerius Leo dressed the asparagus in sauce made from sesame seed called "tahini," which was wildly popular in antiquity—in fact one of the most popular spreads for bread in ancient Rome was a paste made from ground sesame and cumin seed—Caesar's friends might have praised their host instead of decrying his lack of breeding. In the above recipe, I have tried to make good Valerius's lapse of taste by bringing together one of ancient Rome's most popular vegetables—asparagus, with one of its most popular sauces—sesame tahini.

Moreover, for those who would like to taste an asparagus dish created by Plutarch's contemporary, M. Gavius Apicius, I have translated his recipe for *Aliter Patina De Asparagis* ("A Different Dish of Asparagus"). It should be noted that although Apicius wrote down his recipes in the first century A.D., they did not take their present form until the late fourth century A.D. It is entirely possible that Plutarch, who was one of antiquity's great bibliophiles, may have had a volume of Apicius's first century A.D. writings in his library with this very recipe in it.

A Different Dish of Asparagus

(From *De Re Coquinaria*, 1st–5th century A.D., Apicius, Liber IV.)

Adicies in mortario asparagorum praescisuras quae proiciuntur. . . . Toss into a mortar some asparagus tips, which are usually thrown away; pound them, pour wine over them, and strain them through a colander. Grind together pepper, lovage, green coriander, savory, onion, wine, relish, and olive oil. Transfer this mixture with the asparagus into a greased frying pan, and, if you like break eggs over it when it is on the fire, that it may bind the ingredients together. Sprinkle ground pepper over the asparagus, and serve it forth.

Sautéed Soy-Cheese on Toast

1 lb. tofu, firm style
1 large Spanish onion
1 cup vegetable soup stock
Oil for frying
Sea Salt
Toasted whole-grain bread slices
Ground-roasted sesame seeds
Dried figs

Press the tofu by placing it under a cutting board weighted with a five lb. weight such as a heavy skillet and let stand for twenty minutes. When the excess water has been expelled from the tofu, cut it into one-half inch slices. Next place the tofu slices in a mixing bowl and pour in a cup of concentrated vegetable soup stock (obtained from a vegetable bouillon cube, or a dry soup mix such as Nutra-Soup). Let the tofu slices marinate in the soup stock for at least one-half hour.

Meanwhile, chop the Spanish onion into a fine dice, and fry in a heavy skillet. When the onions turn golden, remove them from the skillet with a slotted spoon and let drain on absorbent paper.

Toast the whole-grain bread slices. Then spread each slice with a layer of fried onions and top with the sautéed tofu slices. Serve open-face and sprinkle tofu slices with sea salt and ground-roasted sesame seeds. Serve with dried figs.

Serves four.

Note: In place of milk curds or cheese, which was served at Philo's party (see below), I have substituted bean curd on toast. Although an anachronism here, tofu can be used as a delicious mock cheese that would have been much to Plutarch's taste (moral as well as gustatory).

This recipe was inspired by a dialogue in Plutarch's "Symposiacs" in which Plutarch, his Pythagorean friend Philinus, and Philinus's Pythagorean pupil attend a dinner party given by a physician named Philo. Like contemporary physicians, Philo is conspicuously wealthy, and a big meat-eater. Evidently most of his guests were non-vegetarian too, because Philo grossly underestimates the number of Pythagoreans at his party and neglects to lay in a sufficient supply of vegetarian food for Plutarch and his two vegetarian friends. The best he can muster is some bread and cheese, with some figs. When Plutarch gently reproaches him for failing to consider the needs of his vegetarian guests, he provokes the following exchange, which I have translated from Plutarch's Greek (Moralia, "Table Talk," IV, 1, 660): "This," I [Plutarch] observed, "is what happens to those providing sumptuous and extravagant food, they are given to being careless and are in need of the necessities and the staples of diet." "Precisely," said Philo. "I had forgotten that Philinus was raising among us a young Zoroaster, who they say passed his entire life without taking any other food except milk. But it is likely that the original Zoroaster became a vegetarian after a change of his earlier diet. On the other hand, our young vegetarian unlike Achilles was nourished by his Cheiron straight from birth on bloodless and non-animal food. Doesn't he furnish the classic example of a person's feeding on air and dew just as the cicadas do?"

For those who would like to taste this dish as it was prepared in the first century A.D., during Plutarch's lifetime, simply buy a loaf of whole-grain bread and some goat cheese. Toast the bread and slice the cheese into thin slices. Place the cheese slices upon the toasted bread and serve with figs.

For those who would prefer to taste a slightly more complicated combination of bread and cheese, here is a recipe created by Plutarch's contemporary M. Gavius Apicius (27 B.C.—37 A.D.), who is credited with having written the first western cookbook De Re Coquinaria (On Cookery). (Incidentally, the worlds first cookbook is the Sanskrit book Vasavarayeyam, which is a treatise on vegetarian cookery). Although Apicius wrote down his recipes sometime during the reign of Tiberius, when Apicius was a famous gastrophile and cooking teacher, his recipes were not collected and edited into their final form until they were transcribed by an anonymous Roman into the Latin of the late fourth century A.D. It is entirely possible that Plutarch, who was one of the keenest book collectors in antiquity, may have had a volume of Apicius's first century A.D. writings in his library with this very recipe in it (which I have translated from the Latin).

Cheese Salad Sandwich

(From *De Re Coquinaria*, 1st–5th century A.D., Apicius, Liber IV.)

Panem Alexandrinum excavabis i posca macerabis. . . .
Hollow out a loaf of Alexandrian bread, and soak [the de-crusted pieces] in water laced with vinegar. Mix together in a mortar: pepper, honey, mint, garlic, green coriander, and cow's milk cheese seasoned with salt, water, and oil. [Spread the cheese salad over the pieces of bread.] Chill on snow [refrigerate], and serve.

Serves 4.

(Apicius uses "Alexandrian" as a synonym for "costliest," "of the finest quality," since the Romans imported their most opulent spices from the Egyptian port of Alexandria.)

LEONARDO DA VINCI

Leonardo da Vinci was born in the sleepy hamlet of Vinci, which is about a day's journey by mule-cart from Florence, on April 15, 1452. He was the product of an illicit union between a Florentine lawyer, Ser Piero da Vinci, and his mother, Caterina, who is presumed to have been of noble blood. There was not the stigma attached to being illegitimate in Leonardo's time that there has long been in ours. Some of the most powerful rulers in Renaissance Italy were bastards (like Cesare Borgia, the natural son of a Pope), and were proud of it. Illegitimacy was often regarded as a mark of divine favor.

However, being illegitimate did have its drawbacks: because Leonardo wasn't well-born, his father decided not to pay for him to receive an academic education, and instead sent him to a sort of vocational school. If he had been well-born, his father would probably have sent him to a preparatory school, where he would have been immersed in the study of Greek and Latin, and thence to a university for more of the same. The vocational school that he attended was actually an art studio operated by one of the most accomplished Florentine masters of Leonardo's time, Verrocchio. There, the young Leonardo learned how to draw, paint, sculpt, and cast metal to such good effect that by the time he was in his early teens, he had already outstripped his master and had begun to collaborate with him on paintings.

Some authorities sniffishly deride Leonardo's lack of a classical education* on the grounds that the greatest scholarly works were only just beginning to be translated from Greek and Latin into the vernacular Italian that Leonardo understood. On the other hand, there are many who feel that his lack of a classical education may have been a blessing in disguise; and had he been subjected to the frigid dogmatism of scholastic learning, his genius might have been nipped in the bud.

Prior to Leonardo, the artist had been regarded as a technician, a craftsman, who was on the same footing socially as a goldsmith, or cabinetmaker. His chief patron and source of livelihood was the church, which set him to work decorating cathedrals and lesser religious edifices. But as the church's power and influence began to wane, warrior aristocrats (gorged with plunder), began to vie for the artist's services.

Leonardo was one of the first beneficiaries of this secularization of the arts. As Arnold Hauser notes:

---

*Later, in Milan, as a middle-aged man, he taught himself to read Latin with great fluency, but he never aspired to learn Greek.

The gradual ascent of the artist is mirrored most clearly of all in the career of Leonardo, who is no doubt esteemed in Florence, but still not particularly busy there, who then becomes the pampered court painter of Ludovico Moro, and Cesare Borgia's first military engineer, whilst he ends his life as the favorite and intimate friend of the French King. The fundamental change occurs at the beginning of the Cinquecento. From then onwards the famous masters are no longer the protégés of patrons, but great lords themselves.[1]

But Leonardo never used his position for financial or social self-aggrandizement. Had he contented himself with being a "pampered court painter," he could have become as exalted in social rank as Titian, and as rich in golden ducats as Raphael. Instead, he was as scornful of riches as Pythagoras. He disdained to follow his father's example of becoming a lawyer, and marrying a woman with an immense dowry. What was most precious to Leonardo were not the golden ducats that were his father's ruling passion, but rather time. The free time that he needed in order to paint as he liked, and to carry out his multifarious experiments. In performing his experiments, he ranged widely, ignoring the boundaries between disciplines. He investigated the behavior of flowing water; studied optics, astronomy, aeronautics, hydraulics, gastronomy, anatomy, and ballistics. From his aeronautical researches, he concluded that bats were more airworthy than birds, so he set about fashioning a flying costume to test his theory. Outfitted with huge, batlike wings, he actually had the temerity to fly from a high rooftop into the courtyard at the southeast corner of Milan's Corte Vecchia. Luckily, he survived the attempt without serious mishap. Unfortunately, he did not remain airborne long enough to have beaten the Wright brothers at Kittyhawk. Nonetheless, science historian, George Sarton, regards Leonardo as one of the pioneers of aviation.

Critics such as Kenneth Clark have lamented the fact that Leonardo wasted precious time on pet projects and hobbyhorses that he might better have spent in painting. All his experiments, all the entries in his *Notebooks* (fascinating as they are), cannot be weighed against the *Gioconda* smile. But in taking up so many different studies—anatomy, hydraulics, aeronautics, engineering, mathematics—one feels that he wasn't neglecting his painting so much as he was trying to increase his understanding, so that he could perfect his artistic technique and re-create nature as it had never been re-created before. It is as though he were trying to master every conceivable branch of knowledge to be able to see through nature and penetrate her mysteries so that he could paint the perfect picture— the masterpiece that would endure for all time. With the *Gioconda* it may well be that he did.

Leonardo's absorption in mathematics resulted from his attempts to achieve mathematical precision in measuring the proportions and perspectives in his paintings. His interest in comparative anatomy—which led him to entertain theories about gerontology and evolution centuries before they would be scientifically confirmed—grew out of his passion for accuracy in drawing human and equine anatomy. His love of mountains —which led him to become Europe's first explorer of mountains—sprang from the same urge for perfection: in this case his desire to make accurate drawings of, as it were, the earth's anatomy. It may seem incredible that Leonardo, in the 15th century, should have been the first European to explore the high Alps; but it has to be remembered that until the Romantic movement in the early 19th century, Europeans (abetted by the church) regarded mountains with dread and superstition. They imagined them to be tumors, or wens of the earth that were swarming with demons, gnomes, and goblins. Leonardo, in his reverence for mountains, had more in common with the ancient Greeks (who peopled their mountains with gods and goddesses), and with the Buddhists of China and Japan (who have traditionally associated mountains with divinity, and have always built their most hallowed shrines and temples atop them). In a way, the mountains looming in the background of Leonardo's paintings throw light on his vegetarianism, for it seems fitting that Europe's first mountaineer should also have been one of its first vegetarians. The same independence of mind that bade defiance to the conventional wisdom that mountains are the earth's tumors, also bade defiance to the conventional wisdom that man is innately carnivorous.

Science historian Giorgio de Santillana suggests that Leonardo may have taken his vegetarianism from Ovid, whose *Metamorphosis* gives an account of Pythagoras's life. During the Renaissance, and the revival of classical learning for which it is noted, the neo-Pythagorean writings of such ancient thinkers as Empedocles, Ovid, Plutarch, Prophyry, and Plotinus, among others, were being translated into the vernacular. Their ideas about vegetarianism were becoming the talk of artists and intellectuals in young Leonardo's circle. In fact, one of Leonardo's closest friends from his student days was a vegetarian—alchemist and astrologer, Tomasso Masini, nicknamed Zoroastro. The fact is, he was an even stricter vegetarian than Leonardo, having carried his vegetarianism to the point of refusing to wear articles of clothing made of leather, wool, or fur (which was no mean feat in the 15th century, without the luxury of synthetic substitutes). During Leonardo's formative years, Zoroastro was his closest friend. It seems far likelier that Zoroastro, rather than Ovid, was responsible for setting Leonardo on the vegetarian path. Here is Robert Payne's fascinating description of Zoroastro from his biography *Leonardo:*

> Zoroastro was a colorful figure, sharp-featured, wild-eyed, wearing a magnificent black beard which spread chaotically over his chest. Leonardo designed a dress for him which appeared to be made out of berries, and he was therefore nicknamed "Il Gallozolo," the Berry Man. In Milan he was given another nickname—"L'Indovino," the

Soothsayer. He delighted in all magical things. Alchemy, chiromancy, astrology, physiognomy, and the casting of spells gave him pleasure. He was a great collector of dead men's bones, the ropes with which men had been hanged, the eyes of lynxes, the saliva of mad dogs, crucibles for the distillation of herbs, metals and stones, and herbs and seeds collected during different phases of the moon. He collected relics, and claimed that he possessed the collarbone of King Solomon, together with some swords and daggers used to commit murder and therefore possessed of phenomenal powers. He was a charlatan of sorts but he was also a good-hearted person, an excellent raconteur, and a man of principles. Some of those principles would naturally commend themselves to Leonardo, for Scipione Ammirato tells us that out of respect for created things "he refused to kill·a flea for anything in the world." Like Leonardo, he was a vegetarian; he dressed in linen to avoid having anything on his body that came from animals. Hence he wore no furs in winter, and possessed no leather belts or leather shoes.[2]

In his book-length study of the Mona Lisa, Roy McMullen refers to Leonardo as the "new Pythagoras," and devotes the entire second chapter to a discussion of this epithet: "Elsewhere he justifies his reputation as the new Pythagoras and as a brilliant musician, by maintaining along with many other Renaissance theorists, that music and painting are sister arts, that the proportions in a picture are analogous to a chord, and that objects of the same size receding in space at regular intervals diminish in harmonic progression."[3]

Without wishing to push McMullen's analogy too far, one must admit that between Leonardo and Pythagoras there are some striking similarities. Both Leonardo and Pythagoras are reputed to have been as beautiful physically as they were brilliant mentally. Both were inventors, the sheer number of whose discoveries strains credulity. They believed the study of mathematics to be morally edifying, and preferred to spend their time in privacy, courting the muses. Both lived in an Italy torn by feuding city-states. As a result, both were plunged willy-nilly into the wars and petty disputes that raged around them. Pythagoras was embroiled in the wars between Croton and Sybaris in southern Italy during the 5th and 6th centuries B.C. Leonardo became involved in the wars between Florence and Pisa (and others) during the 15th and 16th centuries A.D.

But the obvious parallel between Leonardo and Pythagoras is, of course, their vegetarianism. The *ostinato rigore* (obstinant rigor) that characterized Leonardo's artistic technique also typified his vegetarianism. Early on he became a vegetarian of such rigor that, as Vasari tells us, it was Leonardo's custom to purchase caged birds from the poultry vendors in town, then take the birds out to the country and release them. His vegetarian sympathies even extended to the bird's eggs, which he disdained to eat. In an entry in his *Notebooks,* he cried out against the eating of bird's eggs: "Oh! How many will they be that never come to birth!—*Of eggs which being eaten cannot form chickens.*"[4] In the earliest printed reference to

Leonardo's vegetarianism, the Florentine traveler Andrea Corsali (writing in a letter sent from India to Giuliano de Medici, in 1515) comments on a group of Indians whose compassionate vegetarianism reminds him of Leonardo's: "Certain infidels called Guzzarati do not feed upon anything that contains blood, nor do they permit among them that any injury be done to any living thing, like our Leonardo da Vinci."[5]

Leonardo openly (and perhaps a bit defiantly) abstained from meat when he was a guest in the house of wealthy patrons. He also did so in the palaces of dukes and kings, even though not to eat of the king's meat might have been looked upon as an act of *lese majesty*. Nevertheless, at a time when court artists were still expected to play the toady, Leonardo remained obstinately and resolutely himself; amid the sumptuous carnage of royal cuisine, he preferred to dine on bread and fresh fruit, or chick-pea soup, or peas cooked in almond milk, or simply a green salad.

In his heyday, Leonardo was as famous for having been a vegetarian as he was for having painted *The Last Supper* and *The Mona Lisa*.[6] When he died in 1519, the cookbook that he had used to prepare his vegetarian meals was found in his library. It was the 1487 edition of *De Honesta Voluptate*, the first modern cookbook. It had been written in 1475 by the first papal librarian, Bartolomeo Platina (1421–1481), an Italian scholar, humanist, and academician, who is best known for his *Vitae Pontificum* ("Lives of the Popes"). Leonard Beck, a collections specialist in the Library of Congress in Washington, and an authority on Platina, was quoted in *The New York Times* (February 25, 1986) as saying: "Leonardo was a vegetarian. If you want to know what he ate, this is the book."[7]

Elsewhere, Mr. Beck has written that Leonardo "had a 1487 edition of Platina in his library. Book VII of that copy answers the question as to the vegetable dishes on which this our Leonardo 'doth feed, that he is grown so great.' "[8]

Fried Figs and Beans

(Faba in Frixorio)
(Beans in the Frying Pan)

1 cup kidney beans (soaked overnight and cooked)
1 cup sun-dried figs (chopped)
1 medium onion, chopped
Sage
Garlic
Kitchen herbs (basil, thyme, rosemary)
Salt and pepper to taste
2 tablespoons parsley, chopped fine

Fabam coctam atque resoluta cum ficis salvia . . .

In a greased frying pan combine cooked beans with onions, figs, sage, garlic, and various kitchen-garden herbs. Fry well in oil. Sprinkle with aromatic herbs and serve.

Serves four.

This is my translation from the original Latin of a recipe in the cookbook that Leonardo used to prepare his vegetarian meals—*De Honesta Voluptate*. It was written by Bartolomeo Platina in 1475 and is considered to be the first modern cookbook. Platina, who is best known for his *De Vitis Pontificum (Lives of the Popes)* was the first Vatican librarian (under Pope Sixtus IV). We know that Leonardo used this cookbook because he praises the recipes of Platina in his notebooks. The 1487 edition of *De Honesta Voluptate* was found in Leonardo's library at the time of his death. Leonard Beck, a collections specialist in the rare book division in the Library of Congress and who is an authority on Platina was quoted in *The New York Times* (Feb. 25, 1986) as saying, "Leonardo was a vegetarian. If you want to know what he ate, this is the book." *Famous Vegetarians and Their Famous Recipes* is the first book to publish recipes actually used by Leonardo, and, so far as I know, this is the first time that Leonardo's recipes have been translated from Latin into English.

Source: Bartolomeo de' Sacchi, called Platina, *Platinae De Honesta Voluptate & Valetudine: Seu de Arte Coquinaria & Cibariis Libri Decem*. (Venetiis: Bernardinus Venetus: Impressit Anno Domini MIID (1498),), Liber Septimus, 03 verso.

Peas Cooked in Almond Milk

(Pisa in Ieiunio)

(Peas for a Fast)

1 cup fresh peas (shelled)
1–½ cups almond milk
Salt and pepper to taste

Condire pisa pro tempore ieiunii cum lacte amygdalino. . . .

You will be able to marinate the peas before the time of the fast with almond milk in the opportune manner that we discussed earlier. Pantagathus Leonicenus* ought to avoid this food, as it must be cooked slowly—not seethed or boiled rapidly lest it increase the black humors (melancholia), and sap one's vigor.

To make almond milk for this recipe: first blanch one cup of fresh sweet almonds by pouring boiling water over the almonds. Let stand for one or two minutes then skim out the almonds and drop them in cold water. Squeeze each almond between thumb and forefinger, and the kernels will easily pop out of their brown cases. Put the almonds in a blender with two cups of water. Liquefy the almonds and pour the mixture through a porous strainer. Filter out the almond meats. Pour the residual almond milk into a bowl with the peas and steep overnight.

"Peas for a Fast" is the literal translation of "Pisa in Ieiunio." Although it seems contradictory to be preparing a dish for a fast, a fast day in the Roman Catholic calendar did not call for a total abstention from food, only from foods of animal origin such as meat, milk, butter, cheese and eggs. (Curiously enough, fish was exempt from the ban). So a fast day was essentially a meatless day.

*Who was Pantagathus Leonicenus, and what is he doing in Leonardo's recipe? Like many medieval and renaissance scholars, the author of Leonardo's cookbook had been influenced by the second century A.D. Greek philosopher and physician, Galen, who was the supreme medical authority in Europe until well into the eighteenth century. Platina composed *De Honesta Voluptate* in accordance with Galen's dietetic theory that everyone has one of four dominant temperaments— sanguine, choleric, melancholic, and phlegmatic—and that certain foods are suitable to each temperament. My guess is that Pantagathus Leonicenus is a made-up name that was meant to refer half-humorously to Galen's dietetic doctrine. A combination of a Greek first name and a Latin surname, it means "every good lion feeder." In other words, a choleric, high-dudgeoned Lionfeeder or meat-eater would not find this dish suitable either to his taste or to his temperament.

Source: Bartolomeo de' Sacchi, called Platina, *Platinae De Honesta Voluptate & Valetudine: Seu de Arte Coquinaria & Cibariis Libri Decem.* (Venetiis: Bernardinus Venetus: Impressit Anno Domini MIID (1498),) Liber Septimus, P3 verso.

Chick-Pea Soup
(Ius in Cicere Rubeo)

1 pound chick-peas
½ ounce flour
1 teaspoon olive oil
20 grains of crushed peppercorn
1 teaspoon ground cinnamon
3 pints water
2 teaspoons sage
2 teaspoons rosemary
2 tablespoons parsley, chopped fine
Salt and pepper to taste

Libram cicerum atque eo amplius aqua calida lavabis. . . .

Soak a pound [the Roman pound equals twelve ounces] of chick-peas for a long time in warm water. Rinse and drain them and place them without water in a cooking pot (cacabum) in which they must be cooked vigorously with half an ounce of flour. Measure out a small amount of oil and salt along with twenty grains of crushed pepper and some ground cinnamon. Mix them together with the cooked chick-peas; then put the pot back on the hearthfire with three measures of water. Enrich the broth with some sage, rosemary, and some finely chopped parsley. Let it boil long enough so that there is enough soup left to fill eight small soup bowls. When it has cooked, pour in drop by drop a small amount of oil. If the soup is being made for someone who is ill, add a small amount of aromatic oil.

Serves six.

Source: Bartolomeo de' Sacchi, called Platina, *Platinae De Honesta Voluptate & Valetudine: Seu de Arte Coquinaria & Cibariis Libri Decem.* (Venetiis: Bernardinus Venetus: Impressit Anno Domini MIID (1498),), Liber Septimus, P2 verso.

Almond Pudding*
(Ferculum Amygdalinum)
(Almond Dish)

1 cup almonds (blanched)
3 cups soft bread cubes
1 cup sugar
4 cups water
Rosewater

Libra amygdalarum albicantium ea ratione qua diximus. . . .

Take a pound [the Roman pound equals twelve ounces] of blanched almonds with a loaf of bread that has had its crust removed, and pound them together in a mortar. Grind them up and blend them with fresh water and pour through a coarse-hair filter into a cooking pot. Cook in the manner described above. Add a half-pound of sugar. This dish likes to be cooked just a little, but a thickness of the cooking liquids is indeed pleasing. Some cooks may wish to add rosewater.

Serves 6.

Note: For the sake of economy, I've taken it upon myself to reduce the quantities proportionately. If one follows Platina's recipe to the letter, it yields about twenty servings (enough to feed an army). By substituting smaller quantities, I've cut it down to six servings.

Source: Bartolomeo Platina, *De Honesta Voluptate*, (Venice: Bernardinus Venetus, 1498), Liber Septimus, P2 verso.

PERCY BYSSHE SHELLEY

Percy Bysshe Shelley was born in England August 4, 1792 at the family estate, Field Place. He was the eldest of five children born to Lady Elizabeth Shelley, and his father, Sir Timothy Shelley (a member of the Whig aristocracy). Although the Shelleys were a family of ancient lineage, Sir Timothy's branch of the family had long since fallen on hard times. They had become the poor relations of the Shelley clan. Sir Timothy's father, Sir Bysshe Shelley, however, had managed to put the Shelleys back on the genealogical map and repair the fading family fortunes. This he did, not by making a killing in cotton, rum, molasses, slaves, or tea (which had been the making of so many other great families), but by the considerably less toilsome expedient of eloping with wealthy young heiresses, and then contriving to outlive them. By the time he was in his sixties, he had buried three wives and amassed an enormous fortune.

Such extraordinary success with the ladies bespeaks a certain amount of dash and comeliness—qualities in which Sir Bysshe is said to have abounded. Unhappily, none of these traits descended to Sir Timothy, but rather seem to have skipped a generation and alighted on Sir Bysshe's grandson, Percy Bysshe Shelley, the poet. Old Sir Bysshe, who had acquired his wealth and position through pluck, guile, and fatal charm, grew to despise his stolid snobbish son, Sir Timothy. It is notable that Shelley, who had inherited so many of his grandfather's admirable qualities, along with a few of his regrettable ones (such as a tendency to elope with nubile women), also shared his grandfather's antipathy for Sir Timothy.

Indeed, if one were pressed to give a single, paramount reason why Percy Bysshe Shelley had become a vegetarian, one would have to say that it was because he hated his father with such a passion that he strove to become as much unlike him as possible. Where Sir Timothy was stolid and dependable, Shelley was madcap and rebellious. Where Sir Timothy was snobbish, and jealous of his rank as a nobleman, Shelley was a flaming radical who wrote poetry and pamphlets decrying the inequities of English society. While Shelley's father was a man who loved nothing so much as a leg of lamb or roast beef *au jus,* Shelley was a vegetarian. Shelley's father liked to drink port wine, but Shelley was abstemious. Even at Oxford, where the drinking of port wine was *de rigueur,* Shelley seldom imbibed. Thomas Hogg, who was Shelley's closest friend, ascribed Shelley's abstinence to his hatred of Sir Timothy:

> I will not be hard upon him, and say that he absolutely disliked port wine—what Oxford man ever did?—but he had unpleasant associations with it. The sight of port wine reminded him of his father, who loved it dearly and drank it freely.[1]

But the issue over which Shelley and his father most violently clashed was religion. Sir Timothy was a deeply pious man, who was never so content as when he was reading his Bible or singing hymns in church. It was doubtless for this reason that Shelley chose, in the supreme act of paternal defiance, to become an atheist. On other matters Sir Timothy was prepared to be indulgent. Before Shelley went up to Oxford, Sir Timothy offered to pay for the upbringing of any illegitimate children Shelley might father (with the tacit understanding that they be sired on girls of equal social rank or better). But when Shelley was expelled from Oxford for writing and publishing a pamphlet entitled "The Necessity of Atheism," Sir Timothy was inconsolable. He cut off Shelley's allowance, and cast him out of the family.

Any hope that father and son might be reconciled was forever dashed when Shelley, isolated from his family and his friends at Oxford, sought to relieve his loneliness by eloping with the vivacious daughter of a London coffee house owner. Harriet Westbrook was a girl whom Sir Timothy regarded as being "of low birth."[2] In Sir Timothy's eyes a misalliance was almost as unpardonable as atheism, or expulsion from Oxford. Matters were not improved when two years later Shelley left his wife to elope with Mary Wollstonecraft Godwin (best known as the author of *Frankenstein*), and her step-sister, Claire Clairmont, with whom Shelley and Mary set up a *ménage à trois*.

Despite Shelley's recalcitrance, he had been a brilliant student at Eton and Oxford. His gift for poetry was so pronounced that he inadvertently wrote his translations of Greek and Latin prose in rhymed meter. In fact, of all the Romantic poets, Shelley was the most learned and by far the best classical scholar. His translations of Plato's *Symposium,* and of Plutarch's vegetarian essays in the *Moralia* are among the best in English. Although Hogg, who was Shelley's alter ego at Oxford, cannot remember what exactly sparked Shelley's conversion to vegetarianism at the age of twenty, it's possible that it may have been prompted by his having read such ancient authors as Plutarch, Ovid, Horace, Plato, and Hesiod—who looked back wistfully to a golden age when all men were vegetarian.

Shelley also had a very strong scientific bent. This seems remarkable in our present age of "the two cultures,"[3] which has pitted science against the arts. His most prized possession was a solar microscope, and nearly all his poetry is shot through with scientific imagery. He was constantly conducting chemical and electrical experiments in his rooms at Eton and Oxford (much to the detriment of the carpeting, the furnishings, and Shelley's clothing). His rooms at Oxford provided a kind of visual pun for his marriage of science and literature: Fuming test tubes, a system of voltaic batteries, and a hand-cranked generator set among jostled piles of precariously stacked books.

Nothing if not precocious, at the tender age of seventeen Shelley published a commercially successful novel that was a pastiche of the gothic horror novels then much in vogue. At twenty-one he published *Queen Mab*, a long philosophical poem in which he gave vent to all his pet "isms": atheism, radicalism, feminism, and vegetarianism. Its first printing went begging in the smart London bookshops, but in 1821 Richard Carlile, a radical publisher, brought it out in a cheap pirate edition, and it became an underground bestseller among the working classes. *Queen Mab* did much to awaken their radicalism, if not their vegetarianism.

In an essay that Shelley appended to *Queen Mab*, he put forth the classic case for vegetarianism. "A Vindication of Natural Diet," which was also published in pamphlet form (1813), owes a great deal to his friend John Frederick Newton's book *Return to Nature, or Defence of Vegetable Regimen* (1810). From Newton, for example, he borrowed the idea of treating the Prometheus myth as a vegetarian allegory. On this showing, Prometheus (mankind) incurs the wrath of Jupiter (nature) by using fire to convert animal flesh (which is malodorous and disgusting in its raw state) into an edible substance through the process of cooking. Thus, as Shelley sees it, the vulture that Jupiter sends by way of punishment to gnaw Prometheus's vitals, symbolizes the diseased state into which man has fallen as a result of his having learned to cook and eat flesh. Newtonian too, is Shelley's thesis that the "forbidden fruit" with which Adam and Eve defile their lips is none other than animal flesh.

Many of the points that Shelley makes under Newton's influence have become classic arguments for vegetarianism that every major writer on the subject has paraphrased. Shelley also cites the scientific findings of the zoologist Georges Cuvier, who was the first to classify vegetarian and carnivorous animals according to their physical characteristics. On the authority of Cuvier, Shelley points out that physiologically and anatomically man bears no resemblance to any carnivorous animal. His closest affinity is with the frugivorous apes.

> Man resembles no carnivorous animal. There is no exception, unless man be one, to the rule of herbivorous animals having cellulated colons. The oran-outang is the most anthropomorphous of the ape tribe, all of which are strictly frugivorous.[4]

Another point that Shelley presciently makes, and one which is being repeated with increasing urgency in this century (in such books as *Diet for a Small Planet*) is that flesh-eating is not only wasteful of life, but is also extravagantly wasteful of arable land.

> The quantity of nutritious vegetable matter consumed in fattening the carcass of an ox would afford ten times the sustenance undepraving indeed, and incapable of generating disease, if gathered immediately

from the bosom of the earth. The most fertile districts of the habitable globe are now actually cultivated by men for animals, at a delay and waste of aliment absolutely incapable of calculation. It is only the wealthy that can, to any great degree, even now, indulge the unnatural craving for dead flesh, and they pay for the greater licence of the privilege by subjection to supernumerary diseases.[5]

By a lucky stroke, while he was in the midst of writing *Queen Mab*, and only nine months after he had turned vegetarian, Shelley was introduced to J. F. Newton, the author of the vegetarian book *Return to Nature*. As well as being vegetarians, Newton, his wife, five children, his sister-in-law Harriet de Boinville, and her two children were all confirmed "naturists" (nudists). Their practice of nudism was in keeping with Newton's theory that a return to an Edenic state of nature should entail a return to an Edenic nudity as well as to an Edenic diet of fruit and vegetables.

With his romantic good looks, his fatal charm, and his gift of gab, Shelley became the cynosure of the "Bracknell set" (the salon named for the house of Harriet de Boinville), where Shelley, the J. F. Newtons, the Boinvilles, and like-minded vegetarians would gather to discuss vegetarianism and allied topics. In his satiric novel *Headlong Hall*, Shelley's cynical friend, Thomas Love Peacock, derides Shelley's vegetarianism, and is merciless in his burlesquing of the "Brackness set."

As luck would have it, Harriet de Boinville had a daughter only a few years younger than Shelley. Not only was Cornelia de Boinville a strict vegetarian, and a beauty, but she was intellectually brilliant besides. Not long after Cornelia had essayed to teach Shelley to read Petrarch in Italian, they fell in love. Had they not been married (though unhappily), and had Shelley not had his head turned a few weeks later by the beauteous Mary Wollstonecraft Godwin, it is probable that he would have eloped with Cornelia Boinville, and produced a dynasty of ardent Pythagoreans.

As it developed, Shelley eloped with Godwin, and her step-sister, Claire Claremont, to Italy. There the cost of living was cheaper; the food for vegetarians, far more palatable; and the attitude towards Pythagorean triangles, far more tolerant.

It would be wonderful to report that Shelley, who came from long-lived forbears, had enjoyed the productive vigor of his fellow vegetarians, George Bernard Shaw and Leo Tolstoy, who lived to a ripe age. But fate decreed that the brilliant author of *Queen Mab, Prometheus Unbound, Julian and Maddalo, Adonais, Ozymandias,* and *A Vindication of Natural Diet,* meet an untimely death. On July 8, 1822, one month before his thirtieth birthday, he was accidentally drowned with two companions while sailing in the Gulf of Spezia. The poet who passionately loved ships and the sea had never learned to swim.

Napoleon's Bean Salad

According to Shelley's best friend and biographer, Thomas Hogg, beans were among Shelley's favorite foods. Unfortunately, none of the recipes for any of the bean dishes that Shelley favored has come down to us. Therefore, I have used poetic license to stretch the point and attribute to Shelley a recipe for bean salad that was favored by one of Shelley's illustrious contemporaries—Napoleon Bonaparte. It was Shelley after all who said that "poets are the great unacknowledged legislators of the world"; so the identification of Shelley with Napoleon is not so far-fetched as it might at first seem. In her delightful cookbook, *Good Things,* Jane Grigson tells us that Napoleon used to have this salad for lunch every other day during his exile on Saint Helena.

½ lb. dried small white beans
2 tablespoons tarragon vinegar
5 tablespoons light olive oil
1 teaspoon French Pommery mustard
1 tablespoon finely chopped shallots
1 generous tablespoon each of coarsely chopped
     fresh parsley, tarragon, and chives
Freshly ground black pepper

In a large bowl soak the beans for two or three hours. Cook the beans for one hour until they are soft, but not too soft. Just before they are done, add sea salt to taste.

While the beans are cooking, make a dressing of the vinegar, oil, mustard, and chopped shallots. Drain the beans and while they are still warm, add the chopped herbs and dressing. Mix the dressing into the salad with your fingers, and let stand for an hour or two before serving so that beans and herbal dressing are well married.

Serves four.

---

*Cited by Rosalie Swedlin in her book *A World of Salads* (New York: Holt, Rinehart and Winston, 1981), 137. The above recipe is an adaptation.

Panada

1 cup dark raisins
3 cups Essene bread or Pythagorean barley bread, crumbled
½ cup sugar
4 cups water
¼ cup margarine, or vegetable oil
1 tsp. nutmeg, ground

Combine the first three ingredients in a mixing bowl and stir until they are thoroughly mixed. Then add ¼ cup melted margarine and a teaspoon of ground nutmeg. Blend thoroughly. Bring the water to the boiling point. Turn off flame and let stand for 5 minutes. Pour the hot water over the bread crumb mixture. Let steep for 5 minutes and serve.

Serves four.

Note: This is a high-enzyme, living food recipe.

---

*In his *Life of Shelley* (London: Moxon, 1858), 2: p. 321, Shelley's best friend, Thomas Jefferson Hogg, tells us that from a Frenchwoman Shelley learned to make panada. "He had been taught by a French lady to make Panada; and with this food he often indulged himself. His simple cookery was performed thus. He broke a quantity—often, indeed, a surprising quantity—of bread into a large basin, and poured boiling water upon it. When the bread had been steeped awhile, and had swelled sufficiently, he poured off the water, squeezing it out of the bread, which he chopped up with a spoon; he then sprinkled pounded loaf sugar over it, and grated nutmeg upon it, and devoured the mass with a prodigious relish."

**"He took with bread, frequently by way of condiment, not water cresses as did the Persians of old, according to the fable of Xenephon, but common pudding raisins." Hogg, *Life of Shelley*, 2: p. 320.

For those who prefer to taste Panada as it was conventionally prepared in Shelley's time, here is a recipe from an English cookbook written in 1813:

Panada (1813)

From *The Young Woman's Companion* (Manchester: 1813), p. 58

Put a large piece of crumb bread into a saucepan, with a quart of water and a blade of mace. Let it boil two minutes, then take out the bread and bruise it very fine. Mix as much water as you think it will require, pour away the rest, and sweeten it to your palate. Put in a piece of butter as big as a walnut and grate in a little nutmeg.

"Queen Mab" Garden Salad

⅔ cup new potatoes, peeled, chopped, and steamed lightly
1 medium turnip, shredded
⅓ cup fresh peas, shelled and uncooked
⅓ cup fresh garbanzo beans, soaked 48 hours and uncooked
2 heads lettuce, red leaf or Boston
1 clove garlic, minced
½ cup olive oil
2 tablespoons vinegar or lemon juice
1 teaspoon mustard
1 teaspoon salt
¼ teaspoon ground fresh peppercorn

Prepare vegetables. Rub minced garlic into the bottom of the salad bowl. Combine the oil, vinegar, mustard, salt, and pepper with the minced garlic in salad bowl. To the dressing, add the shredded turnip, chopped potatoes, garbanzos, and baby peas. Let them marinate in the dressing for fifteen minutes. Meanwhile, wash the lettuce leaves, remove stems, and tear the leaves into bite-size pieces. Dry them in a salad spinner or with a towel. When the lettuce is dry, toss with the marinated vegetables.

Serves four.

Note: This is a high-enzyme, living food recipe.

This recipe was inspired by a passage in Shelley's "A Vindication of Natural Diet," which was originally published as a lengthy footnote to his poem *Queen Mab*. It reads: "The pleasures of taste to be derived from a dinner of potatoes, beans, peas, turnips, lettuces, with a dessert of apples, gooseberries, strawberries, currants, raspberries, and in winter, oranges, apples and pears, is far greater than is supposed." *The Poetical Works of Percy Bysshe Shelley* (New York: Macmillan, 1924, p. 66.

LEO TOLSTOY

Leo Tolstoy was born into one of the oldest families in Russia, on September 9, 1828. His father, Count Nikolai Ilyich Tolstoy, was an impoverished aristocrat, who, in order to save himself from bankruptcy (caused by his father's profligate ways), married an heiress. The heiress, Marya Volkonsky, boasted a sizable fortune and a pedigree of such antiquity that her son Leo could claim kinship with most of the families of highest Russian nobility. On the death of his father, Leo (the fourth of five children) inherited a fortune handsome enough to make him financially independent. He also received the title of Count, and a four thousand acre estate with its attendant human chattel of 330 serfs (scanty by standards of the day when one stops to consider that from his wealthy mother, Tolstoy's friend and fellow novelist, Ivan Turgenev, inherited some five thousand serfs whom he eventually set at liberty).

As a young man, Tolstoy fell heir to the vices as well as to the prerogatives of his caste. At the University of Kazan, he gave himself up to a life of fast living and debauchery that was obligatory in a young nobleman. He cavorted in brothels, got gorgeously drunk every night, and with the fetching wife of a complaisant serf, he fathered an illegitimate son. He raised the boy on his estate as a coachman, cheek-by-jowl with his five legitimate offspring, who were brought up to be coachman-snubbing aristocrats.

Yet unlike most young sprigs of nobility, Tolstoy was cursed with a social conscience. His diaries testify that even as a young college dissolute, he agonized over what he felt to be his moral lapses. So frequent were these lapses and so exquisite his sense of guilt afterwards, that one may be pardoned for suspecting that he delighted in the mental self-flagellation that they occasioned. But his moral outrage at the plight of the serfs was well-founded. So feudal and oppressive was the pre-revolutionary society (holding millions of serfs in thrall), that it is shocking that more of Tolstoy's fellow aristocrats were not appalled by it.

How to square his own opulent and privileged life with the misery and squalor of the Russian serfs was a problem that vexed him all his life. From the *Sevastopol Sketches* (1856), *War and Peace* (1869), and *Anna Karenina* (1877) to *Resurrection* (1899), this theme sounded insistently throughout his works. Personally, he came to terms with his problem by growing more and more to emulate the simple yet spiritually rich lives of the serfs on his estate. He spurned the trappings and blandishments of a glittering Moscow over which, as the celebrated author of *War and Peace* (and as the scion of one of Russia's noblest families), he might easily have reigned.

At the height of his fame as an author, he affected peasant dress, renounced his wealth (in favor of his wife and children), and strove as sedulously to ape the serfs as members of the middle class strove to ape the aristocracy.

For a time he even abandoned literature in favor of the peasant task of cobbling shoes. One of his friends, for whom he had cobbled a pair of boots, put the unworn boots on his library shelf next to Tolstoy's literary works. In emulating the serfs on his estate, it is as though Tolstoy were a wolf, who, having donned sheep's clothing (instead of predatorily falling on the sheep), had tried desperately to become a sheep.

The metaphor, as it turns out, is not an unhappy one; for when he was fifty-seven, Tolstoy's identification with the Russian peasantry (to say nothing of the sheep) became complete. He gave up the meat-rich dishes of the aristocracy and became a vegetarian. Like peasantries everywhere, the Russian peasants were vegetarians perforce. The price of meat was hopelessly beyond their means; black bread and potatoes were their staple fare.

Tolstoy invited the American philosopher, William Frey, to spend three days as a house guest at the Tolstoy estate, Yasnaya, Polyana, on October 12, 1875. Tolstoy was surprised to learn that Frey was a vegetarian, and asked him to expound on the subject. At the end of Frey's talk, Tolstoy embraced him and said, "Thanks, thanks for your wise and honest words! I will certainly follow your example and abandon flesh meat."[1] Feinermann, one of Tolstoy's disciples who was present during Frey's lecture, noted in his diary: "And really from that time Leo Nikolayevitch ate nothing that was slaughtered, and at one time went so far as to live on oatmeal porridge."[2]

It might seem hard to believe that having been such a famous trencherman in his youth, Tolstoy never once faltered in his vegetarianism during the last twenty-five years of his life. But Tolstoy's was a will of iron. Indeed only a man of iron resolution could have conceived and carried through the design of *War and Peace*. Only a man of immense mind power could have taught himself, in the space of three months, and at the age of forty-two, to read ancient Greek to such good effect that he was soon making contributions to the literature of Greek scholarship. Therefore, once Tolstoy had made up his mind to become a vegetarian, there was never any danger of his backsliding (except on those rumored occasions when his wife Sonya artfully spiked his vegetable soup with meat broth).

Yet it must be admitted that Tolstoy, the vegetarian, was not so amiable a fellow as the dashing young count who yielded to no man in his lust for wenching, hunting, and gambling. Though he never lost his sense of humor, his newly acquired odor of sanctity and his repentant attitude towards his wealth, his rank, and his advantages in life made him increasingly the skeleton at the feast. He stopped attending the theater, ceased going to and giving parties, and surrounded himself with earnest disciples or "Tolstoyans" as they were called.

Needless to say, Tolstoy's conversion to vegetarianism and his adoption of peasant ways did not sit very well with his wife Sonya. The daughter of a wealthy physician to the aristocracy, Sonya was acquisitive and socially ambitious. This of course put her at cross purposes with "the Count" as she liked to call Tolstoy. Where Sonya was a social climber who worshipped at the shrine of the aristocracy, Tolstoy (whose exalted lineage few Europeans could claim to surpass) was revolted by his fellow aristocrats, whom he regarded as time-wasting, flesh-eating boors, and parasites upon the labor of the working classes.

Normally, when two people love each other they want to share all of life's pleasures, including that most intimate of substances—food. That Sonya refused to join her husband in his vegetarian diet, and also forbade their children to follow him, suggests that hatred can form as fast a bond between two people as love. From the time Tolstoy turned vegetarian at age fifty-seven, Sonya never ceased bemoaning that she had to make the cooks prepare two sets of meals—meat dishes for herself, her friends and the children, as well as vegetarian dishes for Tolstoy, his friends and disciples.

Despite their differences and the antagonism in their marriage, one wonders whether Tolstoy could have achieved as much as he did had he chosen a more congenial mate. A blissfully married Tolstoy might never have written *War and Peace,* or become a vegetarian. His creative spark seemed to thrive on the tension between himself and Sonya. Doubtless Tolstoy would have been a happier man if he had married, let us say, Sonya's younger sister Tanya (with whom Tolstoy was more compatible, but who was alas too young to be his wife), but literature, the vegetarian movement, and moral philosophy might have been the poorer for it.

Had Tolstoy lived in India instead of Russia, his renunication of the world would scarcely have raised an eyebrow. To this day, it is not uncommon for Indian men-of-affairs, once they have attained middle age and financial security (for one must have capital before becoming a true renunciant), to throw it all up and become wandering holy men (*saddhus*). It is a practice that has the sanction of thousands of years of tradition behind it. The Buddha, who renounced his princely title and comforts to become a wandering *saddhu,* is a case in point. But in late 19th century Russia, it was just not acceptable for Russia's greatest novelist and one of its haughtiest aristocrats to give up everything and become a *saddhu.* Yet this is exactly what he did. When he was at the height of his fame as an author, he transferred all his property to his wife and children, and gave up the copyrights to his literary works. He then began his carefully contrived descent of the social ladder. As nearly as possible, he became one with the serfs on his estate, toiling in the fields by day, and writing essays and pamphlets by night. After his conversion, his writing became increasingly polemical and didactic. Fiction he now wrote mainly to raise money for such humanitarian causes as the setting up of vegetarian food kitchens in villages throughout Russia, as well as the resettling in Canada of an entire religious sect (the Dukhobors). The Dukhobors had been persecuted by the Tsarist government for putting into practice Tolstoy's principles of vegetarian pacifism, which precluded them from serving in the Tsar's army.

A remarkable essay from this period is "The First Step," which is Tolstoy's eyewitness account of conditions in a typical Russian slaughterhouse. Not for the faint of heart or weak of stomach, it is the most powerful diatribe against flesh-eating in all of literature. Tolstoy brings all of his narrative skills to bear in describing the brutal methods used to kill animals in one of the more humane Russian slaughterhouses.

Gandhi, whom Tolstoy considered his most promising disciple, and for whom he predicted great things, understood perfectly Tolstoy's vegetarianism, and his fascination for the life of the *saddhu*. But Tolstoy's wife, relatives, and fellow aristocrats feared for his sanity. A Russian count who did not enjoy carousing, eating meat, and lording it over his serfs must clearly be out of his head. When even his favorite relative, Granny, started to make light of his vegetarianism in front of his children, Tolstoy could no longer restrain himself. As she reached out her hand to take a ham sandwich from a serving tray, he said, "My congratulations, you wish to eat a carcass!"[3] In spite of her best efforts to ignore the remark, Granny was unable to eat the meat.

By contrast, foreign statesmen, scholars, eminent men-of-letters, and newspapermen (for whom Tolstoy was always good copy) traveled thousands of miles for an audience with the sage of Yasnaya Polyana. Among the Russian people, the might of his pen excelled the power of the Tsar himself. They revered him as half-saint, half-oracle, and hung on his every word.

Physically Tolstoy remained a superb specimen well into his seventies, as the distinguished young Italian anthropologist and psychiatrist, Cesare Lombroso, unfortunately found out. Lombroso who called on Tolstoy with a view to studying the behavior of this eccentric sixty-nine year old vegetarian, got a little more than he had bargained for. After watching Tolstoy beat his daughter in a strenuous two-hour tennis match, Tolstoy challenged him to a swimming race. The young psychiatrist nearly drowned trying to keep up with Tolstoy's furious pace. The race had to be stopped so that Tolstoy could help the spluttering wretch back to shore. When Lombroso expressed his amazement at Tolstoy's strength and endurance, Lombroso recalls, "he stretched out his hand and lifted me off the ground as though I were a little dog."[4] Another visitor was equally astounded to see the sixty-nine year old Tolstoy execute a gymnastic feat with more agility than his teenage son. At the age of sixty-seven he had taken up bicycling, which was then just coming into vogue, and until he was in his eighties, Russia's foremost literary genius could be seen crouched over the handlebars, tearing around the countryside.

Soupe Printanière

¼ cup carrots, diced
¼ cup turnips, diced
½ cup fresh, green peas
½ cup green beans, cut into ½ inch lengths
1½ quarts vegetable broth (3 vegetable bouillon
    cubes dissolved in 1½ quarts of water)
Parsley or chervil for seasoning
Salt and pepper to taste

Prepare vegetables. Steam carrots, turnips, and green beans for three minutes. Leave peas uncooked. Bring vegetable stock to the boil. As soon as it reaches the boiling point, remove from flame; stir in the uncooked peas and the steamed vegetables. Add seasonings and serve.

Serves six.

Note: This is a partially cooked, high enzyme dish that is hearty enough to be a meal in itself.

"Soupe printanière" means spring soup, or a soup that contains vegetables that are in season during the spring. This is the classic recipe for "soupe printanière," except that it is usually made with consommé or chicken broth. For consommé I have substituted vegetable broth. I trust that Tolstoy's wife Sonya did the same. If she used consommé, there may be some truth to the canard that she spiked his vegetable soup with beef broth.

We know that "soupe printanière" was on the menu at Yasnaya Polyana every day because Sonya complained about having had to put it on the menu for over twenty-five years: "And now I've got to write the menus again: 'soupe printanière'—Oh, how I hate it! I don't want to hear any more of 'soupe printanière'; I want to hear the most difficult fugue or symphony." (Ernest J. Simmons, *Leo Tolstoy* [Boston: Little Brown: 1946, p. 556].)

For those who would like to taste *soupe printanière* as it was prepared by one of the 19th century's greatest authors and gastronomes—Tolstoy's contemporary, Alexander Dumas—here is his recipe.

Potage Printanière

From *Le Grand Dictionnaire de Cuisine*, 1873, Alexander Dumas, pp. 857–8.

It is made like *le potage à la julienne* (voyez le potage suivant)* except that one adds to it asparagus tips, baby peas, radishes and very small white onions. Take carrots, onions, celery, parsnips, turnips, lettuce, and sorrel in equal amounts. You will then cut your sorrel into fillets. You will then blanch the sorrel in a small amount of water with a pinch of salt. You will cool it, and a quarter of an hour before serving it, you will mix it with the other vegetables. Cut the root vegetables into slices of equal length, reduce them into fillets more or less thick; cut in the same fashion the sorrel, the lettuce, and the celery; rinse all the vegetables in a tub of water, then drain them in a colander; put a quarter pound of butter in a casserole with your root vegetables and your celery; put the casserole of vegetables on the stove and cook until they take on a light color; next fill the vegetable casserole with a good spoonful of bouillon. Add to these half-cooked root vegetables your sorrel; let everything simmer and skim off the skin that forms on the surface of the soup. While the vegetables are cooking, put in a lump of sugar to take away the bitterness. When you are almost ready to serve it, make a broth from bread that has been boiled a long time in salted water and add it to the soup. Mix everything together lightly, and serve.

---

*For the sake of convenience, I have combined the two recipes.)

Baked Macaroni en Casserole

1 lb. whole wheat macaroni (uncooked)
4 tablespoons olive oil or soy margarine
2 medium onions, finely chopped
½ cup sesame tahini
3 cups water
4 tablespoons tamari
Salt and pepper to taste
Pinch of paprika

Bring lightly salted water to a boil. Add macaroni and cook until *al dente*. Drain and set aside.

While the macaroni is cooking, make the sauce as follows: Heat the oil or margarine in a saucepan. Add the finely chopped onions and sauté for two minutes. Pour in one cup of water plus one-half cup of sesame tahini and stir with a wooden spoon until a rich, bubbling sauce is formed. Cook for a bit, then add the tamari. Stir vigorously. Pour in the remaining two cups of water, and let simmer until sauce thickens to a creamy consistency. Remove from flame and set aside.

Into a well-greased casserole dish, pour the cooked macaroni. Add the tahini sauce and mix thoroughly. Put casserole into a 400° oven for twenty minutes. Remove from oven and serve dusted wtih paprika.

Serves four to six.

This recipe is an imaginative recreation of the macaroni dish that Tolstoy used to have for lunch every day. I have taken the liberty of substituting tahini sauce for cheese sauce—(a use of gastonomic and poetic license that I am sure "the Count" would have applauded could he have tasted the result). Doubtless he would have applauded the substitution on ethical grounds as well since there are indications that he might have become a vegan (a strict vegetarian who takes no animal products), had his wife Sonya been a little more understanding. According to Tolstoy biographer Henri Troyat, it was not uncommon for there to be as many as thirty guests for lunch every day at *Yasnaya Polyana* (the Tolstoy residence). As Troyat observes in *Tolstoy* [(New York: Doubleday), 1967, p. 631], "There were two menus: one for ordinary people, and one for the master." While the ordinary mortals, much to Tolstoy's chagrin, invariably fed on meat dishes, Tolstoy's lunch usually consisted of "a soft-boiled egg, raw tomatoes, and macaroni and cheese." For those who would like to taste macaroni & cheese as it was prepared in Europe in the 19th century, here is a recipe from a cookbook written in 1873 by a fellow literary lion, Alexander Dumas—the author of such classics as *The Three Musketeers, The Count of Monte Cristo,* and *The Man in the Iron Mask.* As it happens, Dumas was also a celebrated gastronome, who turned out culinary masterpieces with the same panache and gusto that he brought to the writing of almost 300 volumes—not a few of which have been dismissed by critics as "potboilers." But who could be better suited to the creation of such splendid potboilers than a literary master chef?

In 1873, shortly after his death, Dumas published posthumously his culinary masterwork, *Le Grand Dictionnaire de Cuisine.* What had begun as a diversion from his literary labors, had soon become a ruling passion that took all his free time, and may in the end have killed him. Everything that Dumas wrote is compulsively readable and this cookbook is no exception. Its recipes (nearly all of which are Dumas's own) are interspersed with colorful historical details, humorous anecdotes, and deathless aphorisms such as his famous observation that the discovery of a new dish is of far greater import than the discovery of a new star—for what man can do with a star he has enough already.

It is not improbable that Tolstoy or Tolstoy's cook may have consulted Dumas's cookbook about the preparation of Tolstoy's beloved *soupe printanière,* or his famous macaroni. Tolstoy spoke French as fluently as he did Russian (in fact French was almost his first language), and he was a great admirer of Dumas. It should be remembered that French language and things Gallic enjoyed a great vogue in Russia during Tolstoy's lifetime. In fact the Russian aristocracy talked to each other not in Russian but in French, much as the Roman aristocrats in ancient Rome used to converse in Greek. Dumas was certainly no vegetarian, but fortuitously, neither his recipe for macaroni, nor his recipe for *soupe printanière* contains so much as a sliver of meat. Surprisingly enough, Dumas's cookbook (in its entirety) has never been translated into English. Therefore I have been forced to translate these two recipes myself with apologies to the master.

Macaroni à La Menagère

From *Le Grand Dictionnaire de Cuisine,* Alexander Dumas, 1873, p. 693.

Cook a pound of macaroni in boiling water for three quarters of an hour with a small amount of butter, salt, a small whole onion pricked with a fork, and some cloves. Next, drain the macaroni well and put it in a casserole with a little butter, a quarter pound of grated gruyère cheese and as much parmesan cheese, equally grated, a little nutmeg, peppercorns, a few spoonfuls of cream, and you toss them all together; when your macaroni flows like oil, dress it and serve it.

Russian Beetroot Soup
(High Enzyme, Live Food Soup)

1 small onion, minced
1 Tablespoon olive oil
4 medium beets
1 medium steamed potato
1 medium tomato
2 pints vegetable stock
1 teaspoon salt
1 teaspoon sugar
1 tablespoon lemon juice
chopped cucumbers for garnish

Finely chop the onion and sauté in oil until golden. Remove from flame and set aside.

Peel and quarter beets. Puree in a food processor or blender. Add a few tablespoons of vegetable stock to facilitate pureeing.

While the beets are pureeing, add the tomato and the steamed potato. Keep pureeing and add the vegetable soup stock. When the mixture is thoroughly blended, add the salt and lemon juice, and pour into a soup tureen. Ladle the soup into bowls and garnish with chopped cucumber.

Serves six.

Note: This partially cooked, high-enzyme soup is hearty enough to be a meal in itself.

That Tolstoy regularly ate borscht for dinner is attested again by Troyat: "Toward seven he reappeared, after the rest of the family had already sat down for supper. This time his meal was more copious: borscht, rice or potato dumplings, dessert, and, on very rare occasions, a drop of white wine in a large glass of water." (Troyat, op. cit., p. 634.) This recipe is an inspired recreation.

For those who would like to taste Russian Beetroot Soup as it was prepared by an aristocratic family in Russia in Tolstoy's lifetime during the reign of the last Tsar, here is a recipe for Borscht from a book written by Marie Alexandre Markevitch, called *The Epicure in Imperial Russia* (San Francisco: Colt Press, 1941), p. 22. I have adapted it for the vegetarian kitchen.

Borscht

Make a very strong bouillon. Add to this all the vegetables of a pot roast (very few turnips). When the bouillon is ready, remove all the vegetables. Add to the bouillon thus obtained, a half-pound of very red beetroot, preferably uncooked, cut in little thin sticks about two inches in length, and a white cabbage very hard, cut in the finest possible shreds. Cook from two to three hours.

An hour before dinner, add four tomatoes, or an equal quantity of essence of tomato. At the precise moment of serving, set into the soup a colander containing one quarter pound of chopped beetroot with a few drops of vinegar. Do not let the soup boil any more, so as not to alter the purple color which the beetroot should now have. A sauce tureen of slightly sour cream is passed, and each person should have a good spoonful for his plate. With Borscht, one may serve Kaccha, Vatrouchkis, Pychkis, and miscellaneous Pirojkis.

ANNIE BESANT

In the late nineteenth century Annie Besant was one of the most admired and accomplished women in the world. In her book "Eminent Victorian Women" (Knopf, 1981), Lady Elizabeth Longford writes that "of all great Victorian women Annie Besant was the most extraordinary."[1] Striking-looking, physically; perspicacious, mentally; versatile and many-sided, professionally—in her person she gave promise of what liberated women might achieve in the twentieth century. As a publisher and editor of a widely read Freethought journal, "Our Corner," she was the first to recognize Shaw's genius and publish his novels in serial form. As the country's first laywoman lawyer, she trounced some of England's most respected barristers in court. As a courageous advocate of sex education and birth control, she was a founder of the modern family planning movement. As a pioneering trade unionist, she led England's first successful strike on behalf of female workers (the match girls). In 1889, after joining the Theosophical Society at the age of forty-two, she became Madame Blavatsky's heir apparent, and on the latter's death in 1891, succeeded her as international president of the Theosophical Society with headquarters in Adyar, India.

While in India (where she spent the last thirty-seven years of her life), she used her oratorical skills, and her powerful position as president of the Theosophical Society to spearhead the movement for Indian nationalism and political independence from Britain. Long before Gandhi was even so much as a mote on the political horizon, Annie had called for the Indians to throw off the British colonial yoke, and had drafted a constitution for an independent Indian government that served as a model for the one that was eventually drawn up by Motilal Nehru. A patrician Englishwoman of Irish ancestry, Annie was elected President of the Indian National Congress, the highest elective office ever held by a Britisher in India. As a measure of how serious a threat Annie posed to the British presence in India, in 1916, when she was seventy, on orders of Lord Pentland, then governor of Madras, she was imprisoned for three months at the British hill station in Ootacamund for fomenting Indian nationalism. At the turn of the century, when Englishmen viewed India, as Annie put it, as "a nation of coolies,"[2] Annie proclaimed the cultural superiority of Indian culture over European culture, which she considered barbaric.

At Benares in 1896, Annie founded the Central Hindu College, which was devoted exclusively to the study of Indian religion, mythology and sacred language (Sanskrit). Designed in part to bolster the ethnic and cultural pride of the Hindus, which had been humiliated by its Mughal and

British conquerors, the Central Hindu College was attended by Pandit Nehru, and a whole generation of young men who would become India's leaders in the fight for independence from British colonialism. As an educator, revolutionary firebrand, and spiritual leader, Annie's role in shaping modern India cannot be overstressed.

Not incidentally, when Annie joined the Theosophical Society in 1889, she became a strict Brahmanic vegetarian as well. Shortly thereafter the baggy blouse, frumpy skirt and flaming red neck-tie that she wore in her "Annie Militant" phase, gave way to the flowing white saris of her spiritual phase. Now her unbobbed, curly hair (Annie was the first modern woman to wear her hair bobbed), rippled in waves to her shoulders. As befit a female *saddhu,* she had given up her common-sense shoes, and now walked about India shod in sandals, or, more often than not, went barefoot. In her bungalow in Adyar, near Madras, English furniture had given place to Indian rugs, cushions and charpoys. Seated cross-legged on the floor of her bungalow, Annie ate her Indian vegetarian meals from a large green leaf that served as a plate. As for knives, forks, and spoons, they too had gone the way of bobbed hair, flaming red neckties, and commonsense shoes. Like most Indians, she snapped up her vegetarian food with her fingers.

The only daughter of Emily and William Wood, Annie Besant was born in London on October 1, 1847. Her father had taken his degree in medicine from Trinity University in Dublin, but had his career cut short, when he picked up a tubercular infection while assisting in the dissection of a tuberculosis victim in a London hospital. His sudden death when Annie was five left her mother in the lurch financially. To support her two children—Annie and her older brother Henry—she moved to the London suburb of Harrow-on-Hill where she ran a boarding house for the Harrow School boys. In seeing to it that Henry (who was her white hope) got the best education possible—prepping at Harrow and finishing at Cambridge—Mrs. Wood spared no expense. But when it came to Annie's education, she was parsimonious. Ironically, it was not Henry but Annie who would grow up to cut a figure in the world.

At sixteen Annie had already blossomed into a famous beauty who was the center of male attention at the balls and garden parties given by the young men at Harrow—many of whom applied to her mother for Annie's hand. Years later when Annie learned that her mother had refused these suitors on the ground that Annie was too young, she was shocked. She could never quite forgive her mother for spurning these wealthy, handsome sprigs of nobility in favor of the balding, parsonical mathematician whom she finally picked out for her.

Although Annie protested against the match, her mother insisted that she go through with it. So at the age of twenty, Annie married the

Reverend Frank Besant, a newly ordained minister, and a Cambridge graduate with a first class degree in mathematics. He was seven years Annie's senior.

As Frank's degree in mathematics might suggest, he was possessed of a logical cast of mind that ill-comported with Annie's poetic nature. If Annie's temperament was Byronic, mystical, romantic, passionate, Frank's was more like that of Byron's calculating wife—Annabella Millbanke—who was also a considerable mathematician. To paraphrase Byron's epithet for his own mathematical spouse, Frank Besant was a "prince of parallelograms."[3]

Beneath her husband's cold, logical exterior, however, Annie found to her cost that there smoldered a volcanic temper. Not exactly an extinct volcano herself, Annie admitted that she was "proud as Lucifer," and was not entirely blameless for their Vesuvian rows. But only Frank went the length of using violence to settle their arguments. Once, because she had dared to suggest that they ought to limit the size of their family, Frank, in most unparsonical fashion, kneed her in the abdomen. She was big with child at the time, so Frank's low blow caused her to go into labor, and their daughter Mabel was born prematurely. On another occasion, he threw her over a stile, and in a pet shoved her out of bed so forcefully that she crashed to the floor and was badly bruised. To add insult to injury, when Annie received royalties from articles or stories that she'd had published, Frank would bawl her out for having written them, then pocket her earnings.

In view of Frank's ungallant behavior, it is hardly surprising that Annie should have fled to London with her three-year-old daughter, Mabel, where for a time she supported herself, her daughter, and her mother by working as a governess. Nor is it surprising that she should have renounced her faith to become a Freethinker—a term that in the 19th century had the force of our word atheist.

Eager to make common cause with the Freethinkers against the Frank Besants of organized religion, Annie attended a Freethought lecture, where she met Charles Bradlaugh, the apostle of Freethought. Bradlaugh was notorious for pulling a shocking stunt to get his point across to lecture audiences. (G. B. S. even wrote about it in his introduction to *Back to Methuselah*.) With a great flourish, he would drag out his pocket watch, set it on the lectern, and challenge God to prove His existence by striking Bradlaugh dead within five minutes time. When the time had gone by, and God had declined to hurl a thunderbolt at the world's most notorious atheist, Bradlaugh would draw the obvious conclusion.

Although Bradlaugh may have received no thunderbolts from the Almighty, when Annie Besant made her appearance at his Freethought lecture, he was hit by a bolt from Aphrodite. The attraction was instant and mutual. For his part, Bradlaugh was enchanted with this heartstop-pingly beautiful woman whose intelligence more than matched his own; while Annie was taken with Bradlaugh because he was everything that Frank Besant was not—intellectually brilliant, handsome, idealistic, and unfailingly king.

Gentle and almost motherly as he was towards Annie, Bradlaugh was no milksop. Considered the greatest orator in England, he had frequently to call upon his ability (and his muscles) as an amateur wrestling cham-pion to eject hecklers from his Freethought lectures. When after having been elected to the House of Commons in 1880 by the people of North-ampton, his fellow M. P.s refused to seat him because he was a Free-thinker (atheists were barred from sitting in the House of Commons)—it took fourteen policemen to remove him even though he put up only a pas-sive resistance. Not to be denied, his Northampton constituents kept re-electing him until finally the government backed off from its position and six years later in 1886 Bradlaugh became the first Freethinker to be seated as a Member of Parliament.

With Bradlaugh's encouragement, Annie began to contribute articles to his Freethought journal, "The National Reformer," and to give lectures in public. Soon she found that she had a flair for oratory. In fact she developed into such a spellbinder that she frequently outdrew Bradlaugh at Freethought rallies. George Bernard Shaw, an avid listener, called her "the greatest orator in England, and possibly in Europe."[4]

According to Annie's biographer, Arthur Nethercot, in *The First Five Lives of Annie Besant,* Bradlaugh was a vegetarian: "Bradlaugh was always a stickler for propriety, as well as something of an ascetic. During a recent spirited discussion over whether flesh-eating was immoral, he made it clear that he was a vegetarian."[5] Although Annie didn't become a vegetar-ian until some years later, doubtless her intimacy with Bradlaugh and later with Bernard Shaw helped to smooth the way. That Bradlaugh was as much Pythagorean as Freethinker is further suggested by the name he gave his favorite daughter—Hypatia—the female Pythagorean (and mar-tyr), who for her heresies was torn to pieces by a Christian mob in the fifth century A.D.

Incredible as it might seem in civilized, nineteenth century London, Annie's career came dangerously close to duplicating that of Hypatia the Pythagorean. To be sure, Annie wasn't torn to pieces by a mob for being a Freethinker, but she was nonetheless hounded by the Church and the Government with a vengefulness that would have made dismemberment at the hands of an angry mob seem almost refreshing by comparison.

Her troubles with the Church began in a small way when she ran afoul of her husband, the Reverend Frank Besant, who almost killed her for suggesting that they practice birth control—something so unheretical that the Reverend Thomas Malthus had advocated it way back in 1798 without anyone's raising an eyebrow. In his seminal work, *Essay on the Principle of Population,* Malthus sensibly proposed that couples should limit the size of their family to within their means. Having read Malthus, and having worked in the London slums, Annie was convinced that it was the lack of education about birth control methods that was largely to blame for the misery of the poor. On account of their ignorance of birth control techniques, the poor were multiplying out of all proportion to their ability to feed the children whom they were dragging so carelessly into the world. Herself an upper-class Englishwoman, Annie had first learned about the "birds and the bees" on her wedding night at the knee of Reverend Frank Besant—a teacher who was none too gentle or skillful. How much worse must it be for the benighted poor, whose ignorance of sexual matters, she felt, was connived at by both Church and State, who had a vested interest in keeping them in the dark?

To help set matters to rights, Annie persuaded Bradlaugh, at considerable risk to his career and reputation, to join her in publishing "The Fruits of Philosophy"—a marriage manual with advice on birth control methods. Written in high-sounding prose from the pen of an American clergyman, Dr. Charles Knowlton, the book had enjoyed a steady sale in the puritanical U.S. for over twenty years. It couldn't have been more inoffensive, or in better taste; but just as Bradlaugh had predicted, its appearance in London bookstores prompted the Church to denounce them and the State to prosecute them for publishing obscene materials.

Bradlaugh, one of England's ablest lawyers, had to use all his legal adroitness to keep the book from being suppressed, and him and Annie from being clapped in jail. But the effect of the prosecution was precisely the opposite of what the government had intended—*The Fruits of Philosophy* became an under-the-counter bestseller (selling 185,000 copies in three years), and Annie and Bradlaugh were vindicated on appeal. At a time when most *men* were reticent on the subject, Annie had not only the courage to speak out in favor of birth control, and publish a book promoting it, but also (and most heretical of all) she acted as her own attorney at the obscenity trial. In 1878, a year after the trial, Aletta Jacobs opened the first birth control clinic in Holland. Annie's pioneering efforts had given birth to the modern planned parenthood movement.

As if the trial had not been ordeal enough, Annie was put to an even harder test for the sake of her beliefs. Her estranged husband pounced on the obscenity trial as an opportunity to have Annie declared an unfit parent, and thereby gain custody of their daughter Mabel. As fate would have it, Reverend Besant and his attorney invoked the same law that had been used to deprive another vegetarian Freethinker of his children some sixty years earlier—Percy Bysshe Shelley.

When she insisted on pleading her own case in the custody trial that ensued, Annie electrified the whole of England. Never before had a woman acted as her own counsel, or anyone else's counsel in an English court. Incredible as it may seem, as recently as 1877, no woman had yet been admitted to the practice of law in England. Women were held to be incapable of grasping the mysteries and intricacies of the law. But Annie's widely publicized conduct of her own defense changed all that. So cogent were her arguments, so eloquently did she put her case that the opposing counsel was more an object of sympathy than derision at trial's end. All doubts as to whether a woman was capable of acting as an attorney were silenced. Within a few years of the trial, the first woman was accepted at the Inns of Court to train as a barrister. It was a direct outcome of Annie's having acquitted herself so brilliantly in court.

Unfortunately, the legal outcome was less happy. Judge Jessel, a sober-sided old Tory, found against her, and Mabel was handed over to her father's custody. However, as soon as the children (Frank had retained custody of their son, Digby, from birth) reached their majority (age 20), they chose to live with their mother. Frank then severed all ties with them.

In the midst of her trials, Annie still found time to publish and edit her own Freethought journal, "Our Corner," which is memorable for having included the first edition of George Bernard Shaw's novels, albeit in serial form. When no respectable London publisher would gamble on Shaw, Annie recognized his genius, and paid him handsomely for the privilege of publishing his much-rejected novels.

At Shaw's invitation, Annie joined the Fabian Society to which she gave frequent lectures, and where she came into touch with such vegetarian Fabians as Henry Salt, and his brother-in-law, J. L. Joynes, and of course Shaw himself, with whom she had a brief but torrid love affair.

Through her membership in the Fabian Society, Annie became interested in trade unionism, which was then (circa 1888) just gathering strength. Outraged at the plight of the English match girls, who were overworked and exposed to toxic chemicals (which caused them to lose their teeth and hair), while being paid a beggarly wage—Annie organized them into a union and led the first successful strike on behalf of female workers.

Having accomplished so much, and having spearheaded so many causes, Annie might well have taken a leaf from Alexander the Great, who is said to have sat upon the ground and wept because there were no more worlds to conquer. But as it turned out there was still another world that was beckoning for Annie to conquer it—the spiritual world. Claiming that Freethought could not provide her with the spiritual nourishment that she craved, Annie severed her ties with the Freethinkers and became a Theosophist. Her conversion came about quite fortuitously when W. T. Stead, editor of the "Pall Mall Gazette" (the same paper that employed Shaw as drama and music critic), gave Annie a book to review—*The Secret*

Doctrine by Madame Blavatsky. After reading it, the scales fell from her eyes, the earth moved, and her atheism fell away from her like a tatty old cloak. On May 10, 1899, she paid a personal call on Madame Blavatsky, and entreated her to take her on as her pupil. Flattered to have the most famous woman in London offering to sit at her feet, and realizing that her days as head of the International Theosophical Society were numbered (as she was in failing health), Madame Blavatsky instantly set about grooming Annie as her successor—much as Annie later handpicked Krishnamurti be hers. When Shaw ridiculed her for having become a theosophist, she came back with the witty reply that since she had embraced theosophy after becoming (like Shaw) a vegetarian, that the new diet had probably enfeebled her intellect.

Watercress Salad Sandwich

1 bunch watecress, tough stems removed
½ cup bean sprouts
½ cup walnuts halved
½ cup green onions, chopped
4 tablespoons olive oil
1 tablespoon red wine vinegar
1 clove minced garlic
½ teaspoon salt
½ teaspoon Dijon mustard
Toasted whole-grain bread slices, or
    oven-warmed whole-wheat burger buns

Rinse the watercress and bean sprouts, pick over, and pat dry with a towel. Remove the tough stems from the watercress, and discard. Halve the walnuts and chop the onions, then set aside.

In a large salad bowl, combine the last seven ingredients (excluding bread), and make a dressing. To the dressing add the watercress, halved walnuts, bean sprouts, and chopped green onions. Mix thoroughly, and serve between slices of toasted whole grain bread, or on oven-warmed whole-wheat burger buns.

Serves two.

In her biography of Annie Besant, *The Passionate Pilgrim* [(New York: Coward

McCann, 1931), p. 75], Mrs. Williams records that Annie Besant and her mentor, Charles Bradlaugh, would repair to a riverside restaurant in Kew Gardens, hard by the Thames, where they would have watercress sandwiches and tea.

Mixed Vegetable Curry

4 onions, chopped
4 potatoes, cut in chunks
4 carrots, julienned
1 small cauliflower
1 pound green beans
8 sun-dried tomatoes
1½ cups peas, fresh
1 stick cinnamon
1 teaspoon mustard seed
1 teaspoon coriander
1 teaspoon cumin seed
12 cardamom pods
½ cup coconut milk

Soak the sun-dried tomatoes in one cup of warm filtered water; set aside for one hour. Meanwhile julienne the carrots into thin strips; chop the cauliflower into small pieces; cut the green beans into one-inch lengths and shell the peas.

Steam the potatoes and green beans for three minutes and set aside. Now sauté the onions until golden. Add the spices and cook for two minutes more. Stir in the steamed potatoes, the steamed green beans, the shelled peas and the chopped cauliflower. Turn off flame and stir the vegetables until all the vegetables are coated with the spices. Blend the sun-dried tomatoes in the soak water and add to the vegetables. Add the coconut milk. Stir vigorously and serve. Note that the peas, carrots and cauliflower are left uncooked to preserve their flavor and enzymes.

Serves four.

Hint: If coconut milk is unavailable, blend two tablespoons of dessicated coconut with one-half cup soy milk.

Note: This is a high enzyme, live-food curry.

For the last forty years of her life, Annie was a strict vegetarian. Most of those years she spent as president of the International Theosophical Society headquartered in Adyar, India (a town not far from Madras). Unlike most British residents in India during the raj, Annie had a great admiration for the Indian people. In fact, the British were scandalized that a high-born English woman should identify so thoroughly with the Indians as to dress and eat like them, let alone to agitate for their independence. Here is a description of Annie àt "table" from Gertrude Marvin Williams's biography of Annie Besant, *The Passionate Pilgrim* (Williams, op. cit., p. 232): "At meal times, cross-legged on the floor in her white sari, using her fingers instead of fork and spoon, she ate her Indian food, curries and chapatis, from green leaves or from deep-rimmed plates of shining brass."

1. For those who would like to sample a vegetable curry created by an English woman living in India during the latter part of the 19th century, here is another curry recipe. Curiously enough, the lady who wrote the cookbook from which this dish is taken declined to reveal her identity. She wrote the book under the pseudonym "A Thirty-Five Years Resident."

Khuttah Caree, or Vegetable Curry

(From *The Indian Cookery Book: A Practical Handbook to the Kitchen in India,* (Calcutta: Thacker, Spink & Co., 1880), by a Thirty-Five Years Resident, p. 31.)

Take small quantities of vegetables in season, but the best curry is that made of *kutchoo* or artichoke, sweet potatoes or *suckercund,* carrots, red and white pumpkins and tomatoes.

The vegetables should be cut into large pieces, and boiled in water with the following condiments:—Four teaspoons of ground onions, one teaspoonful each of ground tumeric and chilies, a quarter of a teaspoonful of ground garlic, and one teaspoonful of roasted and ground coriander seed.

Prepare two large cups of tamarind water, slightly sweetened with jaggry, strain through a sieve, and add the strained water to the boiled vegetables with a few fresh chilies. Then melt in a separate pot one *chittock* or two ounces of mustard oil. While the oil is bubbling, fry in it a teaspoonful of the *collinga,* or onion seeds, and when sufficiently fried pour it over the boiled vegetables including the tamarind water. Close up the pot and allow it to simmer for fifteen to twenty minutes, when it will be ready. It is eaten cold.

Serves four.

MAHATMA GANDHI

Mohandas Gandhi was, in a sense, the George Washington of modern India. It may be difficult to reconcile the slight, wiry, loincloth-clad ascetic with the tall, commanding, aristocratic figure of George Washington, but both were "fathers of their country," who devised a new kind of warfare to throw off the British imperial yoke and win independence for their fledgling republics.

Reared in the martial traditions of the West, Washington routed the British with unorthodox tactics that he had learned as an Indian fighter on the American frontier. On the other hand, Gandhi drove the British from India with non-violent tactics that he had developed in his civil rights campaigns against General Smuts and the Dutch Afrikaners in South Africa. Although he got his ideas for civil disobedience and non-violent resistance from Thoreau and Tolstoy, the very fact that he chose non-violent methods rather than the reverse, suggests that his choice of "weapons" was culturally determined. Because he was an Indian, and not an Indian-fighter like George Washington, his methods bear the stamp of the vegetarian peoples among whom he was raised—the gentle Kathiawar Hindus and Jains who prize *ahimsā*, (harmlessness to living creatures).

The term that Gandhi gave to his non-violent "war" against the British was *Satyāgraha* (truth force). The object of a *Satyāgraha* campaign was to use non-violent methods to persuade an opponent of the rightness of one's cause. By stoically and lovingly enduring the full rigor of British wrath, Gandhi believed that he would eventually convert the British to his way of thinking.

The notion of conquering the mightiest military power on earth (which the British still were in the decades before World War II) might seem impossibly idealistic, yet, time after time, Gandhi triumphed over hopeless odds to do just that. In South Africa, he wrung civil rights concessions for the Indians from the racist Afrikaners. On the indigo plantations of Bihar, India, he used civil disobedience to check the greedy English planters' exploitation of the peasants. With hunger strikes and sit-ins, he improved the lot of the Indian "untouchables," and made long overdue reforms in the twenty-five-hundred-year-old caste system.

Novel and startling when he first unveiled them, the non-violent tactics that Gandhi devised for his *Satyāgraha* campaigns have become standard weapons in the armory of civil resisters. The tactics include the "sit-in," the "hartal" (a nationwide strike in which men, women, and children halt their activities for one day), the public burning of identity cards, and the deliberate courting of arrest to protest harsh and unreasonable laws.

Gandhi saw that for an imperial government to function smoothly, it required the tacit cooperation of the subject peoples. Outnumbered though they were by India's teeming millions, the British were yet able to maintain power because the great mass of Indians sleepily acquiesced to British rule. Individuals or conspirators who rose in protest against the British *raj* (reign) were ruthlessly put down. But a whole nation of people, if it could be roused from its apathy, could shake off the British yoke by firmly and serenely refusing to cooperate.

One of the most effective stratagems that Gandhi used against the British was of his own devising, and is now widely employed by civil resisters: the hunger strike. Preposterous and suicidal though it must at first have seemed, every time that Gandhi underwent a "fast unto death" (as he called it) he achieved his aims. Simply by refusing to eat, he quelled riots, settled disputes, got the *pariahs* (untouchables) admitted into Hindu temples, and sent the British army packing.

Imagine if George Washington had announced that he would fast unto death unless George III withdrew British troops from American soil! What would King George have done? Doubtless he would have beefed up the English troop strength, and have done everything possible to speed George's fast. Yet when Gandhi, who was pitted against some of the ablest and wiliest statesmen in English history (including the tough and canny Churchill) threatened to fast to death, King George VI withdrew his troops from Indian soil!

If imperialist powers and colonial rulers tend to be carnivorous, while their subject peoples are docile and submissive vegetarians, then Gandhi's fasting unto death was not only the ultimate form of non-cooperation, it was also the ultimate gesture of vegetarian *Satyāgraha*.

Gandhi credits Tolstoy's *The Kingdom of God Is Within You*, and Thoreau's *Civil Disobedience* with having inspired his program of non-violent resistance and *Satyāgraha*. However, much that is non-violent in Gandhi's philosophy can be traced to the community in which he was raised—a community that was pervaded by an atmosphere of devout vegetarianism and *ahimsā*.

Mohandas Karamchand Gandhi was born on October 2, 1869, the third son of the Prime Minister of Porbander, a principality in the Kathiawar region of northwestern India. A bustling seacoast town on the Kathiawar peninsula, Porbander's population was made up mostly of *vaiśya* (merchant)-caste Hindus (Gandhi was a *vaiśya*), and Jains (who are the strictest vegetarians in India, and for whom *ahimsā* is an article of faith). Although frowned upon in other parts of India, intermarriage between Jains and members of Gandhi's caste were fairly common in Kathiawar. A product of just such an intermarriage was the Jain philosopher, Rajchandra, Gandhi's closest friend and spiritual mentor when Gandhi was in his twenties. Along with Tolstoy, Ruskin and Thoreau, Gandhi counted this obscure Jain philosopher from Kathiawar as one of the four men who had had the greatest influence on him. So, almost from the cradle, Gandhi's thinking was tinged with the devout vegetarianism and non-violence of the Jains. Jains are so scrupulous about *ahimsa* that they strain their drinking water and wear air-filters over their mouths for fear of consuming an insect. For fear of harming insects, Jains are also forbidden to work in agricultural trades, and have been forced to make their way as merchants and traders in cities (where the likelihood of their treading on bugs is rather slight).

The Jains are regarded as being unofficial members of the *vaisya* by other Indians who see everything in terms of caste. This is why it was easier for members of Gandhi's caste to intermarry with Jains. On the other hand, intermarriage between members of Gandhi's *vaiśya* caste and members of the *brāhmana* or priest caste, or the *ksatriya* (warrior) caste would have been unthinkable.

One might expect the brāhmans to have tried to expel the British with prayers and curses, and the *ksatriyas* to have tried to expel the British by direct force of arms. Gandhi's methods—which involved him in economic protests such as the national strike, the refusal to pay taxes, and the boycott of British goods—have a mercantile flavor about them that is characteristic of the *vaiśya* caste into which he was born. Even Gandhi, the great fighter against caste, was unable to escape the imperatives of his own caste.

Of a shy and retiring nature, as a boy Gandhi gave little hint of the powerful leader he would one day become. Despite his obvious mental gifts, he was an indifferent student whose lack of confidence was crippling. Like most boys who suffer from shyness, Gandhi was prone to hero worship. His idol was the star athlete of Kathiawar High School, a young Moslem named Sheikh Mehtab. Popular, fearless, and desperately handsome, Mehtab was the embodiment of everything that Gandhi wanted to be.

Mehtab was a Moslem, and therefore a meat-eater. Was it possible, Gandhi wondered, that Mehtab owed his fearlessness, his good looks, and his athletic ability to his meat-eating? Mehtab gave it as his opinion that it was, and to clinch the argument, he quoted some doggerel verses written half in jest by the Gujarati poet, Naramdashankar:

> Behold the mighty Englishman,
> He rules the Indian small,
> Because being a meat-eater
> He is five cubits tall,
> A host to himself
> A match for five hundred.[1]

Sneaking off with Gandhi to a secluded spot by the river, Mehtab took out from the folds of his garment the Englishman's secret weapon. It was a hunk of goat's meat. Like a young man having his first surreptitious sexual thrill, Gandhi took a bite and lost his virginity.

As in most cases of lost innocence, the thrill was mixed with guilt. Sensible of having broken a deep-seated family and religious taboo, for weeks Gandhi was unable to sleep at night except by fits and starts. In the middle of the night, he would wake up in a cold sweat, having dreamt that he could hear the goat bleating inside his belly (rather like the crocodile in J. M. Barrie's play *Peter Pan*, who, having swallowed a clock, is plagued by the sound of its infernal ticking).

Although his grades were too poor to get him into either Oxford or Cambridge, they were just good enough to satisfy the entrance requirements at the Inns of Court in London. A barrister in the family would be just the thing needed to repair the threadbare Gandhi clan's fortunes. With this in mind, Gandhi's mother reluctantly gave her consent to let him cross the dark waters to England. But first he had to make her a solemn promise—that he would neither touch English food (meat), nor English women (mate).

Having arrived in London to study law, for several months he trembled on the edge of starvation. The English diet was unrelievedly carnivorous, and poor Gandhi wondered if he would be able to subsist for the next three years on overcooked vegetables. He was seriously considering swearing off vegetarianism altogether, when quite by chance, he happened on a vegetarian restaurant while walking home from law school. Picking his way into the dining room, he paused at a display case that featured a number of vegetarian books and pamphlets. For a shilling he bought a copy of Henry Salt's "A Plea for Vegetarianism," then he sat down to "the first hearty meal"[2] he'd eaten since leaving India.

By the time he had finished his meal, he was still engrossed in Salt's pamphlet. Salt's "Plea" put the case for vegetarianism so persuasively that it stiffened Gandhi's resolve to remain a vegetarian (after having been tempted like so many of his Indian friends to give it up). Gandhi had come to England fearing that he would be a beleaguered vegetarian amid the carnivores of London but as he began frequenting the vegetarian restaurants, he was amazed to find that in certain circles the passion for vegetarianism actually ran higher in England than it did in his own country. In fact most Indians, when they came to England, shook off their vegetarianism like the dust of India. They were ashamed of it as though it were some quaint, half-savage custom of a primitive society. Oddly enough, the pressure Gandhi felt to abandon his vegetarianism came not from Englishmen, but from his fellow Indians, who slavishly imitated the English in dress, speech, manners, and diet.

On the other hand, the English (even the most rabid carnivores among them) rather admired Gandhi for sticking to his vegetarian diet. Within the ranks of English vegetarians his rise was phenomenal. Irrepressibly class-ridden, and pedigree-conscious (as what Englishman is not?), the English vegetarians were rather proud to have in Gandhi, the son of a prime minister who could trace his ancestors back to the time when homo sapiens were just coming down from the trees. No sooner did he join the London Vegetarian Society, than he was elected to be a member of its executive committee. For the Society's newspaper he wrote thoughtful articles, and with its editor, Josiah Oldfield, he founded a vegetarian society in the London suburb of Bayswater. Another founding member of that society was the Sanskrit scholar and poet, Sir Edwin Arnold, whose English translation of the *Bhagavad Gita* was Gandhi's introduction to what became his favorite literary work. Had Gandhi chosen to stay on and practice law in London instead of casting his lot in South Africa and India, there is no doubt that he would have become a major force in the western vegetarian movement.

In fact with respect to vegetarianism, the timing of Gandhi's arrival in London was exquisite (1888–91). Not since the publication of Frank Newton's *Return to Nature* in 1810, or Shelley's "A Vindication of Natural Diet" in 1813, had there been so much excitement. Two classics of vegetarian literature had just been published: Howard Williams's *The Ethics of Diet,* and Anna Kingsford's *The Perfect Way in Diet.* Henry Salt, former master of classics at Eton, was penning his brilliant vegetarian diatribes. George Bernard Shaw had just entered the vegetarian lists. Vegetarian societies were mushrooming, vegetarian newspapers and pamphlets were spreading, and vegetarian restaurants were springing up. It was a time when a young vegetarian had a sense of being present at the birth of a new movement that bid fair to spread forth and embrace all of humanity. It was like being one of the early Christians during the reign of Constantine, or an early Buddhist during the reign of Ashoka.

Spicy Chapatis

1 cup chickpea flour
2 cups whole-wheat pastry flour
2 cups corn meal
2 finely chopped chili peppers
1 teaspoon black mustard seed
2 tablespoons poppy seeds
1 tablespoon caraway seeds, crushed
1 teaspoon cumin seeds
1 teaspoon cayenne pepper
1 teaspoon coriander powder
6 cardamom seeds, hulled and crushed
6 cloves garlic, minced
1 teaspoon tumeric
1 teaspoon *garam masala*
½ teaspoon rosemary, crumbled
½ teaspoon basil, crumbled
½ teaspoon oregano, crumbled
1 teaspoon fresh ginger, finely chopped
1 cup yogurt, or soy yogurt
½ cup peanut oil
Piping hot water

In a skillet, heat together the hard spices—the black mustard seeds, poppy seeds, caraway seeds, and cumin seeds. When the mustard seed starts to sputter, add the rest of the herbs and spices and cook for two minutes. Then turn the spices into the flour along with the yogurt. Moisten the flour with enough hot water to make a kneadable dough. Form little balls of dough and roll out until they are flat and circular, like pancakes. Fry on a griddle, or in an ungreased skillet until both sides are golden. Serve spread with soy margarine, or rolled up with soy cheese or soy yogurt.

Serves four.

As a young man Gandhi was greatly addicted to hot, spicy foods. But as he grew older, his passion for spicy food cooled considerably. Therefore this recipe is for a spicy chapati that he would have relished in his youth. Evidence for his love of chapatis is not hard to find. Biographies of Gandhi seldom mention a dish that

Gandhi had eaten without mentioning chapatis in the same breath. Seemingly, chapatis accompanied every curry, korma, salad, and meal that he ever ate. (Robert Payne's *The Life and Death of Mahatma Gandhi* (New York: EP Dutton, 1969), p. 378, "though he would sometimes take light, homemade chapatis.")

Carrot Salad (Gujarati Style)

2 teaspoons peanut oil
1 teaspoon black mustard seed
6 cups finely grated carrots
1 teaspoon salt
4 tablespoons chopped coriander (or chopped parsley)
⅛ teaspoon *hing* (optional)
2 teaspoons lemon juice

Heat the oil in a skillet. Then add a teaspoon of black mustard seed. When the mustard seed sputters, add the shredded carrots, salt, chopped coriander, two teaspoons of lemon juice, and *hing*. Stir vigorously over high heat for one minute, and allow to cook for one minute longer (no more). The carrots should retain their crispness.

Serve with rice or mashed potatoes.

Serves four.

Towards the end of his life, Gandhi simplified his diet considerably. His usual repast consisted of fruit or vegetable salad with chapati, washed down with a glass of goat's milk. Carrot salads became one of his favorite dishes during his later years. See Mahatma Gandhi, *Health Guide* (New York: The Crossing Press), pp. 86, 111. This recipe for carrot salad comes from the Gujarati cuisine of his native region in northwestern India.

Vegetable Korma

1 cup unroasted cashew nuts
½ cup mashed tofu
1 cup fresh coconut, grated
¼ cup filtered water
1 cup cauliflower, chopped fine
1 cup fresh peas, shelled
1 cup string beans, chopped fine
1 cup carrots, diced
1 cup potatoes, peeled and diced
6 tablespoons peanut oil
6 whole cloves
1 stick cinnamon
4 cardamom seeds
½ cup sun-dried tomatoes, soaked
2 cups large white onion, chopped
1 cup unpeeled tomatoes cut into ½-inch cubes
1 teaspoon tumeric
1 teaspoon ground coriander
1 teaspoon ground cumin
2 teaspoons salt
Chopped fresh coriander leaves

Soak the sun-dried tomatoes for one hour in one cup of water. Into a blender or food processor put one cup of cashews with a bit of water and make a cashew-nut puree. Then add the fresh grated coconut, filtered water and mashed tofu and blend to a paste. Set aside.

Prepare the vegetables. Steam the potatoes and green beans for three minutes in a steamer and set aside. Leave the cauliflower, peas and carrots uncooked.

Sauté the spices in the peanut oil until they start to sizzle. Then add the chopped onion and cook until onions turn golden. Turn off flame. Blend the sun-dried tomatoes in the soak water, and add the tomato puree to the pot. Do not cook further. Add the chopped fresh tomatoes, the steamed vegetables and the chopped cauliflower, diced carrots, and shelled peas. Add the cashew-tofu paste. Stir vigorously until the vegetables are coated with the sauce and the spices. Let stand for five minutes. Serve immediately. Garnish with fresh coriander leaves.

Serves four to six.

Note: This is a high-enzyme, live food *korma* dish.

Korma is a technique for braising vegetables in a thick velvety sauce of yogurt and puréed nuts that is traditional in Gandhi's home state of Gujarat. This recipe is probably a reasonable facsimile of othe vegetarian *korma* dishes that were served in the Gandhi household when Gandhi was a boy. Gandhi never lost his taste for the *korma* dishes and the curries of his home state. When he was traveling in Europe shortly before the Second World War, he took along special tiffin carriers that contained his favorite vegetable curries, and *korma* dishes, one of which was made with almond paste. (See Robert Payne, *The Life and Death of Mahatma Gandhi,* New York: Dutton, 1969, page 365.)

GEORGE BERNARD SHAW

George Bernard Shaw was born in Dublin, Ireland on August 26, 1856, and died at "Shaw's Corner" near London in 1950—a life that spanned almost ninety-five years. As an avowed ethical vegetarian, Shaw disdained attributing his longevity to his diet. Nevertheless, both his longevity and his extraordinary creative output as a man of letters reflect no discredit on his fleshless regime. The author of more than thirty plays that have become classics of the modern theater, Shaw also distinguished himself by turns as one of the greatest drama and music critics ever to have put pen to paper. The fifth edition (1954) of Grove's *Dictionary of Music and Musicians,* in its biographical article on Shaw, refers to him as "one of the most brilliant critics, not only of the drama but also of music, who have ever worked in London, or indeed anywhere."[1] But it is chiefly as a writer of plays, and the prefaces to those plays—which critic John Mason Brown called, "one of the glories of the language," and "in the best prose style since Swift"[2]—that Shaw will be remembered.

In the late thirties, Edmund Wilson wrote that Shaw's plays were outliving those of his contemporaries. This is no less true today than it was then. During a recent theater season in New York, three of Shaw's plays were running simultaneously, and playing to packed houses—*Misalliance, Candida,* and *My Fair Lady* (an adaptation of his *Pygmalion* for the musical stage).

In 1925 he was awarded the Nobel Prize for literature. He characteristically donated the entire amount to the Anglo-Swedish Foundation (to spread a knowledge of Scandinavian literature among English readers). On his death in 1950, Shaw left 367,233 pounds. It was one of the largest estates ever left by a writer.

Not bad for an "effete vegetarian."[3] Not bad for a poor Dublin lad whose early life held little promise of the man whom Irving Wardle, theater critic for *The Times* (London), recently called, "the greatest world teacher to have arisen from these islands, the means by which countless adolescents have woken up and learned to think for themselves, the knight-errant intellectual who used his sword for common humanity."[4]

Unlike his contemporary and fellow Dubliner, Oscar Wilde—whose father was a thriving Dublin surgeon—Shaw's father was a notable drunkard and ne'er-do-well with a genius for losing money. In a curious byplay of literary history, Oscar Wilde's father performed a surgical operation to correct George Bernard Shaw's father's permanent squint, but succeeded only in shifting the squint in the opposite direction. Wags have it that Shaw unwittingly avenged his father when he encouraged Frank

"My Life and Loves" Harris to write Oscar's biography—a book that caused its readers to look at Oscar more than a little asquint.

Despite his family's genteel poverty, Shaw could boast—and very often did—that he was well-born. Drunkard and spendthrift though he was, Shaw's father was the son of the high sheriff of Kilkenny, and second cousin to a baronet. Moreover, he was not without virtues. He had an all-embracing sense of humor, a sparkling wit, and a generous gift of gab which he passed on to his son.

Shaw's mother, a talented singer, never ceased to repent of her marriage to Shaw's improvident father. To supplement his meager income, she formed a professional (some say adulterous) liaison with John Vandeleur Lee, a Dublin voice teacher who had devised an infallible method for teaching people to sing. In a sort of ménage à trois, Lucinda Gurly (Shaw's mother), the children, George Carr Shaw (Shaw's father), and John Vandeleur Lee (the music teacher), all lived under the roof of the latter's spacious house in a fashionable quarter of Dublin. Shaw biographers have speculated that George Bernard Shaw (the youngest of his mother's three children), might have been the illegitimate child of Mrs. Shaw and Vandeleur Lee. Whether or not there is any genetic link between George Bernard Shaw and the music teacher (Shaw scoffed at the idea), it is clear that Shaw derived from Lee a love of Mozart, and an encyclopedic knowledge of music (that stood Shaw in such good stead when he became music critic for the London evening newspaper *The Star* in 1889).

Some critics with a Freudian turn of mind have set down Shaw's vegetarianism, his feminism, his abstinence from alcohol, and his sexual prudery (he admitted that his forty-five year marriage to Charlotte Payne-Townshend was unconsummated) as a reaction against his father. But this seems improbable. For Shaw's father was too ineffectual as a father figure (and Vandeleur Lee to benign) to unleash the kind of Oedipal fury that such an analysis presumes. It is quite probable that Shaw became a vegetarian and a teetotaler for the very reason that he gives—that is, because he was inspired by the example of his hero Percy Bysshe Shelley. "I was a cannibal," he writes. "It was Shelley who first opened my eyes to the savagery of my diet."[5]

Although mentally precocious as a boy, Shaw acquired an early hatred of pedagogy and schoolmastering that never left him. "He who can, does; he who can't, teaches" is one of his oft-quoted maxims (from *Man and Superman*) in disparagement of teachers; and it could be applied with equal force to that mounter of soap-boxes and pedagogue supreme—George Bernard Shaw himself. Instead of trying to be the school's best scholar—a distinction that could have been his with little effort—he perversely made a pact with a fellow student to vie for the lowest position in the class. When, out of sheer boredom and financial necessity, he quit school to become a clerk in a Dublin real estate office, his teachers heaved a collective sigh of relief.

It was not until Shaw had given up his post as a real estate clerk (at age twenty), and crossed the Rubicon of the Irish Channel to join his mother who was teaching singing in London, that he began to devote himself to a career as a professional writer. Even so, he spent nine years living in a cramped room in his mother's house (writing five novels that were all hurled back at him by publishers) before his literary fortunes began to turn. Such daunting adversity would have defeated a lesser man, and it doubtless left scars on Shaw's personality for which the dazzling success of his middle and later years could never adequately compensate.

Though Shaw credits Shelley's influence with having moved him to become a vegetarian, there is reason to believe that Shaw's original impulse to convert may have been less high-minded, and may have owed as much to economics as to ethics. For it was during his years as a floundering, financially pinched writer in London (during his mid-twenties) that he began to frequent the vegetarian restaurants that had sprung up like exotic blooms around the British museum. After a morning spent burrowing in the museum library, he would repair to a vegetarian restaurant for a cheap but nourishing meal.

Coincidentally, it was Shaw's vegetarianism that put him in the way of getting his first steady job as a writer. Through his friendship with Henry Salt—whose pamphlet, "A Plea for Vegetarianism," had persuaded Gandhi not to renounce vegetarianism—Shaw was introduced to William Archer, the literary critic for the *Pall Mall Gazette*. Archer began sending Shaw books to review. So witty, so penetrating, so stylishly written were Shaw's reviews that they quickly became the talk of London. Before long, rival papers were bidding for his services, and under his own name as well as a nom de plume he began writing music and drama critiques for the London *Star* and *The Saturday Review* that are regarded as masterpieces of their genre.

From garret to literary great in three years—it was a brilliant passage. By the 1890s Shaw had begun to eclipse his contemporary, Oscar Wilde, whose star had once shone so much more brightly. In 1897, while Oscar was languishing in Reading Gaol (a prison), Shaw was putting the finishing touches on *The Devil's Disciple* (a huge hit in America), and was just getting ready to marry Charlotte Payne Townshend, his "green-eyed millionairess."[6]

Shaw's first success as a playwright came in America in 1900 with *The Devil's Disciple*. It earned him a fortune, and preceded his first London hit by four years. Finally in 1904 with *John Bull's Other Island,* he achieved the London triumph that had eluded him. With their rich intellectual content, their clash of ideas, their brainy repartee and witty dialogue, Shaw's plays crackled with intellectual excitement. They did much to reinvigorate a London theater that had grown fat and enervated on a diet that consisted almost entirely of prettified Shakespeare, creaking melodramas, and vapid drawing room comedies.

Strangely enough, Shaw never raises the subject of vegetarianism in either his plays, or their prefaces. In the prefaces he addressed topics that he felt were too controversial to be broached in his plays—such as marriage customs, creative evolution (his religion), vivisection, medical malpractice, and censorship. In view of his eagerness to take up the cudgels for such unpopular and idealistic causes as alphabet reform, Fabian socialism, and women's suffrage, it is odd·that he should have written so little about vegetarianism. A play from his pen treating of vegetarianism— let's say a vegetarian *Candida,* or a vegetarian *Pygmalion*—would certainly have made it fashionable in London, and might well have sparked a worldwide dietary revolution. Yet in furtherance of vegetarianism he wrote no major essays, no books, no plays. It is a curious omission.

On the other hand, in his private life, Shaw left no doubt where he stood on the matter of his vegetarian diet. And woe betide the hostess or table companion at a dinner party who dared to make light of his vegetarianism. On such occasions the normally jovial and imperturbable George Bernard Shaw could be downright ugly, as the following incident makes plain. Shaw had been invited to a dinner party by the noted English writer, Dame Rebecca West. If Shaw accepted with what might have seemed indecent alacrity, it was only because Dame Rebecca boasted a woman who was considered to be the best vegetable cook in London. The woman's only failing was that she suffered from a mild form of epilepsy called *petit mal,* and was subject to blackout spells that were followed by brief bouts of amnesia. In Shaw's honor, she had just finished cooking a range of tasty vegetarian dishes, and was setting them out to cool on the sideboard, when she had one of her blackouts. After regaining consciousness a few minutes later, she looked around at the vegetable dishes that she had made for Shaw and in a lapse of memory, thought that she had forgotten to put in the meat. So to make good her mistake, she began poking bits of fish and meat into Shaw's dishes.

Came the time for dinner and Shaw was scarcely able to conceal his eagerness to taste the dishes that Dame Rebecca's cook had made for him. Indeed, he fell upon them with unbecoming gusto. It was not long, however, before he found that they had been spiked with meat. Outraged at this deception, and feeling himself to be the victim of a cheap practical joke or worse, he all but accused Dame Rebecca of trying to poison him. It did nothing to mollify him that she was as shocked as he was. Finally, after Dame Rebecca had found out what had happened, she saw to it that he was served with a fresh set of dishes. But it was too late. By then his dark mutterings had cast a pall of gloom over the dinner party that even the return of Shavian high spirits could do little to disperse. No one could question the intensity of Shaw's vegetarian convictions after that.

Casserole of Brussels Sprouts

1-½ lbs. Brussels sprouts
1 medium onion
Butter or soy margarine
5 medium tomatoes
1 cup Cheddar cheese, or 1 cup
    Cheddar-style soy cheese* (made from
    soybeans), grated (optional)

Prepare Brussels sprouts (pick over, wash, and trim). Preheat oven to 325°. Slice onion and sauté in a little butter (or margarine) until transparent. Scald, peel, and slice tomatoes. Arrange sprouts in casserole with onions and tomatoes. Add very little water—about one-half cup. Cover and bake in an oven for forty-five minutes. When sprouts are tender, sprinkle with grated cheese or soy cheese, and place under broiler until golden brown.

Serves four.

This is an actual recipe for a dish prepared for George Bernard Shaw by his personal cook, Alice Laden. It appears on page 63 of her book, *The George Bernard Shaw Vegetarian Cookbook,* by Alice Laden and R. J. Minney (Taplinger Publishing Co., Inc., 1972). Reprinted by permission of Taplinger Publishing Co., Inc.

I have added Cheddar-style soy cheese to enable strict vegetarians like myself (who take no dairy products) to enjoy Shaw's dish.

Savory Rice

½ cup rice
2 tablespoons butter or soy margarine
½ teaspoon salt
Pinch of cayenne pepper
2 tablespoons chopped mixed nuts
2 tablespoons Cheddar cheese, grated, or
    Cheddar-style soy cheese*
2 tablespoons canned tomato sauce
Sautéed tomatoes to garnish
Small triangles of bread, fried in butter
Chutney

Put rice into saucepan and add cold water to one-half inch above rice. Bring to a boil, then cover and simmer gently until rice is cooked and all the water is absorbed. Stir in butter, or soy margarine, salt, cayenne, nuts, cheese and tomato sauce. Serve very hot, garnished with sautéed tomatoes and bread triangles (fried in butter). Serve with chutney.

Serves four.

This is an actual recipe for a dish prepared for Shaw by his personal cook, Alice Laden. (Laden and Minney, op. cit., p. 81) Reprinted by permission of Taplinger Publishing Co., Inc.

*See footnote regarding soy cheese on preceding page.

Lentil Curry

1 cup lentils
2 medium onions, chopped
2 large cooking apples, chopped
2 bananas, sliced
1 cup rice
1 teaspoon brown sugar
1 teaspoon curry powder, or more if desired
1 teaspoon lemon juice
⅓ cup raisins
¼ cup shredded coconut
1 tablespoon chutney, finely chopped

Wash lentils and soak in water overnight, then drain. Put them in a saucepan, cover with boiling water and simmer until soft. Boil the rice in lightly salted water until done. Add to the cooked lentils the onions, apples, bananas, brown sugar, curry powder, lemon juice, and raisins. Simmer for 15 minutes. Strain off excess liquid. Turn onto a hot serving dish and sprinkle with coconut. Ring with the rice mixed with finely chopped chutney. Serve very hot.

Serves four.

This is an actual recipe for a dish prepared for George Bernard Shaw by his personal cook, Alice Laden. It appears on page 85 of her book, *The George Bernard Shaw Vegetarian Cookbook,* by Alice Laden and R. J. Minney (Taplinger Publishing Co., Inc., 1972). Reprinted by permission of Taplinger Publishing Co., Inc.

Nut and Rice Roast*

1 cup chopped mixed nuts
1 cup fresh whole-wheat bread crumbs
1 cup cooked rice
Few sprigs each fresh sage and thyme, finely
    chopped (or ¼ teaspoon each of dried)
1 onion, finely chopped
1 teaspoon salt
⅛ teaspoon pepper
3 tablespoons melted butter
2 or 3 dashes Maggi seasoning
Cumberland Sauce (optional)

Preheat oven to 375°F. Put nuts and bread crumbs through a blender. Mix these well with rice and finely chopped herbs and onion. Blend in seasonings and 2 tablespoons melted butter, moisten with water, and add Maggi. Shape into a loaf and put into a buttered dish. Bake for 35 minutes, basting with a little butter. Serve with Cumberland Sauce.

Serves four.

Cumberland Sauce

Peel of 1 orange
2 tablespoons red-currant jelly
Juice of 1 orange
Pinch of cayenne pepper
Good pinch of dry mustard

Remove pith of orange peel and cut peel into small slivers. Tenderize slivers by covering with boiling water. Drain and mix with remaining ingredients in a saucepan. Boil gently until they are well combined.

Yield: about ½ cup.

This is an actual recipe for a dish prepared for George Bernard Shaw by his personal cook, Alice Laden. It appears on page 70 of her book, *The George Bernard Shaw Vegetarian Cookbook,* by Alice Laden and R. J. Minney (Taplinger Publishing Co., Inc., 1972). Reprinted by permission of Taplinger Publishing Co., Inc.

Section Two
THE VISIONARIES

BRONSON ALCOTT

The life of Bronson Alcott has been largely overshadowed by the fame of his daughter, Louisa May Alcott, whose books *Little Women* and *Little Men* have become classics of American literature. It would appear that he is mainly remembered for being Louisa May's father, but Bronson Alcott certainly deserves a greater claim on our memory than that. After all, he was a pioneer in many fields. He was America's first educational theorist, whose ideas on teaching and child-rearing anticipate those of Gessel and Dewey. He was also, as Emerson called him, the most transcendental of America's transcendental philosophers. In addition, Alcott was a leading abolitionist (than who only William Lloyd Garrison was more militant), and he was one of America's earliest proponents of animal rights and vegetarianism. But the life of the man who would one day be called "the Sage of Concord"[1] and "Emerson's Master"[2] (because his own notebooks and ideas provided the inspiration for many of Emerson's essays) did not have an auspicious beginning.

He was born on November 29, 1799 (the same birthday as his daughter Louisa May Alcott), on a small farm in the western Connecticut city of Spindle Hill—a district from which the aristocrats of Boston were wont to recruit their tall, good-looking coachmen. Although it was only twenty-five miles west of Yale College, Spindle Hill was an impoverished farming community, whose inhabitants viewed reading and book-learning as frivolous pastimes. Schoolmastering was a despised profession, and any time that a boy spent in the schoolmaster's company was time ill-spent. Instrumental as Alcott was in emancipating the child in America, his own childhood was woefully unfree. No sooner had he finished his studies at the little grey schoolhouse, than he was set to toiling on his father's farm. While doing his farm chores, he snatched such leisure time as he could to read Bunyan's *Pilgrim's Progress,* Defoe's *Robinson Crusoe,* and Burgh's *Dignity.*

For his love of learning and his narrow escape from illiteracy, he had his mother to thank. Because Bronson's mother was denied the education that she had always wanted, she saw to it that Bronson had every opportunity (within her pinched means) to improve his mind. She taught him to read, and encouraged him to collect a little library of books. When Alcott turned thirteen, his mother arranged for him to attend a private school (Cheshire Academy) which was run by her brother, the Reverend Tillotson. But Alcott felt ill-at-ease among the boys from well-to-do families. These boys ridiculed his provincial accent and homespun clothes.

Unable to endure their taunts, Alcott quit the school after two months, and flung away his chance to follow his uncle's path to Yale.

There weren't many professional choices open to a young man of Alcott's limited educational background. One could either work in the Seth Thomas clock factory, or stay on the farm. But for young Connecticut men, who were footloose and morally resilient, there was yet another possibility: one might become a peddler. Young men with strong backs were needed to ferry the manufactured goods from the factories in New England to the rural markets of the South. The journeys could be long and arduous, but the chances for turning a profit were considerable. Tin lanterns that retailed in New York for fifty cents were often sold to gullible, rural Southerners for forty dollars; tin toddy sticks, worth a New York shilling, fetched twelve dollars. Doubtless a good deal of the pre-Civil War animosity that Southerners nursed for Yankees could be traced to the glib Yankee peddlers, who left a trail of wooden nutmegs and clocks that would not go.

So while Waldo Emerson was at Harvard reading Homer, Bronson Alcott strapped on a peddler's pack and set off on an odyssey through the Deep South. One week might find him sleeping alfresco under the night sky, while the next might find him quartered in the guest bedroom of a Southern mansion. Unlike the peddlers who swept through the South like a plague of locusts, leaving in their wake little more than rancor and gimcracks, Alcott ingratiated himself with the Southern gentry. He was a man with whom one could hold an intelligent conversation, and there was nothing that Southerners, with their strong oral tradition, appreciated more than a man who could talk. Even the planters' dogs, the bane of postmen, turned from ferocious mastiffs into overgrown, tail-wagging puppies at Alcott's approach. Could it be that, as Alcott suggested in his old age, "those fierce and formidable beasts recognized in him not so much a pedlar as the spirit of Pythagoras come back to earth."[3]

In this way, Alcott spent three-and-a-half years as more of an itinerant houseguest on Southern plantations than as a mere peddler of Yankee notions. Such great Southern families as the Dabneys, the Nelsons, the Tabbs, and the Talliaferros allowed him to browse through and borrow from their well-stocked libraries. They would also invite him to dinner as an honored guest.

By the end of his peddling tour through the South, he had acquired the courtly manners and bearing of an ante-bellum Southern gentleman—a now extinct species that could once bear comparison with an English duke. In fact, a visiting Englishman, Thomas Cholomondely, observed of Alcott that "he has the manners of a very great Peer!"[4] Of course, at the time Alcott was enjoying the amenities of Southern plantation life, slaves were laboring so that Alcott's hosts could lead a life of cultivated idleness. And although his conscience was not pricked at the time, several years later he became a firebrand among the Northern abolitionists. His house was a stop on the underground railroad to freedom in Canada, and many a runaway slave shared a vegetarian meal with Bronson Alcott, his wife, Abby, and daughter Louisa May.

In sum, the South had served Alcott as a sort of finishing school and university combined. From his last peddling expedition in 1823, he emerged as a man of culture and refinement. If, as Thomas Carlyle remarked, "The true university of these days is a collection of books,"[5] then Alcott was as well-read as any university graduate.

With this in mind, it does not seem quite so audacious that a Connecticut rustic, who had only been formally educated through the eighth grade, should have founded three of the most progressive schools in America. Who better to set about reforming a wretched educational system than one of its victims?

Shunning the stiff formality and the condescending manner of the 19th century schoolmaster, Alcott treated his pupils as fellow adventurers in the quest for knowledge. Instead of drilling pupils in rote learning, Alcott stimulated their thinking by using the Socratic method. As a result, Alcott's schools turned out diminutive philosophers who, however deficient they might have been in the three R's, were perfectly capable of bewildering their parents with Socratic questions.

Not unexpectedly, it was the parents who bridled at Alcott's methods, not the children. The parents were not used to having their children think independently, and regard the schoolmaster as a comrade rather than an ogre. During his teaching career, Alcott founded three major schools in three cities: Cheshire, Philadelphia, and Boston. At each school the same pattern was repeated. Children of the local gentry were enthusiastically enrolled by their parents, only to be withdrawn after a few semesters and packed off to a more conventional school.

Ironically, after each failure Alcott's reputation as an educator was enhanced. Two books that were admired in England and Europe emerged from the debacles: *Conversations with Children* and *Record of a School.* In America, however, his educational theories would have to wait until the 20th century before finding their champions in John Dewey and other educational reformers.

It was through his cousin William Alcott, M.D., one of the first American doctors to embrace vegetarianism, that Bronson was introduced to the nutritional theories of Sylvester Graham. So impressed was Alcott with Graham's principles that he, his wife Abby, and their four daughters, all became vegetarians in 1835. Whereas Alcott remained a vegetarian for the rest of his life—refusing to consume milk, eggs, fish, meat, and cheese, or wear leather or woolen clothing—his wife and their four daughters were backsliders.

One could never have mistaken Alcott for one of those fickle vegetarians who changes his feeding habits to suit his company. No matter how socially or intellectually daunting his dinner companions might be, Alcott refused to compromise his principles. At the monthly meetings of the Saturday Club in Boston, Alcott was called the "after-dinner member,"[6] because he invariably joined the other members "for the best of the feast—the nuts and apples, the wits and philosophy abounding—after the abominations were removed."[7] Once when Waldo Emerson was holding forth to his dinner guests on the horrors of cannibalism (while carving a roast), Alcott mirthfully observed: "But Mr. Emerson, if we are to eat meat at all, why should we not eat the best?"[7]

Emerson thought that Alcott personified the "slovenly greatness"[8] of the New World: an ill-educated son of an impecunious farmer, Alcott had yet managed to make himself into one of America's great thinkers and teachers. Such lives were rare in caste-ridden Europe, but in America they were far from uncommon, as the lives of Abraham Lincoln, Mark Twain and Walt Whitman make plain. Would it not be interesting, Emerson thought, for Alcott to meet Emerson's friend Thomas Carlyle and other eminent British intellectuals? So Emerson offered to pay Alcott's passage to England, and arranged introductions with Carlyle and others. Alcott accepted with indecent alacrity, and provisioned himself with enough applesauce, potatoes, and Graham bread to see him through the voyage to the Mother Country.

Once in England, however, Alcott found the country little to his taste. The descendant of an English family that had crossed the Atlantic to settle in America only two hundred years before was actually revolted by what he saw of London. In extenuation of his harsh judgment, it should be pointed out that the London of 1837—Dickens's London—was a singularly unlovely place. As a vegetarian, Alcott was particularly repelled by the gross carnivorism of the English. Wherever he wandered among London's restaurants, his senses were assailed by the odor of roasting flesh. As his biographer, Odell Shepard notes,

> Wherever Alcott went for food, whether to the Cock, the Mitre, or the Cheshire Cheese, he was revolted by the sight and smell of viands, which to him were simply dead animals in various stages of decomposition. It was not bigotry so much as physical repulsion that turned him against all this, and made him think of Englishmen—perhaps with an unconscious recollection of Porphyry "On Abstinence"—as walking sepulchers and perambulating tanks of beer.[9]

Emerson had high hopes for Alcott's meeting with Thomas Carlyle. Both Carlyle and Alcott had risen from humble beginnings to become prominent intellectuals, and both were of the same political coloration. But for some reason, feelings of friendship between Carlyle and Alcott failed to kindle. Most authorities attribute this coolness to Carlyle's impatience with Alcott's vegetarianism. Such a surmise is probably not too far from the truth. One particular incident, recorded by the elder Henry James, is singled out as being fatal to their friendship. Agitated when

Alcott refused to eat the English breakfast that Carlyle's cook had laid before them (because Alcott's vegetarian principles forbade his eating omelets, deviled kidneys, and bacon rashers), Carlyle sent out for some fresh strawberries. When the strawberries arrived, Alcott proceeded to heap up one side of his plate with strawberries, and the other side with fried potatoes, so that the juices from the potatoes mingled with the juices from the strawberries. At the sight of this disgusting "fraternization" of strawberry and potato juices, Carlyle's blood froze; he jumped from his chair and began pacing the room in displeasure.

On the other hand, Alcott's relations with a group of Englishmen couldn't have been more cordial. Although his prophetic educational ideas were without honor in his own country, a number of Englishmen had read *Record of a School* and *Conversations with Children,* and were so taken with Alcott's theories that they formed a sort of Bronson Alcott cult. Under the auspices of James Greaves, a wealthy vegetarian philanthropist, they bought a large tract of land in Surrey, on which they founded Alcott House—a vegetarian commune and progressive school modeled after Alcott's ill-fated experimental schools in America. Unlike their American prototypes, however, Alcott House thrived and prospered. So, not long after his falling out with Carlyle, Alcott made his way to Alcott House, where he was astounded to discover that he was revered almost as though he were an avatar of Pythagoras. Here Alcott was treated as the great sage and mystic that he had always known himself to be. His devotees were all for taking ship to America and setting up a utopian community, based on Alcott's social and dietetic theories, that would be reminiscent of the Pythagorean society in ancient Croton. Alcott frequently read about this society in his favorite book—Iamblichus's *Life of Pythagoras.*

In June, 1843, Alcott, his family, and followers, established America's first vegetarian commune, called "Fruitlands," on a small farm in Harvard, Massachusetts. But the social and economic conduct of Fruitlands honored Pythagoras more in the breach than the observance. Mrs. Alcott and the girls lapsed from vegetarianism. Subsequently Alcott was almost taken away from his wife by an over-ardent disciple. This action ran counter not only to Pythagoras's teachings, but to Abigail Alcott's emotions. After a violent quarrel with the disciple, Charles Lane, Abigail left Fruitlands in a huff. Crestfallen, Alcott flew to her side, and Fruitlands fell into a state of neglect from which it never recovered. The primary cause of Fruitlands' failure, however, was that the communards had waxed conversational and contemplative when they should have been planting crops. Come autumn there was scant food to be harvested, even for the most ascetic, self-denying vegetarian.

Transcendental Potatoes and Rice

> 3 tablespoons olive oil
> 1 cup raw rice
> 2 cups potatoes, peeled and chopped
> 2 cups water
> 1 teaspoon salt
> 1 bunch fresh parsley, chopped

In a large saucepan heat the olive oil and add to it the potatoes and rice. Stir constantly over a high flame for about five minutes. Then pour in the two cups of water, parsley, and salt. Bring the water to a boil, then lower the flame and let simmer for about twelve minutes. Test the potatoes and rice to see if they are tender. If not, add a bit more water, stir, cover, and cook gently until done.

Serves four.

"So taken was Bronson by Graham's ideas (which were similar to those of his cousin, William Alcott, now also writing books of advice on health and marital relations) that he became at this point a convinced vegetarian—a position from which he never deviated the rest of his long life. Eating his Graham diet of rice and boiled potatoes, Bronson began extolling his latest hero." (Madelon Bedell, *The Alcotts* (New York: Potter, 1981), p. 121)

For those who would like to taste a potatoes-and-rice combination created by one of the nineteenth century's preeminent vegetarian cooks, here is "Potato and Rice Soup" by the wife of Dr. John Harvey Kellogg—Ella Eaton Kellogg—from her vegetarian cookbook *Science in the Kitchen:*

Potato and Rice Soup

(From *Science in the Kitchen* (Battle Creek: 1892), Ella Eaton Kellogg.)

Cook a quart of sliced potatoes in as little water as possible. When done, rub through a colander. Add salt, a quart of rich milk and reheat. If desired, season with a slice of onion, a stalk of celery, and a little parsley. Just before serving, add a half-cup of cream and a cup and a half of well-cooked rice with unbroken grains. Stir gently and serve. Cooked vermicelli may be used in place of the rice.

Serves four.

Fruitlands Apple Pan Dowdy

Filling

6 large apples, peeled, cored, and cut into chunks
1 cup Barbados sugar or dark brown sugar
1 teaspoon cinnamon
½ cup cider
4 tablespoons soy margarine

Crust

1 cup flour
2 teaspoons baking powder
¾ cup soymilk
1 teaspoon salt
3 tablespoons soy margarine
Dollop soy ice cream

Take an eight inch square baking dish and grease it with soy margarine; then fill it with the apple chunks. Sprinkle the apples evenly with a teaspoonful of cinnamon and the cup of Barbados sugar. Pour cider over the seasoned apples and put aside.

To make the crust, sift together the flour, salt, and baking power in a mixing bowl. Using a pastry blender or a pair of knives, cut in the soy margarine with the flour mixture until it forms little pea-size bits. Add the soymilk and stir into a smooth batter. With a wooden spoon or spatula, spread the batter evenly over the apple slices. Bake in a pre-heated 400° oven for about forty-five minutes. Serve topped with a dollop of soy ice cream.

Serves four to six.

"Later that evening, as she set about cutting the flannel to make the baby's frock, Abby confided her troubles to her friend and burst out crying. But then her spiritis rallied and she was bright again. The next morning before daylight Hannah heard her bustling about the house, singing away as merry as a child. Great events were in preparation; the baking of a 'Pandora Pie' (now known as apple pan dowdy) for Christmas. No turkey or other trimmings of course." (Bedell, op. cit., p. 164).

Bronson Alcott and his wife Abigail May were inveterate diarists and record keepers; so it is surprising that there is no recipe for 'Pandora Pie' in Abigail's receipt book (recipe book), which has come down to us. These recipes of Abigail May Alcott (wife of Bronson and mother of Louisa May) were found pasted in a scrapbook dated 1856 in the attic of the Alcotts' house in Walpole, New Hampshire. A facsimile edition of Abigail's receipt (recipe) book (the original is on display at Orchard House in Concord, Mass.), was edited by Nancy Kohl, and published by the Louisa May Alcott Memorial Association of Concord, Mass. in June, 1980. In her introduction to the 1980 edition, Nancy Kohl makes the following observation: "As the Alcott's followed a vegetarian diet, the recipes are primarily puddings, cakes, and breads that do include eggs, milk, and butter." Here is a recipe from Abigail Alcott's little cookbook that most closely resembles "Pandora Pie:"

Apple Cake

From Abigail May Alcott's *Receipts & Simple Remedies*, (Walpole, New Hampshire, 1856), Abigail May Alcott, p. 10.

One pound flour, half a pound sugar, quarter of a pound of butter, these to be well rubbed together, eight or ten good sized apples, pared or not, cut up without stewing into eight to ten pieces and then mixed in with the flour and other ingredients. A teaspoonful of soda in as much milk as will just wet the whole mixture and spice to taste. Mix as dry as you can.

Ginger Snaps

(From Abigail May Alcott's *Receipts & Simple Remedies* (Walpole, New Hampshire, 1856),Abigail May Alcott, p. 4.)

Half pound butter, half [cup] sugar, two and one half [cups] flour, 1 pint molasses, teaspoon soda, caraway seed or ginger.

Roll very thin and bake a few minutes.

Half pound butter
Half [cup] sugar
Two and one half [cups] flour
1 pint molasses
1 teaspoon soda
Caraway seed or ginger.

Roll very thin and bake a few minutes.

Cake without Eggs

(From Abigail May Alcott's *Receipts & Simple Remedies* (Walpole, New Hampshire, 1856), Abigail May Alcott, p. 2.)

1 cup of butter
2½ cups sifted sugar
1 pint sour cream or buttermilk
1 quart flour
1 spoonful of saleratus [baking soda]

Bake ¾ hour.

Biscuit without Milk

(From Abigail May Alcott's *Receipts & Simple Remedies* (Walpole, New Hampshire, 1856), Abigail May Alcott, p. 7.)

Rub a piece of butter the size of an egg into a quart of flour. Add teaspoonful of salt, scatter in two teaspoonfuls of cream of tartar. Have ready a large pint of cold water in which teaspoonful of saleratus has been dissolved, pour it into the flour stirring quickly with your hand then add flour enough to mould it smooth. Roll out an inch thick and bake quickly.

These recipes of Abigail May Alcott (wife of Bronson and mother of Louisa May) were found pasted in a scrapbook dated 1856 in the attic of the Alcott's house in Walpole, New Hampshire. A facsimile edition of Abigail's receipt (recipe) book (the original is on display at Orchard House in Concord, Mass.), was edited by Nancy Kohl and published by the Louisa May Alcott Memorial Association of Concord, Mass. in June, 1980. In her introduction to the 1980 edition, Nancy Kohl makes the following observation: "As the Alcotts followed a vegetarian diet, the recipes are primarily puddings, cakes, and breads that do include eggs, milk, and butter."

SYLVESTER GRAHAM

Although his memory survives chiefly through the whole-wheat products that bear his name (graham crackers, graham flour, and graham gems), in mid-19th century America "Sylvester Graham" was a household word. He was the first in a long line of self-appointed food reformers who thought that nutrition was too serious a matter to be entrusted to the medicos and the commercial food producers.

Trained as a minister, he crisscrossed the country to preach the gospel of vegetarianism, temperance, and the virtues of home-baked whole-wheat bread. Some of America's most impenitent carnivores actually got religion during Graham's lectures, and became lifelong vegetarians. Horace Greeley, founder of the *New York Tribune* and the greatest newspaper editor of his time, is a case in point. After attending one of Graham's lectures, Greeley swore off alcohol and coffee, and became a "closet vegetarian" for the rest of his life (Greeley took pains not to publish the fact after being derided in print by rival journalist James Watson Webb, for practicing vegetarianism). Greeley even met his future wife, Mary Cheney, at a Graham boarding house. In the wake of Graham's cross-country fulminations against the eating of meat and the baking of over-refined white bread, Grahamite boarding houses sprang up like mushrooms after a thundershower. Here Grahamites could gather to eat vegetarian food and air vegetarian views without being ridiculed or rubbernecked by fellow diners.

It is worth quoting Greeley's biographer, James Parton, writing in 1855 on the subject of his conversion to Grahamism:

> Graham arose and lectured and made a noise in the world, and obtained followers. The substance of his message was that We, the people of the United States, are in the habit of taking our food in too concentrated a form. Bulk was necessary as well as nutriment; brown bread is better than white. Graham was a remarkable man . . . one of the two or three men to whom this nation might, with some propriety, erect a monument.
>
> Horace Greeley, like every other thinking person that heard Dr. Graham lecture, was convinced that upon the whole he was right. He abandoned the use of stimulants and took care in selecting his food, to see that there was the proper proportion between its bulk and its nutriment; i.e., he ate Graham bread, little meat, and plenty of rice, Indian meal, vegetables and fruit.[1]

Another one of Graham's vegetarian proselytes was Bronson Alcott. "So

taken was Bronson by Graham's ideas, that he became at this point a convinced vegetarian—a position from which he never deviated the rest of his long life."[2]

Sylvester Graham was born July 5, 1794, in Suffield, Connecticut. A descendant of two generations of clergymen, it was virtually foreordained that someday he should become a man of the cloth. But his route to the ministry took many unconventional turns. Graham was the youngest of 17 children. His father's first wife died after producing 12 children. Graham's father remarried. His wife bore him 5 children, then went mad and had to be committed to an asylum. Then his father died. Orphaned at seven, he was passed from one penniless relative to another. Throughout his childhood he was plagued with incipient tuberculosis, and long sieges of illness interrupted his schooling. Without parents to provide for him, his education was further protracted by his having to support himself at odd jobs. Consequently, when he arrived at Amherst College at the age of twenty-nine, he was ten years older than his fellow classmates, and suffered from a massive inferiority complex.

At Amherst, Graham tried to compensate for what he felt to be his social and educational inadequacies by overcompensating. He sought to impress his professors with his hastily acquired erudition, and in a theatrical manner he pontificated half-baked ideas to his fellow classmates. While these may have been commendable traits in a man who would soon be thundering homilies from the pulpit, they did nothing to endear him to either faculty or students. In fact, Graham's presence became so irksome that the students conspired to have him expelled on a trumped-up charge.

Graham left Amherst under a cloud. As a cashiered student, his chances of getting a degree in theology were nil, so his hopes of becoming a minister seemed forever dashed. He promptly suffered a nervous breakdown. But the cloud was not without its silver lining: Sarah Earl, the woman who nursed him back to health, at length became Sarah Graham.

Despite the black mark of having been tossed out of Amherst in 1826, he somehow managed to get himself ordained as a Presbyterian minister in the presbyter of Newark, New Jersey. A fanatic teetotaler, he used his pulpit to inveigh against the evils of drink—to such good effect that he was offered the job of General Agent for the Pennsylvania Society for the Suppression of Ardent Spirits. While carrying out his duties in that august office, he met the Reverend William Metcalfe, founder of the first vegetarian church in Philadelphia—The Bible Christians. Metcalfe's church preached abstinence from animal flesh as well as from alcohol. At Metcalfe's suggestion, Graham gave vegetarianism a try. His health and outlook (both of which were abysmal) improved so much as a result, that he became an enthusiastic convert. He even became convinced that a vegetarian diet could cure alcoholism—his particular *bête noire*. So, in his campaign to suppress Ardent Spirits, he urged the adoption of a vegetarian diet.

To Graham, alcohol was a criminal misuse of grain that might otherwise have gone toward the production of bread and other foodstuffs. The brewing of beer alone used up millions of loaves of barley each day. Worse still, the process of fermentation converted wholesome and nutritious foods such as grain, apples, potatoes, corn and grapes into a seductive poison.

It outraged him to see that commercial bakers were working the same wicked alchemy on flour as were the distillers on grain. In order to give bread a fashionable whiteness, and to increase their profits, the bakers were foisting on the public a bread whose flour was bleached, over-refined and adulterated. But what angered Graham most was that they were using a flour that had been "bolted" (sieved) through a cloth made of silk gauze, called a "bolting cloth." The bolting cloth was designed to filter out the bran, which imparts to whole grain bread its speckled brown color. By removing the bran, however, the bakers were robbing the bread of its primary source of nutrients, as well as the roughage that promotes digestion and bowel regularity.

With all the indignation he could muster—and he was capable of mustering a great deal—he called for the bakers to "put back the bran!"[3] White bread may have been more visually appealing; it may have been more palatable; it certainly had more social cachet—but it lacked the dietary fiber that gave whole grain bread its purgative powers. The medieval European peasant, who lived almost exclusively on whole-grain bread, had a digestive tract that resembled the town drain.

Constipation—that scourge of the rich and mighty who feed on fiberless foods such as white bread and animal flesh—held no terror for the poorer classes in Europe and America because they were constantly being reamed out by the roughage from the bran in whole grain bread, and the fiber in their largely vegetarian diet. Not until the 20th century (when the poor could first afford to take white bread and animal flesh as their daily bread) did they suffer from bowel cancers, and what Dr. T. L. Cleave calls "the saccharine diseases"[4] that plague the rich and well-born.

It is important to notice that in Graham's day, bread was something more than the bleached fluff into which it has lately degenerated. In fact, for the ordinary person whole-grain bread was the chief article of diet. Whereas today the average American consumes less than six ounces of bread per day, in the 19th century he consumed a minimum of one pound of bread per day. For most people, bread was truly the staff of life—as it had been from time out of mind. Had not Hippocrates in the 7th century B.C. extolled whole-wheat bread "for its salutary effect upon the bowels?"[5] And was it not Pliny who recorded that unbolted whole-wheat bread had sustained the Romans in their days of grandeur? Yet it was this same brown bread that the bakers were debauching.

Not suprisingly in a man who had lost his mother at such a tender age, Graham had an acute mother complex that shaped his dietary theories in a curious way. He had almost Proustian recall of his childhood years up to the age of seven. In particular, he associated the aroma of home-cooked, whole-grain bread with the mother love and cohesive family life that he had known as a small boy. He could remember with nostalgia how his family had been whole and happy when his mother and older sisters used to bake whole-grain bread. Thus for Graham the commercialization of bread-making was not just an affront to the great goddess of bread-stuffs—Demeter herself, but, it also symbolized the break-up of the family and the loss of mother love. To revive family values, and to reinvigorate the health of the nation, bran must be put back in the bread; and bread-making, back in the family.

Graham realized that his efforts to reform the practices of the bakers, through moral suasion, were not very likely to succeed. But he refused to be discouraged. Invoking the memory of the Roman matron for whom the baking of bread was a sacred ritual, Graham urged families to buy their own unbolted flour, bake their own bread, and restore to the home-baking of bread its sacred character. On no account were people to use sifted flour: "the ripe sound berry of wheat or rye, being ground to the requisite fineness, should in no manner be sifted, but should be made into loaves, and eaten precisely as the mill stones deliver it."[6]

In 1835, Graham delivered a series of inflammatory lectures in Boston in which he called the physicians "vampires,"[7] and accused the bakers of stretching their flour with such foreign materials as bean flour, pota-toes, chalk, and pipe clay. He also accused them of using alum and sul-phate of zinc as bleaching agents to whiten inferior flour. The butchers he denounced for the horrors that he had witnessed in the local abattoirs. In the wake of his lectures, the price of bread and meat plummeted on the Boston market. The butchers and the bakers were so incensed that they vowed to stone Graham to death if he dared to give another lecture in the city of Boston.

Refusing to be intimidated, Graham immediately scheduled another lec-ture series at Amory Hall. But the owners, fearing reprisals, went back on their word. However, the proprietors of the Marlborough Hotel, the first temperance hotel in America, were made of sterner stuff, and they granted Graham the use of their hall. On the night of the lecture, just as they had threatened, a mob of butchers and bakers gathered outside the hotel, armed with the implements of their trade. When they had worked themselves up to a pitch of frenzy, they stormed the hall, intent upon tear-ing Graham to pieces. But the Grahamites were ready for them. From the hotel roof, they emptied huge wooden troughs filled with slaked lime onto the milling bakers and butchers below. No sooner had they been drenched in lime (a poetic bit of justice, as Graham had condemned the Boston bakers for extending their flour with lime-based plaster of Paris), than another group of Grahamites burst from the building, and hurled themselves at the sputtering, flour-white ruffians. Reeling from the slaked lime and the blows of the Grahamites, the bakers and the butchers were routed, and Graham proceeded with his lecture as if nothing had happened.

Although Graham's beliefs were held in contempt by the medical establishment of his day, recent studies show that his fears were not misplaced; his branding of the bolting cloth as America's "shroud"[8] was more than just a figure of speech. In 1962, T. L. Cleave, a retired surgeon-captain in the British Navy, began publishing his epoch-making works on what he called "the saccharine disease." Incidentally, the term "saccharine," which means "related to sugar" (rhymes with "Rhine," or "vine"), has nothing to do with the chemical sweetener "saccharin."

It was Dr. Cleave's theory—which has now been widely accepted by medical authorities—that there is a single master disease, the "saccharine disease," which links many of the modern diseases of Western man such as diabetes, coronary thrombosis, cancer of the colon, diverticulitis, hypertension, varicose veins, and hemorrhoids to the consumption of fiberless foods such as animal flesh and refined carbohydrates. Cleave holds that these diseases are the result of the autointoxication (internal poisoning) that occurs, when man's digestive tract has not been sufficiently stimulated by the consumption of foods that contain dietary fiber. The white-bread, meat-and-potatoes diet of the typical Westerner is almost wholly devoid of dietary fiber. Hence the paradox—prosperous, flesh-gorging Europeans and Americans in full pursuit of the good life are ravaged by diseases to which the poor of rural Africa and Asia, living on a high-fiber, vegetarian diet, enjoy a charmed immunity.

If there is one substance that might be considered a cure-all for the saccharine diseases, it is bran. Hence the recent spate of high-fiber cookbooks containing ingenious recipes for introducing bran into one's meals. Essentially all are popularizations of the work of Dr. Cleave and his colleagues, and by extension, Sylvester Graham. The bolting cloth, to say nothing of the butcher's smock, has indeed become the shroud of Western man.

Graham Flour Bread

4 cups whole-wheat or graham flour
1 teaspoon salt
1 teaspoon sugar
1 package dry yeast
½ ounce soy margarine
1 cup water
Cracked wheat

Add salt and sugar to one cup of warm water. Stir until dissolved. Then add the yeast, and set aside until yeast starts to foam.

Meanwhile, cut the soy margarine into the flour. Then add the yeast and water to the flour mixture, and mix until a dough forms. Turn the dough out on a lightly floured board, and knead by hand until it becomes elastic and smooth.

Put the dough in a bowl, cover lightly with a cloth, and leave in a warm spot to rise. When it has doubled in bulk, knead it and shape it to fit into a nine-inch by five-inch loaf pan. Cover and allow to rise again (about forty minutes). Set the oven at 450°. Sprinkle cracked wheat over the loaf, and place in the oven for forty minutes. The bread is cooked through if it makes a hollow sound when lightly tapped on top.

Serves four.

Graham Muffins

3 cups graham flour
1 cup cracked wheat
1 teaspoon salt
2 tablespoons sugar
1 package dry yeast
1 tablespoon softened soy margarine
1 cup warm water
3 cups soy milk

Stir together the graham flour, cracked wheat, salt, and sugar. Cut in the softened soy margarine and set aside. Dissolve the yeast in a cup of warm water. Then add the water and the soy milk to the dry ingredients, and mix thoroughly. Cover lightly with a cloth and leave to rise. Pour into well-greased muffin pans. Bake at 425° for eighteen to twenty minutes.

Serves four.

Graham Crackers

4 tablespoons soy margarine
1 teaspoon egg replacer
2 teaspoons water
4 tablespoons dark brown sugar
4 tablespoons maple syrup
½ teaspoon baking soda
2 teaspoons water
1 teaspoon salt
1¾ cups graham flour
¾ cup all purpose flour

Melt the soy margarine in a saucepan. Dissolve a teaspoonful of egg replacer in a cup containing two teaspoonsful of water; then combine the soy margarine, the egg replacer, the dark brown sugar, and the maple syrup, and whisk vigorously until light and foamy. In a small cup containing two teaspoonsful of water, dissolve the baking soda, and turn it into the maple syrup margarine mixture. Gradually add the salt, the graham flour and the all-purpose flour to the mixture, combining gently but thoroughly. Mix until well-blended.

On a surface dusted with graham flour, roll out the dough until it is about an eighth of an inch thick. With a small sharp knife, cut the dough into sections that will fit onto your cookie sheet. Using the same knife, pre-cut the dough into 2½ inch squares without separating them from the dough section. With a toothpick, fork, or trussing needle, prick several holes into each square. Transfer the sections of pre-cut cracker dough to an ungreased cookie sheet with the aid of a spatula. Bake in a pre-heated, 350 degree oven for nine minutes on one side, and for seven or eight minutes on the other. Cool on a wire rack. The pre-cut squares in the baked cracker dough should now separate easily into individual graham crackers.

Yield: 36 graham crackers.

DR. JOHN HARVEY KELLOGG

How is it that the life of the inventor of America's most quintessential foods—peanut butter and cornflakes—is so little known? John Harvey Kellogg was the Edison of the epigastrium, the Einstein of the colon. Not only was he America's most prolific food inventor, but in his heyday, in the latter part of the nineteenth century, he was also the greatest abdominal surgeon in the world. Yet today he is remembered, if at all, because his name adorns the packages of America's best-selling breakfast cereals.

A perfectionist in his surgical specialty as he was in everything else, he used to beguile the time on train journeys by stitching samplers—not because he loved to sew, but rather because he wanted to improve his speed and accuracy in sewing up incisions during the countless gastrointestinal operations that he was called upon to perform. He even took drawing lessons, and frequently practiced sketching—not because he was a frustrated artist, but rather because he felt that drawing trained the hand to follow the eye—the best possible exercise he thought (apart from sewing samplers) for a surgeon.

Although Kellogg was a brilliant surgeon, throughout his long career, he remained a most reluctant and uneasy one. He recoiled at the thought of having to cut into another person's flesh, and never overcame his lifelong aversion to the sight of blood. In fact he was so squeamish that he did not begin to study surgery until well after he had left medical school, and was chief physician at the Battle Creek Sanatarium.

Appalled by the high mortality rate (twenty per cent) in abdominal surgery, he was convinced that he could do better. So he took a leave of absence from the Battle Creek Sanatarium, where he had been appointed physician-in-chief at the age of twenty-four, to study under the greatest surgeons in Europe: Theodor Billroth of Vienna (who invented modern gastric surgery); Sir Arbuthnot Lane of London; and Lawson Tait of Birmingham, England. At the time Kellogg served as his surgical assistant, Dr. Lawson Tait had set a record of 116 successive operations without a fatality. (This was in the days before surgeons wore sterile rubber gloves.)

Dr. Lawson Tait's record was unsurpassed until Kellogg bettered it with over 165 operations without a fatality. Kellogg attributed his extraordinary record in large part to his practice of putting his patients on a strict vegetarian diet a few weeks before and after each operation. To prevent relapses, he strongly urged his patients to give up meat, alcohol, and tobacco altogether.

A firm believer in Hippocrates's dictum that "Our medicine should be our food, and our food should be our medicine,"[1] Dr. Kellogg held that

149

a low protein diet strengthened resistance to disease, promoted longevity, and increased physical and mental endurance; whereas a high protein diet overtaxed the kidneys and liver, and contributed to the accumulation of toxins in the intestines. The result—those abominable abdominal disorders, which, if one were lucky, could be repaired by Dr. Kellogg's surgical skill. However, Dr. Kellogg regarded surgery as a last resort, and made it clear to his patients, and to his overflow lecture audiences, that if they embraced a vegetarian diet before the onset of disease, then they need never wear a "Kellogg scar."[2] Admired by surgeons for their neat stitchwork, "Kellogg scars" had become something of a status symbol among the well-to-do (high protein consumers) at the turn of the century.

At the height of his career as a surgeon (he performed more than 22,000 operations in his lifetime; the last at age eighty-four), Dr. Kellogg estimated that he had earned fees in excess of $400,000; and this was when the dollar was worth twenty times what it is today. Had he hoarded up his medical fees and the royalties from his food inventions, he could have become an American Croesus—not unlike Charles "Post Toasties" Post, a former charity patient at the Battle Creek Sanitarium, who became one of the richest men in America by copying (Dr. Kellogg had a blunter word for it) Dr. Kellogg's food inventions. However, Post's suicide at the age of sixty (from a self-inflicted gunshot wound) provided an object lesson (wealth alone does not bring solace) that Dr. Kellogg of all people did not need.

Money, Kellogg believed, should be spent on improving the lot of the unmoneyed. So he plowed his fees and royalties into charity work. He built orphanages, and established missions for the poor in the slums of Chicago. He himself was the father of forty-two adopted children. One third of all the surgery he performed were charity cases. In the skid rows of America, he set up a chain of vegetarian restaurants where a poor man could buy a meal for a penny; Dr. Kellogg then distributed meal-ticket books to the wealthy citizens of the city, which they were to carry on their person; so that when they were set upon by panhandlers trying to cadge the price of a drink, they could give them tickets for vegetarian lunches instead.

John Harvey Kellogg was born in Tyrone, Michigan on February 26, 1852, the first son of John Preston Kellogg, and his second wife Anne. He had four step-siblings from his father's second marriage; but he was closest to his younger brother Will Keith ("Only the Original Has This Signature") Kellogg, whose signature and motto adorned boxes of Kellogg's Cornflakes for over fifty years.

Fittingly enough, John Harvey's advent coincided with his parents' Adventism. Six months after he was born, his parents forsook their Baptist faith to become Seventh-day Adventists. The effect of his parents' conversion upon John Harvey's development was fateful and decisive. It meant that his diet, in keeping with Ellen White's food-reform vision of Otsego, Michigan, would be vegetarian; and his schooling perfunctory. For in site of the miscarriage of William Miller's prediction that Jesus Christ would return to earth on October 22, 1844, many of the early Adventists still believed that Christ's return to earth was imminent. John Harvey's father, like many other early Adventists, saw scant reason to have his children educated when at any moment they might be carried up to heaven.

Fortunately, John Harvey's lack of formal education did him no great harm because he had early acquired an appetite for books, which he read omnivorously. Before he was ten he had devoured the books in the libraries of his parents, his relatives and his neighbors; he even sorted broom corn in his father's broom factory so that he could earn enough money to start a small library of his own. Books on shorthand, botany and astronomy; a second-hand set of Farr's *Ancient History,* foreign language grammars and dictionaries crowded his shelves and bespoke an intellectual curiosity that was quite remarkable in such a young boy.

Word of Kellogg's mental acuity and manual dexterity (he outdid adults at sorting his father's broomcorn) reached James and Ellen White, who were looking for a young man to help them with the typesetting at the Review and Herald Publishing Association in Battle Creek. Since the Adventists believed that God communicated with them through the prophecies of the Church's founding mother, Ellen White, the Review and Herald had been set up to publish the Lord's views on health and nutrition as they were revealed to Mrs. White in her visions.

Kellogg leapt at the chance to work for two such pillars of the Adventist Church—and to learn the printing trade (shades of the young Ben Franklin) as a boy apprentice. One of the perquisites of working for the Whites was that it enabled him to absorb the health teachings of Mother White directly, and to read the great nutritional tomes of the nineteenth century, such as the works of Sylvester Graham, L. B. Coles, and James Caleb Jackson—which the Whites kept on hand as reference books in the office library.

Reading these works, which he did voraciously, confirmed Kellogg in his Adventist-bred vegetarianism, and kindled his interest in nutrition.

Over the years the Whites waxed fond of Kellogg. It was said that James White had become more of a father to him than his own father; and that Ellen White had adopted him as a protege. Once she had a vision in which she divined that someday he would occupy an important place in the Church and in the world as a physician. Accordingly, they offered to lend him the money to attend medical school. Despite his awkward tendency to swoon at the sight of blood, he accepted with alacrity. After studying for a year at the University of Michigan medical school, in 1875 he took his degree in medicine from Bellevue Hospital Medical College in New York, then regarded as the country's leading medical school.

It was actually while he was a medical student in New York that he started to experiment with making ready-to-eat breakfast cereals and meat analogues. The exigencies of his diet forced him to cook his own meals and to devise dishes that put nut meats and cereal grains to imaginative new uses. Although he was still many years away from making the discoveries that gave rise to flaked breakfast cereals such as corn flakes, and such mock meats as Nuttose, Protose and Battle Creek Steaks, the ingenious nut and cereal dishes that he concocted for himself were clearly the germ of a great idea. The year before he graduated from medical school, he gathered these student recipes of his into a cookbook that sold more than 30,000 copies. In many of these recipes one can glimpse the seeds of his later food creations.

As soon as he had gotten his M.D. he was asked to take the reins of leadership at the Health Reform Institute in Battle Creek, Michigan. The Institute had originally been founded at the behest of Mother White, who had a vision in which she saw that the Adventist Church should have its own medical facilities where Adventist patients could receive treatment that comported with their dietary and spiritual needs. One of John Harvey's first administrative acts on becoming physician-in-chief was to rename the Health Reform Institute, "The Battle Creek Sanatorium" (he coined the term "sanatorium") and to free it from its narrow sectarian aims by throwing open its doors to the general public.

Prior to his stewardship, the "San," as it affectionately came to be known, had fallen on hard times, but within two years of his taking charge he built the San into one of the most popular hotel spas in the world. A typical guest list reads like a "Who's Who" of the period. Everyone from presidents to motion picture royalty used to stop at the San to get revitalized with a crash course in Dr. Kellogg's "Biologic Living"—which consisted of a grain-based vegetarian diet, courses in hygienic cookery, vigorous exercise, hydrotherapy, plenty of fresh air and sunshine, emphasis on improving one's posture and mental outlook, and as a last resort—expert surgery. Notable among Dr. Kellogg's patients were former President William Howard Taft; pianists Percy Grainger and Jose Iturbi; Arctic explorers Vilhjalmur Stefansson and Roald Amundsen; world travelers such as Richard Halliburton and Lowell Thomas; industrialists like Alfred Dupont and John D. Rockefeller; grape juice king Edgar Welch; Yale economist Irving Fisher; playwright George Bernard Shaw; retailers S. S. Kresge, J. C. Penny, and Montgomery Ward, among many others, who returned to the San year after year; often sending their friends, relatives and employees to learn Dr. Kellogg's health secrets.

It was really in an effort to wean the San guests from their meat-centered diets that Dr. Kellogg developed ersatz meats, ready-to-eat cereals (a substitute for the all-American breakfast of ham 'n' eggs, or bacon 'n' eggs), and peanut buttter (a byproduct of his quest for the perfect nut cutlet and the perfect butter substitute).

In 1896 he produced America's first meat analogue, or ersatz meat, which he called "Nuttose." It was made from an emulsion of finely ground peanuts and water that had been thickened with flour and steamed or retorted until set. The nut cutlet that this process yielded could be flavored to taste like chicken, beef, or salmon, and was featured on the San menu as a mock-meat entree.

Dr. Kellogg soon followed Nuttose with such other meat analogues as Protose, Battle Creek Skallops, and meatless wieners—all of which, in health food stores, are still selling like hot cakes. These products differed from Nuttose in that they combined peanuts with varying amounts of wheat gluten.

Although Kellogg had made his meat analogues out of peanuts rather than the soybean, which is the principal ingredient in most modern meat analogues, he was very much aware of the soybean's possibilities, and predicted that it "would play a large part in the feeding of America's millions."[3] In fact his last major food invention was a soybean product—soy acidophilus milk, which he patented in 1934—just in time to save the life of Marie, the youngest of the Dionne quintuplets. At four months, she had contracted an intestinal infection that Dr. Kellogg's soy milk was instrumental in curing.

The story of Dr. Kellogg's discovery of a successful ready-to-eat breakfast cereal (i.e. Kellogg's Cornflakes) is most edifying—but it's not without its humorous aspects. Dr. Kellogg's first ready-to-eat was a confection that he called "Granola." Although its name, "Granola," has prospered (it's even in the dictionary), Kellogg's original formula has (mercifully) not survived. Little more than crumbled multigrain biscuit, it was hard to swallow and harder to chew—especially as Dr. Kellogg urged that it be eaten dry. Nonetheless, he might have been content to serve Granola to the San guests until the next Advent, had not an embarrassing incident taken place in the San dining room that put his scheme for making flaked cereals on the front burner, so to speak. In keeping with his belief that proper digestion begins in the mouth, with vigorous chewing, he asked that each guest chew a small portion of dry Granola before each meal—to stimulate the salivary flow. One morning an irate dowager burst into his office, shouting that the Granola had cracked her dentures! She demanded that Dr. Kellogg pay her on the spot for a new set of false teeth. Mortified, he took out his wallet, counted out the money in crisp bills, and immediately set to work trying to develop a chewable cereal.

After months of trial and error in his wife Ella's kitchen, Dr. Kellogg seemed to be getting nowhere. Then in a fortunate chain of events that recall Charles Goodyear's absent-minded discovery of the vulcanization of rubber (when he accidentally mixed sulfur and rubber on a hot stove), Dr. Kellogg absent-mindedly hit upon the principle of 'tempering," which is vital to the process of cereal flaking. Called away on an errand from Ella's kitchen, he inadvertently let a batch of cooked wheat stand for several hours. When he came back, he found that the wheat had turned rancid. But Dr. Kellogg was too thrifty to let such a large batch of wheat go to waste even if it had gone a little funny. So, rather than throw it out, he decided to run it through a pair of laundry-wringer-like rollers that he had been using to try to flake wheat. To his surprise the gamey, slightly moldy batch of wheat emerged form the rollers as distinct flakes of wheat—one discrete flake to each wheat berry. Dr. Kellogg had produced the first edible flakes in an endless snowfall of flaked cereals that has been pouring down on the American breakfast table for almost a century.

The author of more than fifty books, the father of forty-two adopted children, world class surgeon, and food inventor extraordinaire, Dr. John Harvey Kellogg, who lived to the ripe age of ninety-one, was a living testimony to the value of a vegetarian diet.

Protose Fricassee

4 tablespoons vegetable oil
1 teaspoon basil
1 medium onion, chopped
6 medium tomatoes, skinned
1 tablespoon peanut butter
1 can Protose, cut into chunks
Salt and pepper to taste.
Kellogg's Toasted Corn Flakes

Fry onions and basil until brown. Add the skinned tomatoes, peanut butter, and Protose. Cook gently for twenty minutes. Serve garnished with Kellogg's Toasted Corn Flakes. Mashed potatoes or boiled rice make a handsome complement.

Serves four.

"Protose"—a combination of wheat gluten and nutmeats—is commercially produced by Worthington Foods, which now markets many of Dr. Kellogg's ersatz meats, and is available in health food stores.

"Protose Fricassee' brings together three of Dr. Kellogg's major food inventions: mock meats (made from cereals and nut meats); peanut butter; and flaked, ready-to-eat cereals (e.g., Corn Flakes). This recipe is adapted from a recipe for "Protose Fricassee" in a cookbook written by Dr. Kellogg's wife, Ella, titled *Healthful Cookery* (Battle Creek, Michigan: 1904), p. 78. In her cookbook, Mrs. Kellogg tried to incorporate as many of her husband's food creations as possible.

Asparagus on Toast
(with Soy-Cream Sauce)

12 asparagus spears (trimmed and scrubbed)
6 slices whole-wheat toast
6 pats soy margarine
1 teaspoon sea salt
1 cup boiling water

Cream Sauce

2 tablespoons soy margarine
2 tablespoons flour
¼ teaspoon nutmeg
½ teaspoon sea salt
½ pint soy milk
¼ cup asparagus cooking liquid (obtained
    by boiling asparagus)

Wash trim and scrub asparagus spears. In a skillet bring to a boil one cup of salted water. Add asparagus spears. As soon as the water resumes boiling, lower heat, cover, and let simmer for five minutes. Be careful not to overcook! When tender, remove asparagus from the skillet, and drain. Reserve the asparagus cooking liquid for the cream sauce. Spread pats of soy margarine on the toast. Cut the spears into four-inch lengths, and cover the buttered side of the toast slice with asparagus pieces.

Cream Sauce: Melt the soy margarine in a saucepan. Stir in the flour, nutmeg, and sea salt. Combine the asparagus liquid with the soy milk, and gradually beat into the margarine and flour mixture. Stir over a low flame until mixture thickens. When it reaches a thick, creamy consistency, pour (piping hot) over the asparagus and toast.

Serves four.

This recipe is adapted from a recipe for "Asparagus On Toast," which appears in a vegetarian cookbook (Kellogg, op.cit., p. 14), written by Dr. Kellogg's wife, Ella. As the inventor of soy acidophilus milk, Dr. Kellogg was a great believer in the virtues of soy milk and championed its use in recipes such as this.

Breakfast Cornflakes

2 cups Kellogg's Cornflakes
1 cup apple juice, chilled
½ cup bananas, raspberries, or
    strawberries (optional)
2 tablespoons choped nutmeats (cashews,
    peanuts, brazils) (optional)

Pour 2 cups Kellogg's Cornflakes into a cereal bowl and add 1 cup of chilled apple juice. Peel a banana and slice it into rounds ¼ of an inch thick. Arrange the banana rounds (or raspberries, or strawberries) in a layer on top of the cornflakes. Sprinkle over it some chopped nutmeats. Allow the cornflakes to stand for a few minutes to absorb the apple juice, and serve.

Serves one.

Raised as a Seventh-Day Adventist and consequently as a vegetarian from birth, Kellogg invented cornflakes as an alternative to the American breakfast of bacon 'n' eggs, which he considered to be nutritionally unsound. As a result of his having invented cornflakes, millions of people now enjoy a meatless breakfast.

Fresh Peanut Butter

½ cup shelled, fresh peanuts or other fresh nuts
such as almonds, hazelnuts, walnuts, Brazil
nuts or cashew nuts—all of which yield a
delicious nut butter.
1¾ cups vegetable oil such as peanut oil or
safflower oil, or soya oil
Sea salt to taste

Pour ½ cup of nuts into a blender and add to it 1¾ cups of vegetable oil. If you like your peanut butter to have a crunchy taste, then grind just enough to yield a chunky paste in which the peanut fragments are still discernible. If on the other hand, you prefer a peanut butter with a creamy taste, then grind until all the peanut particles have been pulverized into a smooth, featureless paste. From time to time you should wipe down the sides of the blender with a spatula so that the nut butter has an even texture. Season with sea salt, and keep in a screw-top glass jar, or a plastic container. Store in the refrigerator.

Serves eight.

Oddly enough, the fact that Dr. Kellogg invented peanut butter is not widely known. One would think that the name of the man who invented America's most popular food (some 600 million pounds are consumed annually; that's eight pounds of peanut butter per person per year) would be as famous as Thomas Alva Edison's, or Alexander Graham Bell's. But it is not. In fact, in an otherwise informative article on peanut butter in *The New York Times* (Florence Fabricant, "Peanut Butter: An enduring Passion," *The New York Times,* May 21, 1986, pps. C1,4.), the reporter, Florence Fabricant, was unable to name the inventor of peanut butter, saying, "Its creator is known among peanut butter authorities only as a St. Louis doctor." A Battle, Creek, Michigan doctor would have been nearer the mark. Dr. Kellogg's biographers, Gerald Carson and Richard Schwarz, have established beyond cavil that Dr. Kellogg is the inventor of peanut butter. His purpose in doing so was the same as that which prompted him to invent Nuttose, Protose, and Battle Creek "Steaks"—to create a viable meat substitute. It is a measure of how far he has succeeded that countless millions of students, office workers and factory workers eat peanut butter sandwiches as a meatless meal.

(See Gerald Carson, *The Cornflake Crusade* (New York: Rinehart & Co., 1957), p. 107; and Richard W. Schwarz, *John Harvey Kellogg, M.D.* (Nashville: Southern Publishing Association, 1970), pps. 120, 121, 243.)

HENRY SALT

Like his countryman Jonathan Swift, Henry Salt was capable of drawing blood and laughter in equal measure with his "rapier" pen. In Salt's autobiography *Seventy Years Among Savages,* which cast him as a vegetarian Gulliver among the carnivorous yahoos of England, Salt obviously owed a debt to Swift's *Gulliver's Travels*—to say nothing of Swift's essay "A Modest Proposal," which, for satiric effect, exploited the idea of cannibalism in the British Isles.

It is important to notice that *Seventy Years Among Savages* appeared at a time when the British empire was at its fullest flood (1921). Engraved in the heart of every Englishman was the Kiplingesque notion of one's solemn duty to take up the white man's burden and extend the benefits of English culture to the benighted Hindus of India and the pagan Buddhists of China and Southeast Asia. But wait! There was Henry Salt, old Etonian, telling his fellow countrymen that they themselves were barbarians and cannibals, and that the vegetable-eating Buddhists and the cowloving Hindus were truly civilized.

Like Prince Siddhartha (who became the Buddha) or Mahavira, the founder of the vegetarian Jains, Henry Salt was born (in 1851) into an Indian military family. Had he been Hindu instead of the Anglican son of an English army officer, he would have been a member of the *ksatriya* (warrior) caste (like Siddhartha and Mahavira). That the warrior caste should have produced three such implacable vegetarians and pacifists is the keenest of ironies. To compound the irony, Salt's father had won rapid promotion through the military ranks for his skill and ruthlessness in putting down the Hindus, whom he regarded as a race of dusky savages.

To Salt's father, an officer in the Royal Bengal Artillery, Henry was an enigma. Think of it—officer Salt's son a vegetarian pacifist! How could Salt, a professional warrior, have sired such a freak? It was the same question that Sir Bysshe Shelley must have asked himself when his son Percy became an atheist, got himself expelled from Oxford, married a woman of "low birth," and became a full-fledged poet and vegetarian.

In fact, it was to Shelley that Salt largely attributed his own vegetarianism. While Salt was influenced by Shelley's poems and pamphlets on vegetarianism, he was even more inspired by the force of Shelley's personal example. After being asked to translate Shelley's "The Cloud" into Latin verse (while a student at Blackheath school), Salt became hopelessly besotted with its author—so much so that one might be pardoned for thinking that Salt had tried to turn himself into a carbon copy of Shelley.

159

Like Shelley, Salt was a brilliant classicist at Eton and Oxford, a writer by profession, a socialist, an atheist, and a vegetarian who was at odds with his own father.

If there had ever been any danger of Salt's wavering in his admiration for Shelley, such danger was forever dispelled by the Eton headmaster J. J. Hornby's frequent and intemperate denounciations of Shelley. On one occasion Hornby gave a speech in which he regretted that Shelley had not attended Eton's arch-rival, Harrow. Harrow already had one romantic poet and libertine to its credit—Lord Byron. Nothing, however, could have been more calculated to ensure that Salt would remain a worshipper at Shelley's shrine than headmaster Hornby's disapproval.

If Salt was never the social outcast at Eton that Shelley had been, it was because Salt could play a creditable game of "fives"—an Eton game considered to be the forerunner of squash racquets. Students at Eton were esteemed more for their athletic ability than for their intellectual prowess. Studies were an unpleasant interlude between games of cricket and the killing of animals for sport—a practice that Salt, as both an Eton master and crusading alumnus, had tried to abolish, with negligible results.

After Eton, Salt, like Shelley, went on to Oxford. But Salt's career as an undergraduate was considerably more subdued than Shelley's. Shelley was expelled for publishing a treatise on atheism. By contrast, Salt stayed the course and graduated with first-class honors in Greek and Latin. In his senior year he won the gold medal for Greek epigram and compiled an academic record of such distinction that he was invited by Eton's headmaster to teach the boys.

Patient, unfailingly kind, good humored, and idiosyncratic, Salt (in spite of his curious views about animals and food reform) was an exceedingly popular master. One of his most endearing eccentricities (for his pupils, at any rate) was his willingness to allow his students to use a "crib" or translation when they were doing their Greek or Latin assignments. To other masters this would have smacked of cheating, but Salt felt that his students could profit from copying a skillful translation.

Salt's most salient eccentricity, and the one that earned him the gentle mockery of boys and masters alike, was, of course, his vegetarianism and his opposition to such time-honored Eton sports as hare coursing and fox hunting. It should be noted, however, that Salt was never discouraged by any of this. In the parry and thrust of verbal exchanges he always gave as good as he got. His repartee was sparkling, yet deadly. For example, when a fellow Eton master and distinguished scientist once asked Salt, "Don't you think that animals were *sent* us as food?" Salt shot back the killing reply: "The invoice has not yet been received."[1]

Surprisingly, several Etonians from Salt's time as a master (even some who had held him up to the most savage ridicule) went on to become vegetarians later in life. One Etonian, Dr. Edward Lyttelton, who had been a lowly assistant master during Salt's tenure, became Eton's first vegetarian headmaster—much to the chagrin of Old Etonians who shook their wattles and rued the day that their beloved Eton had elected a vegetarian headmaster: "What is Eton coming to?"[2] they cried. Salt's account of Dr. Lyttelton's election in his *Seventy Years Among Savages*, is worth quoting:

> A vegetarian was of course regarded as a sheer lunatic in the Eton of those days. Twenty-five years later Eton had a vegetarian headmaster in Dr. Edward Lyttelton, who was an assistant there in the 1880s. "Little did I think," he wrote to me, "when we used to chaff you about cabbages, that it would come to this!"[3]

Although there was much about the life of an Eton master that appealed to Salt—the intellectual companionship and the steady income—there was also much that appalled him. As he neared his mid-thirties his spirit began to chafe at the school's narrow-minded orthodoxy; its glorification of cricket, rugby, and bloodsports over scholarship; and its stultifying intellectual atmosphere that did not tolerate new ideas and fresh thoughts. As luck would have it, just when Salt had despaired of ever having enough money to be able to leave Eton and strike out on his own as a writer, he discovered the works of Henry David Thoreau. *Walden*, with its paradoxical message that one can live a richer and more fulfilling life by reducing one's store of material possessions and by simplifying one's life, was to Salt a revelation.

Having saved enough of his salary to provide a modest income, Salt and his wife, Kate, decided to take their leave of these "cannibals in cap and gown"[4] as he jokingly styled his fellow Etonians, and retire to the hills of Surrey near the town of Tilford. They took up residence in a former laborer's cottage on a small parcel of land. There Salt and Kate tried to put into practice the ideas and principles that they had gleaned from *Walden*. As though to dramatize the finality of their move (for the tug of Eton life was still strong), Salt set up a scarecrow in his vegetable garden and covered it with his Eton cap. His flowing academic gown, he cut into strips which he used to fasten some vines to the wall.

That an Eton master should throw up a coveted teaching post to live as a vegetarian rustic excited much comment in the public prints. Old Etonians were as much scandalilzed by Salt's vegetarianism, as Old Concordians were by Thoreau's. The conservative papers upbraided Salt for his socialism, his Shelleyanism, and his vegetarianism. These papers regarded the whole enterprise as a waste of a beautiful education. On the other hand, the radical papers were positively enchanted with the idea, and confidently predicted that Salt's example would inspire Eton masters to take to the countryside in droves. Though this never happened, the publicity did have the effect of inducing a great many like-minded artists and writers, such as George Meredith, William Morris, Edward Carpenter,

Havelock Ellis, Lowes Dickinson, and George Bernard Shaw to make the pilgrimage to the hills of Surrey and drop in on this Etonian Thoreau. Encouraged by all the publicity, Salt began to pen a stream of books about subjects that were dear to him—vegetarianism, animal rights, naturalism, and the lives of neglected and misunderstood writers like Shelley, Thoreau, De Quincey, and Melville. If their names are familiar now it is in no small measure because Salt helped to put them on the literary map. By virtue of the fuss that Salt's quitting Eton had kicked up, his books sold at a fairly brisk pace—well enough, at any rate, to keep Henry and Kate in vegetables and writing materials.

A frequent guest at Salt's cottage was the up-and-coming playwright, George Bernard Shaw. Despite Shaw's brilliance, his formal education had been rather sketchy, and he felt somewhat awed in the presence of a man of Henry Salt's scholarly attainments. Vegetarian and socialist though he was, Shaw was secretly intrigued by the trappings of social success (he was a bit of a social climber), and Eton, which was the nursery of the English aristocracy, especially fascinated him. Through his friendship with Salt—who was the quintessence of Etonism—Shaw was able to acquire the patina of an Eton education by association (this may have helped Shaw cut even more of a dash in English society).

Both Salt and Shaw were members of the Shelley society, and meetings of that society frequently brought them together. Unfortunately both Salt and Shaw held views of Shelley that were, to put it mildly, at variance with those held by other members of the society. Most members liked to think of Shelley as a sort of biscuit box cherub, who wrote charming ditties about autumnal zephyrs and chirruping skylarks. Conveniently forgotten were Shelley's fiery poems on the rights of workers, feminism, freethought, animal rights, and vegetarianism. So, at a meeting of the Shelley society, when Shaw announced to the other members that "Like Shelley I am a socialist, an atheist, and a vegetarian,"[5] it was all that Salt could do to restrain one of the members from taking a poke at Shaw for blaspheming the poet's memory. In 1887, Salt wrote the first of his books on Shelley. His Shelley studies became the basis for a critical reevaluation that helped restore Shelley to the front rank of English poets, and helped win him recognition as the poet-prophet of a new age of social, economic, and dietary reform.

After Shelley, Salt's grandest literary passion was for Henry David Thoreau, and essentially, Salt performed the same service for Thoreau that he had done for Shelley. Until Salt wrote his biography of Thoreau (which is still compulsively readable after ninety years), Thoreau was little known in England beyond a small circle of admirers. Not only did Salt's biography gain him a wide following in England, but it also played a role in the break-up of the British Empire.

If this last statement seems a bit grandiose, it is meant to be. For Salt was responsible for putting Thoreau's writings into the hands of one of the most powerful political leaders of the century—Mahatma Gandhi. It is surely one of history's great ironies that a retired classics master from Eton, whose father had helped subjugate the Indians to the British, should be the instrument for providing the leader of India's *swarajist* (self-rule) movement with the means for defeating the British. Yet this is exactly what happened.

Many of the tactics of non-violent resistance that Gandhi used against the British colonial government in India and the Dutch colonial government in South Africa had been anticipated by Thoreau in his essay "Civil Disobedience." Thoreau was one of the first political thinkers to realize the importance of symbolic protest, and he recognized that symbolic gestures of defiance—such as the resfusal to pay taxes, the burning of identity cards, and the courting of arrest through non-cooperation with draconian laws—could be far more effective in bringing down an unjust regime than acts of violence.

Although Gandhi claimed not to have read Thoreau before formulating his own theory of civil disobedience (circa 1907), scholars now believe that through the writings of Henry Salt, Gandhi had become familiar with Thoreau's ideas much earlier—in 1890, to be precise. During that year Gandhi was a law student in London, and Salt's *Life of Henry David Thoreau* was published.

Two years before Salt's biography of Thoreau came out, Gandhi had sailed from Bombay to study at the Inns of Court in London. Walking home from the Inns of Court one evening, he happened on a vegetarian restaurant. He was picking his way toward the dining tables, when his eye was caught by the title of a pamphlet in a display case. The pamphlet was "A Plea for Vegetarianism" by Henry Salt. Paying the shilling that it cost, he took the pamphlet to one of the tables and devoured it as greedily as he did his vegetarian supper, which was his "first hearty meal in England."

Salt's "Plea" opens appropriately enough with a quote from Henry David Thoreau, whose own vegetarianism, unhappily, was not so thoroughgoing as the quote would make it seem.

> I have no doubt that it is a part of the destiny of the human race, in its gradual improvement, to leave off eating animals, as surely as the savage tribes have left off eating each other, when they came in contact with the more civilized.[6]

In his "Plea," Salt had put the case for vegetarianism so forcefully that by the time Gandhi had finished reading it, he became, for the first time in his life, a vegetarian by choice rather than heredity. When, in 1931, Gandhi returned in triumph to England as head of India's *swarajist* movement, the first person he asked to see was Henry Salt. At a meeting of the London Vegetarian Society on November 20, 1931, he expressed his debt to Salt as follows:

It was Mr. Salt's book, "A Plea for Vegetarianism," which showed me why, apart from a hereditary habit, and apart from a vow administered to me by my mother, it was right to be a vegetarian. He showed me why it was a moral duty incumbent on vegetarians not to live upon fellow animals. It is therefore a matter of personal pleasure to me that I find Mr. Salt in our midst.[7]

Walnut Rissoles

2 ounces margarine
1 small spring onion, chopped
1 stalk celery, diced
2 teaspoons marjoram and thyme
1 tablespoon all-purpose flour
½ cup apple juice
½ lb. grated walnuts
1 teaspoon yeast extract
4 ounces whole-wheat bread crumbs
Crushed cornflakes
Salt and pepper to taste

Melt the margarine in a saucepan. Add the chopped onion, celery, marjoram, and thyme, and fry gently. Stir in the flour; then add the juice, yeast extract, walnuts and whole-wheat bread crumbs. Cook for about seven minutes, stirring constantly. Remove from flame. As soon as the mixture has cooled sufficiently, form into round shapes and roll in crushed cornflakes. Bake in moderate oven, or fry gently in a skillet. Serve with mashed potatoes.

Serves four.

These dishes, which were among Henry Salt's favorites, were provided by his widow Catherine Salt, who is a spry ninety and lives in England. They were obtained through the good offices of Salt's literary executor Jon Wynne-Tyson.

Apple Fritters

4 medium cooking apples
4 ounces all-purpose flour
2 teaspoons baking powder
1 teaspoon cream of tartar
½ cup apple juice
1 teaspoon vegetable oil
Salt and pepper to taste
Oil for deep-frying

Peel and core the apples and cut them into wedges about one-half inch thick. Set aside, and prepare the batter.

In a mixing bowl combine the flour with the baking powder and cream of tartar. Add the apple juice and stir vigorously with a spatula. When the ingredients are thoroughly mixed, add the vegetable oil.

Dip the apple wedges into batter and deep-fry them.

Serves four.

ESMÉ WYNNE-TYSON

Esmé Wynne-Tyson tasted fame earlier than any of the other vegetarians in this book. At the age of thirteen she was hailed as one of England's most successful child actresses. In fact, it was while she was playing the star part of Rosamund in *Where the Rainbow Ends* that she struck up a friendship with an equally precocious young player who had been cast in a minor role—a twelve-year-old named Noël Coward.

At first she and Noël didn't take to each other; relations between them were rather frosty. But after they had appeared in a few performances together, the ice melted. From then on, until Esmé married, she and Noël were inseparable. So inseparable in fact that Esmé's fiancé, Lynden Tyson, nearly broke off his engagement with Esmé when, during a sojourn with Noël and Esmé at a country house, Lynden was shocked to see the pair emerge from the bathroom, arm-in-arm. Noël's biographer, Sheridan Morley, recounts the event as follows:

> Nevertheless, the ménage à trois seems to have worked out except for one moment of crisis when Esmé and Noël were discovered by Lynden Tyson as they sailed simultaneously out of the bathroom. For Lynden this was almost the last straw: "I knew that intellectually Noël and Esmé were very close, and though I wasn't able to understand their non-sexual relationship, I was getting a bit jealous of Master Noël."[1]

Given Noël's sexual proclivities, which were quite evident early on, his relationship with Esmé was necessarily platonic. But that didn't stop them from touring in plays together, taking baths together, skinny-dipping in the sea together, or capering through the woods, looking for all the world like two disheveled disciples of the great god Pan.

Noël gives credit to Esmé for sparking his interest in writing. She was forever dashing off novels, plays, and verses. Her industry and output were daunting. Soon Noël too was scribbling furiously—plays, novels, epics, and doggerel verses leapt from his pen like imps from an inkwell. Though most of what Esmé and Noël wrote during this period of late adolescence they would later have cheerfully burned, these early effusions were curtain raisers for the great works that each would produce in maturity—his in the field of musical comedy, hers in the field of belles-lettres and comparative religion. His works, which have become classics of the 20th-century English theater, include *Design for Living, Blithe Spirit, Private Lives,* and *Fallen Angels.* Hers include such novels as *The Gift,* and *Riddle of the Tower;* biographical studies like *The Best Years of Their Lives* (biographies of women who began new lives after forty); and such works of comparative religion as *Mithras: The Fellow In The Cap* (1958), *The*

Philosophy of Compassion: The Return of the Goddess (1962); and *The Dialectics of Diotoma* (1970). In her introduction to Porphry's *On Abstinence from Animal Food*, which she edited in 1964, she employed a formidable erudition to show that there is a forgotten tradition of vegetarianism at the very wellsprings of Western culture. If Noël put his genius at the service of Thalia, the muse of comedy, then Esmé put hers at the service not of Melpomene, the muse of tragedy, nor of Mnemosyne, the mother of the muses; but of the great Goddess herself, the Mistress of Animals (The Lady of Wild Things), who ruled the earth before there were male gods, fratricidal wars, plague, and famine. The Mistress of Animals ruled in that golden age hymned by the classical poets, Hesiod, Vergil, Ovid—when all men and women were vegetarians.

Apart from stimulating each other mentally, collaborating on stories and plays, and serving as each other's muse, Noël and Esmé also drew upon their shared experiences for the subject matter of their literary work. There appears to be more than a hint of the Noël Coward-Esmé Wynne-Tyson platonic triangle in the drollest, yet darkest of Noël's plays, *Design for Living*. Similarly, the themes of platonic love and the androgynous male sound insistently throughout Esmé's great work, *The Philosophy of Compassion: The Return of the Goddess*. The heroes of the book include Pythagoras, Buddha, Christ and Plotinus—all men who were notable for their tenderness, gentleness, and compassion (qualities that are traditionally associated with women). In other words, these godlike men stand as exemplars for the androgynous ideal of strength-tempered-with-compassion that Esmé felt all men and women should aspire to. Doubtless it was Noël Coward—the androgynous genius of the English theater—who first made Esmé aware of the creative potential that is available to a man who had the courage to cultivate his feminine side, rather than the obnoxious swagger and the false-hair-on-the-chest of masculine convention.

Esmé was born in the proverbial "trunk" on June 29, 1898. Her parents were both involved with the stage, and Esmé grew up in the magical world of the theater. Although it may not have been prevalent in other branches of English society at the turn of the century, in the English theater equality of opportunity existed as much for women as for men. If anything it was dominated by women, and was probably more matriarchal than any other English institution—save the monarchy. Certainly the great leading ladies of the period—Stella Campbell, Ellen Terry, Sybil Thorndyke—reigned as indisputably over the British stage as Queen Victoria ruled over the British Empire. Because Esmé grew up in this heady, enchanting, electrically charged atmosphere of a world dominated by powerful, gifted, and beautiful women, one can easily see how she might have entertained the notion that the world itself was once governed by such women.

This is precisely the thesis that Esmé puts forward in her magnum opus

The Philosophy of Compassion: The Return of the Goddess. The book presents the theory that the earth originally was inhabited by peace-loving vegetarians, who practiced a Mother Goddess religion and reckoned their descent through the female line. But their golden days were numbered. In harsher climes, warlike societies sprang up that made a cult of masculinity, and ate the flesh of animals. With contemptible ease, these warriors swept down upon the vegetarian peoples, dethroned their Mother Goddess, and set up male gods—gods of war and plunder—in Her place.

As Esmé views Her, the primeval Goddess was a Lady of Wild Things whose compassion extended to all living creatures. Neither the oppression of women nor the degradation of animal life (so prevalent in our own time) ever reared its head during the reign of the Goddess. Despite the triumph of patriarchal religions, it is Esmé's belief that the Mother Goddess religion never wholly died out. It lives on in such compassionate religions as Hinduism and Buddhism with their emphasis on the sanctity of life and the essential oneness of all living things. She also finds evidence of its staying power in the writings of such modern philosophers as Hegel and Schopenhauer—especially Schopenhauer, who blasted the Christian churches for denying that animals have souls, even though he himself stopped short of becoming a vegetarian: "We may observe that compassion for sentient beings is not to carry us to the length of abstaining from flesh like the Brahmins."[2]

In the closing chapters of *The Return of the Goddess,* Esmé draws upon a wealth of material to suggest that Christ was a member of the ancient Jewish religious sect known as the Essenes. Like the Pythagoreans and the Neoplatonists, the Essenes were a society of pacifists and vegetarians, whose philosophy, Esmé believes, derived from the ancient Mother Goddess religion that was driven out by the patriarchs. Christianity, she feels, missed its chance to revive the wisdom of the Goddess when the apostle Paul and the church fathers tampered with the Essene spirit of Christ's teachings. They tried to make it more palatable to the masses by grafting on to it the more crowd-pleasing and sensational features of its chief rival during this period—the masculine, militaristic religion of Mithraism, which had as its central mystery the redemption of the world through the ritual sacrifice of a bull.

In contending that the vegetarian, goddess-worshipping cultures of prehistory were overthrown by patriarchal peoples who worshipped warlike male gods, Esmé anticipated by two decades the feminist anthropological writings of Elizabeth Gould Davis (*The First Sex*), Merlin Stone (*When God was a Woman*), and others who have brought to bear compelling archaeological evidence that shows that a violent overthrow of peaceful, vegetarian matriarchies did in fact occur in the not-too-distant past.

Red Cabbage en Casserole

1 medium size red cabbage
1 large onion, sliced or diced
2 cooking apples
1 tablespoon brown sugar
1 teaspoon cinnamon
½ teaspoon ground cloves
½ teaspoon allspice
1 tablespoon margarine
Seasoning

Slice cabbage. Place layers of cabbage in a casserole dish, then mix the apples and onion. Repeat layers and finish with cabbage. Sprinkle sugar and spice and season well. Cover with water and add margarine. Place lid on dish and cook gently in a moderate oven.

Butter Bean Soup

8 ounces white butter beans (lima beans)
2 pints water
1 medium size onion
2 heaping teaspoonfuls Marmite, or
      Yeastrel, or other yeast extract
Knob of margarine
Chopped parsley
Salt and pepper to taste

Soak white butter beans overnight and then cook until tender. Increase the water that the beans have cooked in until the quantity is roughly two pints. Cook again gently with onion, two large teaspoons Marmite, knob of margarine, and seasoning. Garnish with chopped parsley.

Serves four.

SWAMI PRABHUPADA

Ex Oriente Lux is a Latin phrase that means light or wisdom comes from the East. The same might be said for the phenomenon of vegetarianism itself. The cradle of vegetarianism is India. Every philosophy or religion associated with vegetarianism has had its origin in India. Each wave of vegetarianism that has broken upon Western shores has either directly or indirectly come from India. It could be argued that the same wave that brought vegetarianism to the U.S. in the 1960s had bobbing on its surface the freighter that carried the most improbable world teacher that the West had ever known.

After chugging into New York Harbor on September 19, 1965, the Indian freighter *Jaladuta* disgorged a most unusual passenger. Clad in a saffron-colored *dhoti* and *chadar;* wearing white rubber shoes; wielding an umbrella and a battered typewriter, the old man looked as if he should be treading the dusty roads of Mathura (Krishna's birthplace), instead of padding about the mean streets of Manhattan. Was this the man who with only a few rupees in his pockets and no apparent prospects believed that he could travel to America and teach the members of this coarse, materialistic, animal-eating society how to cook and eat vegetarian food? Was this the man who would open Vaishnava temples and vegetarian restaurants in every major city of the world? Was this the man who would establish the first Eastern religion on Western soil since the days of the Roman Empire (the likelihood of which theologian Harvey Cox put at one in a million)? Yes, this was he, the *dhoti*-clad savior that the Western world had been pining for since the death of Pythagoras and Porphyry. This was the man who would teach them not to kill and eat animals, but to eat the *prasadam* of Lord Krishna.

With his saffron-colored *dhoti* cinched at the waist; his *chadar* wound round his chest; the *shika* (tuft of hair) bristling at his nape, the two whitish vertical *tilaka* striping his forehead; the strand of beads slung round his neck, His Divine Grace A.C. Bhaktivedanta Swami Prabhupada's appearance as he strode down the gangplank of the *Jaladuta* was almost defiantly outlandish. For unlike the bogus swamis who swooped down on New York by jet from India, sporting Western garb and spouting a streamlined version of Hindu dharma, Prabhupada putt-putted into Gotham in an old tub. He stoutly refused to wear Western clothes; eat Western non-veg. food, or water down his teachings for Western audiences. Polite he was—almost to a fault, but he was also fiercely and uncompromisingly himself; and he saw himself as the divinely chosen instrument for spreading the dharma of Lord Krishna to the West.

Happily for Prabhupada, Krishna's charismatic powers were to prove as potent for Westerners as they had always been for Hindus. Fact is, Krishna's effect on Westerners had been compelling from the very start (circa 150 B.C.). The first Westerner of whom we have any record to fall under His spell was Heliodorus, a Greek ambassador to one of the regional courts of India. Heliodorus erected a pillar proclaiming himself to be a *bhagavata* (devotee) of Lord Krishna in 150 B.C. The first modern Westerner to have fallen under Krishna's sway was the great English jurist and Sanskritist, Sir William Jones. During the summers, when court was out of session, "Oriental Jones" (as he is still affectionately called) stayed with his wife in a little bungalow in the aptly named town of Krishnagar just north of Calcutta in Bengal and with the aid of a patient *pandit*, he became the second Englishman to learn Sanskrit. (This was in the early days of the Raj, circa 1793.) In addition to being a distinguished jurist, who compiled a seven-volume digest of Hindu law, he authenticated the first date in ancient Indian history. As if this were not enough, he discovered the Indo-European family of languages, conveyed to the West the riches of Sanskrit and—one of his most enduring achievements—founded the Asiatic Society. In the little spare time that he could snatch from his busy schedule, Sir William diverted himself by reading widely in the *Puranas* in which Krishna and the Gopis—His love-swacked cowgirls— figure prominently. To his wife and his friends, Sir William confessed that he was "charmed with Krishna" and "in love with the Gopis"—so much so, that he seriously entertained the idea of becoming a Hindu convert; he was particularly drawn to the doctrine of reincarnation, which seemed "incomparably more rational, more pious, and more likely to deter men from vice than the horrid opinions inculcated by Christians of punishment without end." Moreover, since vegetarianism is a corollary of a belief in reincarnation, it's not surprising that Sir William flirted with the notion of becoming a vegetarian. Who knows? —had he not died at the unripe age of 49, he might have become a *Gaudiya Vaishnava* and chanted *Hare Krishna!* with the followers of Lord Chaitanya (Prabhupada's 16th century mentor) in the streets of Calcutta. If such a great sahib as Sir William Jones could become besotted with Krishna, then how could Swami Prabhupada's Krishna Consciousness mission fail to capture the imagination of the spiritually famished millions in the West?

Prabhupada's desire to preach did not begin to stir in him until he was in his mid-fifties. Through sheer dedication and hard work, he had parlayed a small pharmacy in Bombay into a thriving business; but as he approached mid-life, he found that being a successful businessman no longer held any charm for him. What he really wanted to do was to go out and preach Lord Chaitanya's message to the world, as his spiritual master Swami Bhaktisiddhanta had entreated him to do way back in 1922 (when Prabhupada was 26).

Swami Prabhupada was born in Calcutta on September 1, 1896. Although members of the caste into which he was born—the *vaisya* or merchant caste—were traditionally forbidden to study Sanskrit, which was a jealous possession of the *brahmin* elite—Prabhupada had the good fortune (or karma) to be born into a *Gaudiya Vaishnava* family—(a family who worshipped Lord Krishna after the manner of the 16th century Bengali saint Chaitanya Mahaprabhu). In this branch of Vaishnavism, caste and social rank are viewed as distinctions to be earned, not privileges of birth; so Prabhupada's parents, recognizing their son's great mental gifts, saw to it that he had an education befitting a *brahmin* of the highest rank. From the primary grades on through college, he studied Sanskrit and English; in college he studied a trio of subjects—Philosophy, Sanskrit and English that would contribute to the panoply of skills that he would need to spread the message of Lord Chaitanya throughout the world.

His study of Philosophy helped him to understand Western thought processes, which are based on the syllogism. His knowledge of Sanskrit enabled him to translate the classical texts of Vaishnava religious literature into English. His knowledge of English which he spoke with an infectious Bengali lilt, enabled him to write and speak in a language that was fast becoming the *koine* or lingua franca of the world. Furthermore, probably due to the cultural interchange that invariably takes place between a colonial power and its subject colony (until 1945 India had been for amost 200 years a colony of England), English was becoming the language of the vegetarian idea. (More books have been written in English on the subject of vegetarianism than in any other tongue.) So Prabhupada himself speaking his immensely charming Bengali English and unlimbering his hefty English translations of Indian sacred literature (that would soon be hawked at airports throughout the world)—would play a leading part in that curious process whereby the colonizing nation is pacified and civilized by its former subject nation. Because of men like Prabhupada the English speaking world, which was once the most carnivorous tribe on the planet, is now converting to vegetarianism at a furious pace.

Also propitious for Prabhupada's mission (although he was unaware of it at the time) was it that Europe and America in the mid-1960s were passing through a period of cultural upheaval. As a result of the "baby boom" in the post-WWII years, Western youth accounted for a disproportionately large segment of the population. An entire generation seemed to be experiencing the collective *weltschmertz* of late adolescence. Suddenly they began calling into question the bourgeois values to which they owed their privileged, affluent but spiritually empty lives. Owing to technological advances in methods of animal slaughter, animal flesh had become cheaper, with the result that flesh consumption among members of this age group had reached a critical mass. Indeed, more dead animals had passed down the gullets of Western youth in this period than those of any other generation in history. Consequently a wave of inner revulsion swept through this group that drove them to seek absolution for their unconscious guilt in radical politics, utopian living schemes, and other idealistic experiments. Many felt in the spirit of the times that some great sage from the East would come to teach them new rituals of eating, loving, living and worshipping—because the traditional Western modes of doing these things were steeped in blood. The trendsetters among this generation who sought spiritual guidance in the East were pop musicians and film stars like Paul McCartney and George Harrison of the Beatles. They actually traveled to India and sat at the feet of Indian gurus. (How ironic that descendents of Britishers who had drilled it into the Indians that they were a second-rate nation were now traveling to India to be healed and shriven!)

It's worth noting that prior to the late 1960s, Western spiritual seekers usually had to travel to India to find a guru. This was because the true *sadhus*, or holy men would rather die than travel to the West, which they regarded as a truly barbarous place—coarse, animal-eating, and materialistic. Swami Bhaktisiddhanta, Prabhupada's own spiritual master, had sent several *Gaudiya Vaishnava* teachers to the West hoping that they would impart the message of Lord Chaitanya; but within a few months they had crept back to India. Only Shrila Prabhupada, who was just one year shy of his seventieth birthday was able to do the impossible—to travel to America and establish a living branch of *Gaudiya Vaishnavism* on American soil. Of Prabhupada's achievement, the great Indologist A.L. Basham wrote that the Hare Krishna movement represents "the first time since the days of the Roman Empire that an Asian religion is being openly practiced by people of Western origin in the streets of Western cities."

Before Prabhupada could board the freighter in Calcutta that would transport him to New York and worlds beyond, he had to convince the ship's owner, a bountiful lady shipping magnate named Sumati Morarji (who had already helped to finance the publication from Sanskrit into English of the *Shrimad Bhagavatam*) that he was equal to the journey. At 69 years, Prabhupada was in delicate health and the sea journey from India to America on a freighter without stabilizers could be treacherous. She was afraid that he might not survive the voyage. (As it turned out, her fears were not misplaced—Prabhupada had three heart attacks on the first leg of the outward voyage, but fortunately they weren't disabling.) However, Prabhupada was nothing if not determined, and he was so insistent that she finally gave in. "All right," she said reluctantly, "I will make the arrangements to send you by our ship." She then set about finding a captain who would be sympathetic to the needs of a devout vegetarian and a bona fide Vaishnava saint—if not an avatar of Lord Krishna Himself.

All was arranged, and the *Jaladuta* was scheduled to sail on the 13th of August from Calcutta, the capital of West Bengal. The place of departure was not without a certain resonance; for it had been in Bengal that Lord Chaitanya—whom Prabhupada revered—had revitalized Krishna worship in the 16th century. It was Chaitanya who had popularized the *kirtan* and the *bhajan*—the public dancing and chanting in praise of Lord Krishna in towns and cities throughout Northern India. But Chaitanya was no mere street minstrel—he was a Sanskrit scholar of immense erudition, who routinely worsted *brahmin* pundits in public debates.

Similarly his heir in the disciplic succession (albeit at a 400 year remove), Swami Prabhupada taught his American devotees to dance and chant in adoration of Lord Krishna, but like Chaitanya he was also a deep student and scholar of the Vaishnava tradition. His roundly admired translations of the classics of Vaishnava religious literature have made these works available to Westerners for the first time.

Also like Lord Chaitanya who used to smack his lips over his favorite vegetarian dishes—each of which was recorded in almost Proustian detail by his biographer Krishnadasa Kaviraja Goswami—Prabhupada had a highly developed palate. Furthermore, he was also a talented cook who trained Yamuna Devi (author of the culinary classic *Lord Krishna's Cuisine*) and other devotees to become world-class Indian vegetarian cooks. In fact many of the early Krishna devotees in America made no secret of the fact that they had initially been attracted to Prabhupada's lectures by the sumptuous vegetarian *prasadam* meals that he used to cook for them afterwards.

In so many ways, Prabhupada in the final most productive decade of his life had become Chaitanya Mahaprabhu's worthy successor. In some ways he may have even excelled him; for not only did Prabhupada revitalize Krishna worship throughout India in the style of Lord Chaitanya but he also spread Vaishnavism, Krishna worship and vegetarianism throughout the world.

Pishima's Stuffed Okra

1½ pounds tender okra, preferrably 4-inch pods, washed
  and thoroughly dried
2 tablespoons coarsely crushed coriander seeds
1 tablespoon coarsely crushed cumin seeds
2 teaspoons fennel seeds
½ teaspoon freshly ground pepper
1 tablespoon *garam masala*
¼ teaspoon cayenne pepper or paprika
¼ teaspoon yellow asafoetida powder *(hing)*
½ teaspoon turmeric
1 tablespoon ground almonds
½ teaspoon *amchoor* powder or ½ tablespoon lemon juice
5 tablespoons sunflower oil
½ tablespoon salt

Slice off the stem end and ⅛ inch off the tip of each okra pod. Slit each one lengthwise, leaving ¼ inch unslit at both ends, taking care not to cut the pods in half.

Combine the crushed coriander seeds, cumin seeds, fennel seeds, black pepper, *garam masala*, cayenne or paprika, asafoetida, turmeric, ground almonds, *amchoor* powder, if you're using it. After mixing the ingredients together, drizzle in the lemon juice (if you haven't used *amchoor*) and 2 teaspoons of oil, and crumble through your fingers to blend well into a dry, oatmeal consistency.

Using a teaspoon or knife, ease about ¼ teaspoon of the stuffing evenly into each slit. Working one at a time, stuff, then press the cut edges closed and set aside, covered, until ready to cook.

When you are ready to fry the okra, place the oil in a heavy-bottomed 12-inch frying pan over moderately high heat. When it is hot but not smoking, add the stuffed okra and spread the pods into one layer. Cover, reduce the heat to moderate and cook for five minutes. Remove the lid, gently turn the okra to ensure even browning, and fry, turning frequently, for 20–25 minutes or until the okra is tender, golden brown and crisp. Depending on the size of the pods, cooking time will vary. Transfer the okra to paper towels, salt and gently toss. Serve piping hot.

Serves 4.

This recipe was supplied by Swami Prabhupada's personal cook Yamuna Devi, who had in turn learned it from Prabhupada's sister Pishima, hence the name.

Pleasingly Bitter Vegetable Stew
(Shukta)

1 inch piece fresh ginger root, scraped and coarsely chopped
2 teaspoons black mustard seeds
2½ cups vegetable stock or water
2 teaspoons cumin seeds
½ teaspoon fennel seeds
4 tablespoons *ghee* or vegetable oil
⅓–1 teaspoon fenugreek seeds
1 small cassia or bay leaf, crumbled
½ teaspoon turmeric
½ tablespoon brown sugar
3 medium-sized waxy boiling potatoes (¾ pound), peeled
  and cut into 1-inch cubes
2 medium-sized tomatoes (about ¾ pound), peeled, seeded,
  and chopped
1 medium-sized sweet potato (about ¾ pound), peeled and
  cut into ¾-inch cubes
2 cups fresh green beans (8 ounces), trimmed and cut
  into 2-inch lengths
2 small Japanese eggplants (about 6 ounces), cut into
  1-inch cubes
¼ cup shelled lima beans or fresh peas
2 tablespoons chopped fresh coriander or parsley
1½ teaspoons salt

Combine the ginger, black mustard seeds and ½ cup of stock or water in a blender, cover and process until the seeds are crushed. Pour in the remaining liquid and process for 30 seconds, then set aside.

Place the cumin seeds and fennel seeds in a small, cast-iron frying pan. Dry-roast over low heat until they darken a few shades. Let cool for a few minutes, then coarsely crush and set aside.

Heat the *ghee* or oil in a 4-quart pan over moderate heat. When it is hot but not smoking, add the fenugreek seeds and fry until they darken a few shades to golden brown. Drop in the cassia or bay leaf, turmeric, sugar and potatoes. Fry the potatoes, tossing with a wooden spoon, for about 4–5 minutes. Add the tomatoes, sweet potato and green beans, stir-fry for a few minutes, then pour in the mustard-ginger water and bring to a full boil. Add the eggplants, lima beans or peas, half of the minced herb and the salt. Reduce the heat to low, cover and simmer for 30–35 minutes or until the vegetables are fork-tender. Check from time to time to see if the vegetables are cooking in sufficient liquid.

Before serving, sprinkle with the remaining fresh herb and the dry-roasted seeds.

Serves 4.

This recipe was supplied by Swami Prabhupada's personal cook Yamuna Devi, who assured me that it was his very favorite.

WILLIAM SHURTLEFF
AND AKIKO AOYAGI

Tofu (*Tōfu*)—in 1975 few Americans had even the vaguest idea of what it was. Now it is sold in countless supermarkets and health food stores, and its name as well as its substance is on everyone's lips. Credit for this extraordinary surge in popularity must go to William Shurtleff and his Tokyo-born wife Akiko Aoyagi. They are the authors of *The Book of Tofu*, which has become the Bible for tofu enthusiasts.

It is incredible that tofu (which is derived from soybeans) should have remained so long neglected and ignored in America, especially when one stops to consider that the U.S. has for years been the largest producer of soybeans in the world, and that the soybean was introduced to America by the same man who gave us the lightning rod, the rocking chair, bifocal glasses, and the first circulating library—Benjamin Franklin.

The Japanese call the soybean "the meat of the fields." This title is appropriate since the soybean yields more protein per acre of land at a cost that is 60 percent less than that of animal flesh. It is one of the cheapest protein sources known to man, and one of the richest. Soybeans contain a higher concentration of protein (35 percent) than occurs in any other unprocessed plant or animal food. Moreover, soy protein includes all eight essential animo acids in a form that is easily assimilated by the human body.

A staple of Chinese cooking since at least 1100 B.C., tofu is as commonplace a food in the Orient as it was once rare in the U.S. In Japan there are some thirty-eight thousand tofu shops that supply the average Japanese with seventy-eight cakes a year. This figure is comparable to the average American consumption of bread, which is seventy loaves per person, per annum. But too close an analogy with Western bread would be misleading, for tofu is far more nutritious than bread—particularly the devitalized pap that passes for bread in most countries of the West.

High in protein, low in cholesterol, calories, and cost, tofu is one of the world's most nutritious and versatile foods. Made from milk that has been extracted from soybeans, and then curdled, cooled, and compressed, tofu bears an uncanny resemblance to cottage cheese. But tofu is far more adaptable than cottage cheese. So obligingly does tofu take on the flavor of the spices and vegetables with which it is cooked, that it can be made to mimic almost any food. It can even be made to mock the taste and texture of both meat and dairy products. In fact, one form of tofu called *yuba* lends itself so readily to the mocking of meat dishes that there are shops

in Japan that specialize in making mock meats out of this tofu. To pass a *yuba* shop in Kyoto and see displayed in the window perfect replicas of hams, sausages, plucked poultry, boar's head, and fish (complete with fake fins, gills, eyes, and mouth) is an eerie experience. So deceiving are the *yuba* replicas to the eye and even to the palate, that they can easily be mistaken for the real thing.

In America, enterprising kosher caterers have been quick to seize upon tofu's protean ability to mock meat and dairy products as a way of getting around dietary laws that forbid combining the two. For instance, a cheeseburger would ordinarily be taboo to a kosher eater—but a tofu burger topped with melted tofu cheese violates no religious scruples. In California, vegetarian restaurants and delicatessens serve such tofu-derived meat analogs as tofUNA (fake tuna), and tofu burgers side by side such tofu-derived dairy analogs as tofu ice cream, tofu pizza, and tofu lasagna.

The man who is chiefly responsible for making tofu a household word in America—William Shurtleff—is an ardent vegetarian, who subscribes to the diet-for-a-small-planet philosophy that man is imperiling himself and the planet by living too high on the food chain. He wrote *The Book of Tofu* to entice Western man into eating at the bottom rather than the top of the food chain. His rationale for wanting to see tofu replace meat in the diet of Westerners is ecologic and humanitarian as well as economic. Not only would such a diet reduce the number of animals slaughtered for food, but it would also free the pastures for the cultivation of grain and soybeans. As previously mentioned, cultivated land could feed many more times the number of people than land used for the pasturing of cattle. Says Shurtleff: "I would be happy if tofu replaced thirty percent of the meat in American diets."[1]

William Shurtleff and Akiko Aoyagi, who are man and wife as well as co-authors, grew up on opposite sides of the Pacific. Shurtleff was born on April 28, 1941, in Lafayette, California. His father headed a successful construction company, and his mother was a housewife. In 1963, Shurtleff graduated from Stanford University with honors in humanities, physics, and engineering. After College, he served for two years in the Peace Corps in Eastern Nigeria (Biafra). A stark contrast to the agricultural luxuriance of Southern California, famine-stricken Biafra was Shurtleff's first encounter with the agony of starving humans—an experience that stirred him so profoundly that he determined to dedicate his life to conquering world hunger.

Back in the States, he lived for two years in the Peace and Liberation Commune, while taking his Masters in education at Stanford. Shortly thereafter, in 1968, he entered the Tassajara Zen Mountain Center in Big Sur, California to study under Zen master Shunryu Suzuki *roshi,* who was then head abbot. Tassajara is the same Zen Center that gave rise to the ever popular *Tassajara Bread Book*—a collection of Buddhist vegetarian recipes. Although seemingly remote from the agony of Biafra, Tassajara aided Shurtleff in gaining the knowledge that would help him realize his dream of alleviating world hunger, for it was in the kitchen at Tassajara that Shurtleff discovered tofu. Working as a cook at the Zen Center, he learned how to prepare tofu, *miso* (fermented soybean paste), and whole soybeans for the community meals. Once each year he helped in the preparation of a fifty-gallon batch of red *miso*.

Inspired by his experience at Tassajara, Shurtleff sought to learn more about Zen meditation and Buddhist vegetarian cuisine by continuing his studies in Japan. In Japan, as a financially strapped student, his knowledge of tofu cookery came in handy. By living mainly on a diet of tofu and *miso*, he found that he could subsist on as little as thirty cents a day.

There is a wonderful symmetry in Shurtleff's traveling to Japan to study Zen meditation and tofu-based Zen-Buddhist cuisine. For it is believed that tofu was first brought to Japan by Buddhist monks and priests who plied the waters between China and Japan. At this time (*circa* 800 A.D.) all Buddhist monks were strict vegetarians and tofu was their daily bread, so to speak. Until well into the Kamakura period (*circa* 1200 A.D.), all of Japan's tofu shops were operated exclusively by Buddhist priests and temple cooks within the sacred precincts of the temples and monasteries.

The spread of tofu in Japan accompanied the spread of Buddhism. In the Kamakura period, the carnivorous, or more precisely, the piscivorous Japanese nobility as well as the redoubtable *samurai* (warrior caste) embraced a tofu-based vegetarianism when they converted to Zen-Buddhism. After his conversion to Zen Buddhism, the ruling *shogun* (military governor) gave up river fish (to which he was greatly addicted) in favor of tofu, and in the *samurai's* ritual breakfast dish of hot soup, tofu cutlets and deep-fried tofu pouches ousted fish as the chief ingredient. In feudal Japan the *samurai* were a sort of warrior aristocracy who set the fashions in feeding as well as in finery. So, when the *samurai* became tofu-eating Zen Buddhists, it wasn't long before tofu found its way out of the Buddhist temple shops and refectories and into the *haute cuisine* of the Japanese people.

Some months after arriving in Kyoto, in December of 1971, Shurtleff met his future collaborator and bride Akiko Aoyagi. To his delight, he found that she shared his interest in Zen meditation and most important of all, tofu cookery. However, Akiko was a little taken aback at the intensity of Shurtleff's interest in tofu. For the Japanese, as for most Orientals, tofu is a culinary commonplace. It was rather like a Japanese student coming to America and being agog with curiosity about the potato or corn-on-the-cob.

Born on January 24, 1950, in Tokyo, Japan, Akiko was educated at the Quaker-run Friends School, and at the Women's College of Arts, where she majored in fashion design. Her training as an artist and her culinary skills stood her in good stead when it came to co-authoring *The Book of Tofu*, whose pages are packed with her illustrations and recipes.

Not long after they had met, Akiko initiated Shurtleff into the delights of the seven varieties of tofu, which she cooked to a turn. She also introduced him to Kyoto's *haute cuisine* tofu restaurants. At these ersatz fleshpots, he and Akiko could savor a twelve-course meal in which tofu was the *pièce de résistance* of each course for as little as three dollars for two. In fact, it was over dinner at one of these temples of tofu gastronomy that Shurtleff and Akiko got the inspiration for doing a tofu cookbook that would show Westerners how to prepare tofu. The only trouble was that they were both stone-broke. By taking on this monumental project, which would take years to complete, they knew that they were tempting Providence. But as Bernard Shaw once remarked, "Providence likes to be tempted!"[2] Sure enough, within two weeks of their overhasty decision to do *The Book of Tofu*, they found a publisher in the shape of Autumn Press, a small American publisher based in Japan. Autumn Press specialized in putting out books on Eastern philosophy and new age foods. By another stroke of luck they were hired by an American firm (with offices in Japan) to act as interpreters. This gave the couple enough money and free time to spend the next four years researching and writing *The Book of Tofu*.

The research for *The Book of Tofu* was as exhausting as it was exhaustive. It often involved Shurtleff and Aoyagi in back-packing into the hinterlands and journeying to remote islands where few, if any Americans had ever set foot, in order to ferret out traditional tofu recipes and techniques that had all but vanished from the urban centers. Although the great tofu masters were reputed to be secretive about their methods, they were so impressed with Shurtleff and Aoyagi's sincerity and desire to learn, that they imparted their knowledge to them willingly.

The Book of Tofu was published in 1975. Since tofu was virtually unknown in America at this time, a cautious printing of 5,000 copies was essayed. It was too cautious by half. Within a month, it had completely sold out its entire print run. So in February of 1976, a more optimistic 10,000 copies were printed. By early 1979, sales of *The Book of Tofu* had exceeded 100,000 copies, and by 1980 over 250,000 copies had been sold.

Encouraged by the extraordinary response to their first book, the Shurtleffs set about writing a comprehensive series of books on soyfoods. Their second book, *The Book of Miso*, which treats of fermented soybean paste, duplicated the success of *The Book of Tofu*. Their third, *The Book of Tempeh*, which deals with a form of tofu popular in Indonesia and throughout the Far East, was also wildly successful.

Living and working at The Soyfoods Center, their home-cum-office in Lafayette, California, Shurtleff and Aoyagi make a comfortable living as consultants to the growing international soyfoods industry that they have done so much to propagate. A typical day at The Soyfoods Center will bring telegrams and queries from as far afield as Paris, Rome, Athens, Tokyo, and Bombay; and from as nearby as Los Angeles, San Francisco, and Palo Alto. The Soyfood Center boasts the largest library on soyfoods in the world. Recently Shurtleff unveiled SOYA, the world's most comprehensive computerized database. It was ten years in the making, and is international in scope. SOYA provides information on soybean processing, marketing, nutrition, and history. SOYA contains references to over 18,000 publications on soybeans that range from 1100 B.C. to the present. It features over 1700 references to tofu alone, some dating from as far back as 900 A.D. Currently, Shurtleff and Aoyagi are also at work on their forthcoming book (fourth in their series of books on soyfoods)—*The Book of Shoyu* (soy sauce)—the world's most popular seasoning. It augurs well to become another best soy-seller.

Homemade Tofu Burgers

You won't believe the wonderful flavor of these easy-to-make meatless entrées. We like to make a big batch and freeze the leftovers.

30 ounces tofu, pressed then squeezed*
6 tablespoons grated carrots
4 tablespoons minced leeks, scallions,
    onions, or ginger root
2 teaspoons (ground) roasted sesame seeds,
    sunflower seeds, peanuts, or chopped nutmeats
¾ teaspoon salt
Oil for deep-frying
Shoyu (natural soy sauce)

Combine the first five ingredients in a large shallow bowl, mix well, then knead mixture for about three minutes as if kneading bread. When "dough" is smooth and holds together well, moisten your palms with a little oil or warm water and shape dough into eight patties, each three to three-and-a-half inches in diameter.

Fill a wok, skillet, or deep fryer with two to two-and-a-half inches of oil and heat to 300°. Slide in patties and deep-fry from four to six minutes on each side, or until crisp and golden brown. Drain briefly on absorbent toweling, then serve hot as is, topped with a sprinkling of *shoyu,* or placed on a bun with your favorite burger trimmings.

Serves four.

---

*Chinese-style firm tofu requires no pressing. However, in case you are not using firm tofu, simply wrap the tofu in a towel, place on a slightly tilted cutting board, and cover with a two pound weight for one or two hours. For squeezing: place the firm or pressed tofu in the center of a dry dish towel, gather the ends together to form a sack, then twist the sack closed, and knead the tofu for two or three minutes to expel as much water as possible.

(Note: I have found that it is necessary to add a half cup of bread flour to the tofu mixture as a binder—R.B.)

"Homemade Tofu Burgers" from *The Book of Tofu* by William Shurtleff and Akiko Aoyagi (Ballantine Books, 1980), page 267. Reprinted by permission of the authors.

Tempeh "Mock Chicken" Salad

6 ounces tempeh
4–5 tablespoons mayonnaise (tofu or other eggless)
1 stalk celery, chopped fine
2 tablespoons minced dill pickles
2 tablespoons minced onion
2 tablespoons minced parsley
1 teaspoon prepared mustard
1 teaspoon *shoyu*
Dash of garlic powder

Steam tempeh for twenty minutes. Allow to cool, then cut into three-eighth inch cubes. Combine all ingredients, mixing lightly but well. Serve as a sandwich filling or mounded on a bed of lettuce.

W. S. & A. A.

Serves three.

Eggless Egg Salad Sandwich

11 ounces tofu, mashed
¼ teaspoon tumeric
1 stalk celery, chopped
¼ cup minced onion
1½ tablespoons mayonnaise (tofu or other eggless)
1 tablespoon minced parsley
1 tablespoon nutritional yeast
½ teaspoon dill leaves
½ teaspoon salt
¼ teaspoon dry mustard
¼ teaspoon celery seed
5 slices bread, buttered or margarined
1¼ cups alfalfa sprouts

Combine the first twelve ingredients in a bowl and mix well, then spread on the buttered bread. Serve topped with fresh alfalfa sprouts. Yummy!

Serves four to six.

W. S. & A. A

Tofu Cheesecake
with Fruit Topping

A close relative of this delectable recipe was developed by the Spruce Tree Baking Co. in Belair, Maryland, and is now a favorite throughout New England.

Shell: Use your favorite cheesecake crumb crust (whole-wheat flour and oil, or graham crumbs and butter) or the following:

½ cup whole-wheat flour
1 cup unbleached white flour
½ cup margarine

Filling

17 ounces tofu
3 to 4 tablespoons sesame tahini
½ cup pure maple syrup
2 tablespoons lemon juice
½ teaspoon sea salt
1½ teaspoons pure vanilla extract

Strawberry Topping

1 cup whole strawberries
10 tablespoons apple juice
3 tablespoons pure maple syrup
⅛ teaspoon salt
1½ teaspoons cornstarch

Sift together both flours. Cut in, then rub in margarine with fingertips until mixture resembles coarse sand (add no water). Wrap and chill for one hour or more, then, using fingertips, press into an eight inch pie tin to make a crust of even thickness. Prick bottom with a fork and bake at 450° for ten minutes.

Purée tofu in two batches in a blender until smooth, then mix in a bowl with the remaining filling ingredients. Spoon into a prebaked shell and bake at 350° for thirty to thirty-five minutes, or until filling has set, maybe risen a little, and is golden yellow on top. Allow to cool to room temperature.

For topping, combine strawberries, one-half cup apple juice, maple syrup, and salt in a small saucepan; bring to a boil. Dissolve cornstarch in the remaining two tablespoons juice. Stir quickly into fruit mixture until thick and clear, then pour topping over cooled pie. Allow topping to cool and set. Serve cheesecake chilled.

Serves six.

W. S. & A. A.

FRANCES MOORE LAPPÉ

Marshall McLuhan, the social critic and media pundit, predicted in the early 1960s that as soon as men were able to view the earth as an entirety, it would become an art object. Since one of the main feelings that an art object evokes is the desire to nurture and protect it for posterity, then the modern ecology movement and the trend to vegetarianism, which emerged in the late 1960s, may be seen as a fulfillment of McLuhan's prophecy.

In 1968 the Apollo 8 mission was the first manned space flight to leave the earth's orbit and enter into orbit around the moon. It also marked the first time that men saw the entire earth with their own eyes, and took pictures of it. When these pictures were flashed around the world, the effect was electric. Almost overnight the international ecology movement and the vegetarian movement seemed to spring up from the earth like the sown men of Greek legend. It was as though they had risen up to put an end to the misuse of the planet's resources and to preserve its beauty for posterity.

It is ironic that it took a manned space voyage to the moon to give earth dwellers a heightened aesthetic appreciation for the planet. But the revelation that the planet is a small and fragile *objet d'art* seemed to call forth a maternal instinct in the inhabitants of the globe. All at once people of contrasting political views were ready to forget their differences and cooperate in saving the small planet from extinction. McLuhan's comparison of the planet to an art object is especially apt, because the impetus to save the earth from doom was reminiscent of those international campaigns to restore the crumbling works of a quattrocento master, to rescue Venice from sinking into the sea, or to recover the lost frescoes of Leonardo.

In addition to Stewart Brand, whose *Whole Earth Catalogue* (Brand got the idea for his book from seeing the pictures of earth that had been taken from space), helped give rise to the back-to-the-land movement of this period, there was another book whose author, however inadvertently, seems to have been inspired by the Apollo 8 mission's photograph of the earth in its entirety. This was Frances Moore Lappé, author of the epoch-making book *Diet for a Small Planet*. With its emphasis on the diminutive size of the planet, and its suggestion that the earth's food resources are finite, the title of her book is almost a verbal correlative of the cover photo that appeared on Brand's *Whole Earth Catalogue*, which showed a small jewel-like planet set in a sea of darkness.

191

Lappé admits that it was her sudden perception of the earth as a small and fragile planet that set her on the vegetarian path: "Why food? In part I was influenced by the emerging ecology movement and the 'limits to growth' consciousness. The first Earth Day was in 1970."[1]

The title as well as the tenor of Lappé's book captured the public's imagination as no previous vegetarian tract ever had. Its first edition sold over two million copies and its second edition, which was published in 1982, bade fair to surpass it. As much as it is a serious discussion of ecology, geopolitics, economy, and nutrition, *Diet for a Small Planet* also serves as a practical cookbook that the reader can use to reform his own eating habits and strike a blow for ecological sanity.

It is ironic yet appropriate that the most successful debunker of what Lappé calls "the Great American Steak Religion"[2] should have been born and bred in Texas (in February, 1944), which is the capital of beef production in America. But then having grown up in a cattle culture must have given Lappé a unique insight into "the great American Steak Religion" as well as a healthy disrespect for the false values that it fosters. The profligate waste of land, the glorification of violence and false virility, the lust for wealth, the subjection of women, the cult of youth, prurient interest in sex, and the exploitation of animals—these are typical manifestations of cattle cultures throughout history, and which, unfortunately, have their apotheosis in Texas. Lappé learned to see through these false values when she was growing up. Perhaps this is why she deliberately shed her North Texas drawl in her first semester at the small Quaker college that she attended. Doubtless it was part of an attempt to exorcise the baleful influences wrought upon her by a culture that is based on the exploitation of animals.

Cattle herding peoples have traditionally been inimical to civilization and culture. This has been evident ever since the cattle-herding Aryans invaded the vegetarian, art-producing high cultures of India, Asia Minor and Europe in the second millenium B.C. One might say that the history of civilization in the millenia since has been a continuous struggle between settled agriculturists and nomads or stock-breeders, the steppe against the sown, flesh-eaters versus vegetarians. Cattle-raising is a flight from the land and a denial of its virtues and limitations. But as Apollo 8's photos showed, the earth is neither a vast abattoir, nor an endless cattle pasturge. Rather, it is an oasis in space, a magical graden floating in a sea of blackness, which it behooves us (as it did Voltaire's Candide) assiduously to cultivate. *Diet for a Small Planet* is a space-gardener's manual that shows us how to go about it.

Lappé shed her cattle-country accent in college, and in graduate school at Berkeley she shed her cattle-culture diet. Ensconced in her basement library she discovered three facts that gave her the idea for the book that would start a worldwide dietary revolution and seal the fate of the cattle culture in the West. The first was that over half the harvested acreage in the U.S. goes to produce livestock feed. The second was that Americans eat twice as much protein as their bodies can use. The third was that by combining plant foods one may obtain a protein that is equal if not superior in quality to animal protein. She worked this data up into a one-page handout that grew into a 70-page booklet that grew into a two-million copy best-seller.

Not content to rest on her laurels, Frances Lappé used the royalties that she earned from *Diet for a Small Planet* to found the Institute for Food and Development Policy, which publishes books and pamphlets that promote global nutritional awareness. More recently, she started a news gathering service called the American New Service, of which she is now Editor-in-Chief. In sharp contrast with the daily diet of mayhem served up by the daily press, the American New Service furnishes the electronic and print news media with stories that focus on civic problem solving, high achievement, and human triumph—an apt summary, one might say, of the life of Frances Moore Lappé.

Sweet and Pungent Vegetable Curry

⅔ cup soybeans, kidney
    beans, or limas (or
    a mix of the three)
1 cup brown rice
¾ cup bulgur
2 or 3 tablespoons oil for
    sautéing
4 carrots, sliced diagonally
2 onions, thinly sliced
1 zucchini, sliced (opt.)
1 tablespoon hot curry
    powder (or more, to
    taste)
¼ cup flour
¾ cup raisins
¾ cup raw or roasted cashews
3 tablespoons mango chutney
    (or more, to taste)

Cook the beans and reserve one cup of the cooking liquid. Cook the brown rice and the bulgur. Heat oil and sauté carrots, onion, and zucchini until onions are translucent. Add curry powder and flour and sauté one minute. Add beans and reserved bean cooking liquid (or water) and simmer until carrots are tender but not soft. Add raisins, cashews, and chutney, and more liquid if necessary (sauce should be thick). Taste for seasoning and simmer until raisins are soft. Serve over the cooked grain.

Serves six.

A delightful combination—perfect for the most festive occasion. It can be prepared well in advance.

F. M. L.

Tofu-Apple-Nut Loaf

1 cup tofu
2 cups applesauce (if using
    unsweetened applesauce,
    increase honey to ½ cup)
½ cup oil
¼ honey
Grated rind of 1 lemon
1 tablespoon lemon juice
½ teaspoon cinnamon
¼ salt (opt.)
2 cups whole-wheat flour
1½ teaspoons baking soda
½ to ¾ cup chopped walnuts
1 cup raisins

Preheat oven to 350°. In a blender, combine tofu, applesauce, oil, honey, lemon rind, lemon juice, cinnamon, and salt, and purée until smooth. Sift together flour and baking soda and combine with puréed ingredients in a large bowl. Stir in walnuts and raisins. Pour into a well-greased nine-inch ring mold or large loaf pan and bake until a toothpick comes out clean, about fifty minutes. Cool for five minutes in the mold or pan, then remove. Serve hot or cold.

Variation: For banana bread, substitute 2 to 3 mashed bananas for the applesauce.

This recipe is a favorite of Bill and Akiko Shurtleff of the Soyfoods Center in Lafayette, California. They write, "This delectable, slightly sweet whole wheat bread . . .has a light, well-risen texture but requires the use of no eggs, milk, or other dairy products. The secret lies in the use of tofu."

F. M. L.

Fried Spiced Tofu

1 lb. tofu
1 tablespoon oil
½ teaspoon turmeric
½ teaspoon each sweet basil, thyme,
    ground cumin, and curry powder
2 cloves garlic, minced
2 tablespoons soy sauce
2 tablespoons nutritional yeast

Drain tofu, pat dry, and cut into one-half-inch cubes. Heat oil (in a wok, if you have one) and sauté tofu over high heat for five minutes. Pour out excess water, reduce heat, and add turmeric; stir until tofu is uniformly yellow and add basil, thyme, cumin, and curry powder. Add garlic (and perhaps a little more oil to prevent sticking) and increase heat; then add soy sauce and yeast. Sauté until golden brown. Taste and add more soy sauce, if desired.

Good hot or cold in sandwiches or tacos, or as a side dish.

Serves three to four.

A favorite of Eric Dunder of Greenbush, Maine. We served this at an Institute potluck while testing recipes for the Tenth Anniversary Edition. It was gone in minutes.

F. M. L.

Brazilian Evening

Menu

Feijoada (Tangy Black Beans)
Rice with Green Chili Sauce
Greens with Sesame Seed Topping and Orange Slices

Feijoada (Tangy Black Beans)

Oil for sautéing
1 large onion, chopped
2 cloves garlic, minced
2 green onions, chopped
1 green pepper, chopped
1 tomato, chopped
1 teaspoon cilantro (opt.)
1 cup black beans
3 cups Seasoned Stock (or
    substitute wine for up to
    half the stock)
1 bay leaf
¼ teaspoon pepper
1 teaspoon vinegar (omit if
    using wine)
1 orange, washed but unpeeled,
    whole or halved
½ teaspoon salt
2 stalks celery, chopped
1 tomato, chopped
1 carrot, chopped (opt.)
½ sweet potato, diced

Heal oil in a large heavy pot and sauté onion, garlic, green onions, green pepper, tomato and cilantro until onion is translucent. Add beans, stock, bay leaf, pepper, and vinegar. Bring to a boil, reduce heat, and simmer for two minutes. Take off stove and let sit, covered, for one hour.

Add remaining ingredients and simmer, with lid ajar, for two to three hours more, until beans are tender. Remove a ladleful of beans, mash them, and return them to the pot to thicken the mixture.

Serves six.

I have done the whole thing in a pressure cooker, after first sautéing the onion and garlic. It is much quicker and still very good.

This recipe is one of my favorites. A Brazilian friend embellished it for this edition.

F. M. L.

Rice with Green Chili Sauce

Rice

2 tablespoons olive oil
1 onion, chopped
3 cloves garlic, minced
2 tomatoes, peeled, seeded,
    and coarsely chopped
About 4½ cups cooked brown rice
    (2 cups uncooked)

Heat oil and sauté onion and garlic until onion is translucent. Add tomatoes and simmer a few minutes. Stir in the cooked rice and keep warm over low heat.

Sauce

1 tomato, peeled and seeded
California green chiles,
    seeded, to taste (start
    with half a 2-ounce can)
1 teaspoon salt
2 cloves garlic
Juice of 1 lemon
1 onion, cut in chunks
Scallions and parsley to taste
¼ cup vinegar

In a blender, purée tomato, chiles, salt, and garlic until smooth. Add lemon juice, onion, scallions, parsley, and vinegar, and blend coarsely (do not purée). Just before serving, stir in a little liquid from the Feijoada pot.

Serves six.

Greens with Sesame Seed Topping and Orange Slices

1½ lbs. trimmed greens
(turnip or mustard greens,
collards, etc.)
Olive oil for sautéing
1 clove minced garlic
½ cup toasted sesame seed meal
Garnish: 1 orange, sliced

Steam greens until barely wilted. Heat oil and briefly sauté greens with garlic. Sprinkle one heaping tablespoon sesame seed meal on each serving and garnish with orange slices on top or around edges.

Serve the rice with sauce along with the beans and greens for a splendid three-course Brazilian dinner.

Serves six.

Section 3
CONTEMPORARIES

PAUL AND LINDA McCARTNEY

In the mid-1960s, America was invaded by swarms of English rock groups such as The Hollies, The Dave Clark Five, The Who, and the Rolling Stones. Spearheading this invasion was a Liverpool rock group with the silliest name of all—The Beatles. Absurd name! horrible pun! to be sure, but there was nothing silly about their music. In 1964, eight of the top ten songs in America belonged to the Beatles. For more than a decade their records dominated the American charts with hit after hit after hit. Not even Elvis, the uncrowned king of rock 'n' roll, had held such undisputed sway over the American record buying public. The Beatles were more than a rock group, more than a quartet of cuddlesome teddy boys, they were a four-man cultural revolution. Each member of the group was deified into a rock demigod whose taste in clothes, hair-styles, food, and entertainment was carefully watched and copied by his adoring fans. In the mid-1960s after the Beatles made their American debut wearing long hair, hitherto crew-cut American males began to cultivate their tresses and locks. In 1966, when the Beatles took to wearing psychedelic clothes, hitherto conservatively clad Americans and Englishmen started arraying themselves in a riot of brilliant colors. In 1967, when Paul announced that he had taken LSD, the whole of America seemed to be collectively ingesting LSD. When in 1968, Paul and George traveled to India to sit at the feet of Maharishi Mahesh Yogi, and subsequently became vegetarians, millions of Americans copied them. There can be no doubt that the enormous upsurge of interest in vegetarianism in the West is due in no small part to their example.

Born in Liverpool, England, on June 18, 1942, Paul McCartney is the elder of two sons from the marriage of Mary McCartney, a professional midwife, and Jim McCartney, a salesman in the Liverpool cotton exchange. That Paul's father was a cotton salesman is not without a certain symbolic significance. Cotton (still a major import), the slave trade, and privateering helped establish Liverpool as England's second largest port. Picked by black field hands in America's rural South, cotton was shipped in English bottoms to Liverpool. From Liverpool the cotton was sent on to the Lancashire mills, to emerge as textiles and cloth for wearing apparel.

Cotton fields and the Negro churches of the Deep South were the cradle of such African derived music as jazz, blues, and rock 'n' roll. No humble pieties or tranquil hymns were intoned in these cotton country churches. On the contrary, the hymns were so frantic and rousing that, like as not, the preacher himself would be cutting capers, while the congregation was shouting and rocking in the aisles. An Anglican bishop would no doubt have been shocked to the depths of his being at such a spectacle. But any red-blooded rock concertgoer would have felt right at home. In fact, as a boy growing up poor in Mississippi, the king of rock 'n' roll, Elvis Presley, used to attend black revival meetings and gospel singings. He was fascinated with the boisterous singing, and the jitterbugging that not so much accompanied the service as formed the essential part of it. ("The preachers cut up all over the place, jumping on the piano, moving every which way.")[1] There is a good deal of truth in the seemingly glib observation that Elvis was instrumental in popularizing rock, because he was the first white man who could sing and move like a Negro. But Presley was too hyperkinetic and sexually lubricious to make rock respectable to the middle class. That task fell to Paul McCartney and the Beatles. For they took raw rock music from the cotton lands of the South, and transmuted it into a sound that was palatable to the middle class, much as the Lancashire mills converted raw cotton into the stuff of English haberdashery.

In 1954, when Paul was twelve, the BBC, the state-owned radio monopoly in England, had sternly set its face against rock 'n' roll and had banished it from the airwaves. But thanks to pirate radio stations anchored offshore, and "Cunard Yanks," who smuggled this subversive new sound into Liverpool like so much contraband (thereby heightening its sex appeal to the young), Paul McCartney and other Liverpool lads were gyrating in sympathy to the anarchic strains of Little Richard singing "Long Tall Sally," and Chuck Berry singing (rather prophetically as it turned out), "Roll Over Beethoven."

Although Paul and the other Beatles were from Liverpool's lower middle class, they grew up speaking the King's English (albeit in thick Liverpudlian), and were by modern standards tolerably well-educated. Indeed, one of the striking things about the Beatles was how witty and articulate they all were. This was especially startling to American audiences of the early sixties, who had formed the impression that rock 'n' roll singers were all mindless exhibitionists, who could do little more than wiggle their hips and mouth lyrics that had been written for them by others. But not only did Paul McCartney and John Lennon write nearly all of the Beatles' hits, they also wrote hit songs for other vocalists and groups. Many of the McCartney-Lennon songs are as memorable as those of such other great songwriting teams as P. G. Wodehouse and Jerome Kern, Rodgers and Hart, or Lerner and Loewe.

From primary school right through to the early grades of high school, Paul McCartney was always at the top of his class academically. It was his father's fondest wish that Paul should go on to college and become a teacher. Paul gave every appearance of heading in that direction by compiling a 95 average in Latin, as well as equally high marks in his other subjects. But then fate took a cruel turn. When Paul was fourteen his mother died of cancer, and Paul completely lost his bearings. Shortly after her death, he begged his father for a guitar. As soon as Paul got it he began to play obsessively. As his brother Michael remembers it, "he played it in the lavatory, in the bath, everywhere." His brother theorizes that the guitar provided some kind of balm that eased the memory of their mother's passing.

Be that as it may, one thing is certain: his compulsive guitar playing made Paul into one of the best guitarists in Liverpool. When a friend introduced him to John Lennon (then at sixteen the lead guitarist and singer in the embryonic Beatles group called the Quarrymen), John asked Paul to play "Twenty Flight Rock," of which John declared himself to be a connoisseur. So deftly did Paul play that he was summarily drafted into the Quarrymen, even though John had to expel a good friend to make way for Paul.

Despite their meteoric rise in the mid-1960s, the Beatles spent many ill-paid years toiling in the bowels of Liverpool. They performed in such converted basements as the Casbah Club, the Cavern Club, and the other dank cellars to which rock music had been relegated. It was not until they began to play nightclubs in Hamburg, Germany (the Germans were precociously besotted with rock 'n' roll), that the Beatles started to forge a sound and an identity that was distinctly their own.

At length Paul and the Beatles were discovered by Brian Epstein, who managed a record shop in Liverpool. Requests for a record by a group whose name was an entomological pun, aroused his curiosity, so he went to the Cavern Club to hear them play. Intrigued as much by their colorful personalities as he was by their playing, he offered to become their manager. They agreed, and Brian wandered from record company to record company in his vain bid to get their music recorded. Invariably, as he was being shown the door, he would deliver himself of the prophecy that someday the Beatles would be bigger than Elvis. The record company executives simply sniggered up their sleeves.

The last laugh was on them, however, when Brian found an obscure London record company, Parlophone (specializing in the production of comedy records such as Peter Ustinov's "Mock Mozart," and the Goon records of Spike Milligan and Peter Sellers), that was willing to take a chance on the Beatles. Their first record "Love Me Do" climbed into the top-twenty, but their second "Please Please Me," vaulted to the top of the British pop charts, inaugurating a reign of chartbusters that is unrivaled in rock history.

Paul's songs are notable for their genial optimism, their nostalgia ("Penny

Lane" and "Honey Pie"), and their unabashed appreciation of femininity, as displayed in such hits as "Girl," "Here, There, and Everywhere," "Eleanor Rigby," and "Hey Jude." The Dark Lady of the Beatle love songs was Paul's ex-fiancée, actress Jane Asher. In his collaboration with John Lennon on such classics as "A Day in the Life," John's mordant humor acted as a brake upon Paul's tendency to be overly sentimental (even, at times, mawkish), while Paul's irrepressible high spirits often kept John's songs from tumbling over the edge of cynicism into despair.

In 1967 the Beatles' album *Sergeant Pepper's Lonely Hearts Club Band* contained songs such as "Lucy in the Sky with Diamonds," and "Strawberry Fields Forever" that were lit with phantasmagoric visions. If they seemed a touch hallucinatory, it was probably because, as Paul admitted in an interview on the BBC, he and the other Beatles had been dosing themselves with LSD. This revelation provoked a tremendous public outcry. The Reverend Billy Graham prayed for the Lord's intercession to prevent millions of teenagers from aping the Beatles and addling their brains with LSD.

Suddenly, as if Billy's prayers had been answered, Paul's flirtation with LSD ended as quickly as it had begun. Through Patti and George Harrison, Paul was introduced to Indian culture and the Maharishi Mahesh Yogi. At the Maharishi's behest, Paul stopped taking LSD, and became a vegetarian. The following year, in February of 1968, Paul and the Beatles traveled to Rishikesh, India to receive religious instruction from the Maharishi during a three month stay at his *ashram* (religious retreat). Although Paul and the Maharishi have long since parted company, Paul is today a staunch vegetarian.

In 1969, Paul married Linda Eastman, a talented photographer, who has published *Linda's Pictures,* and other volumes of her photographs. The daughter of Manhattan attorney Lee Eastman (who looks after Paul's financial affairs), Linda has contributed vocally instrumentally, and inspirationally to Paul's post-Beatles rock group, Wings—which has garnered so many gold and platinum records as to have won it a place in *The Guinness Book of World Records.* Together, she and Paul have two daughters, Mary and Stella, and a son, James. There is also a daughter from Linda's previous marriage, Heather, whom Paul has adopted. Despite their crowded schedule, Paul and Linda pride themselves on raising their children without nannies or governesses. Paul babysits, and Linda, who is also a vegetarian, does the cooking.

It has to be admitted that in the early years of their marriage, Paul and Linda frequently lapsed from their vegetarian diet. But then one evening while the family was in the middle of a roast mutton dinner, one of their lambs wandered into the kitchen. "That," as Paul says, "was it!" "Now, we don't eat anything that has to be killed for us. We've been through a lot coming through the sixties with all those drugs and friends dropping like flies, and we've reached the stage where we really value life."[3]

As a measure of how seriously the McCartney's take their vegetarianism, when the McCartney's donated Christmas hampers from the posh London department store, Fortnum & Mason, to the women nuclear protesters at the cruise missile base at Greenham Common in Berkshire, Paul and Linda took the precaution of carefully removing the meat from each hamper.

Green Pea Soup

1 lb. green split peas
½ lb. orange lentils
3 large onions, quartered
1 head of celery (approx. 8 stalks), including
    leaves, cleaned and chopped
4 peeled tomatoes
4 leeks
½ lb. soy margarine
Crushed peppercorns and sea salt to taste

Place the first six ingredients in a large cooking pot, and cover with water. Bring water to a boil, then lower flame and continue simmering until the lentils are soft. When ready, add the one-half pound margarine, and crushed peppercorns and sea salt to taste.

Serves four.

Mrs. Mac's Cabbage Salad

¾ of a small head of cabbage
5 ounces olive oil (extra virgin preferred)
4 ounces red wine vinegar
Juice of one lemon
Salt and freshly ground pepper to taste
½ cup chopped fresh parsley

1. Place the sliced cabbage in a large mixing bowl.
2. Combine the remaining ingredients, and blend thoroughly. Season to taste. Pour over cabbage and toss well.

Yield: 6 to 8 servings.

GEORGE HARRISON

One day George Harrison's mother came home to find George hunched over a sheet of paper, carefully drawing what appeared to be designs for a spacecraft. Never had she seen him draw anything with such concentration. Closer inspection would reveal that George was not designing a spaceship after all, but rather a far sleeker, far more practical vehicle that would someday rocket him out of the Liverpool slums, and the social cul-de-sac to which he had been consigned at birth. It would carry him to a magic land where he had but to open his mouth and money would cascade to his feet. Here, girls would rend their garments and tear their hair in anticipation of glimpsing him; there, beautiful women would fling themselves at his neck and offer themselves up to be his paramour.

The craft would someday transport him to India where he would learn to question the spiritual values and the very food on which he had been nourished as a boy, and where he would disembarrass himself of the awful Liverpudlian diet of bacon rashers, black puddings, kidney pie, bread and drippings, and fish 'n' chips in favor of Indian cuisine and vegetarianism. What on earth might it be, that it could loft a poor Liverpool lad to such dizzying heights? Finally, his mother recognized, or thought she recognized what it was. It was an electric guitar.

George had just returned from a concert where with bated breath he had watched Lonnie Donegan, an English caricature of Elvis Presley, play his hit song "Rock Island Line" on an electric guitar. Even though George had never shown any interest in music, as soon as he saw Donegan's guitar, he simply had to have one. Touched by his earnestness, for three pounds his mother bought him a guitar. The guitar was that of a friend at school who'd become bored with it. Within a short time George had outgrown this guitar, so his mother helped him buy an electric guitar for thirty pounds—a tidy sum in those days. George paid her back by working on Saturday mornings as a delivery boy for a Liverpool butcher.

Although George's parents encouraged his guitar playing, they were not at all pleased when he began adopting the defiant hairstyle, loud clothes, and insouciant manner of a Liverpool Teddy Boy. And they were more than a little perturbed with him for not applying himself in school. For of all the Harrison children—there were four altogether—George showed the most intellectual promise. He was the only one of their children who qualified for admission to the selective Liverpool Institute, where John Lennon and Paul McCartney were also enrolled.

Unlike Paul, who shone in his schoolwork and was one of the Liverpool Institute's brightest pupils, George was one of the worst students. He

barely eked out his education, which, considering that he slept through his classes, was a backhanded tribute to his intellectual potential. Not infrequently would he wake up at five o-clock in the afternoon to find that the teachers and students had all gone home. This is not to suggest that George wasn't bright—only that he was deeply bored. Schoolwork he regarded as being irrelevant and pointless, the teachers, as high-handed and overbearing. "They're all trying to transfigure you from the pure way of thought as a child, forcing their illusions on you. All those things annoyed me. I was just trying to be myself. They were trying to turn everybody into rows of little toffees."[1]

For their part, the teachers held him in contempt. His drainpipe trousers; his blue-suede, winkle-picker shoes; his pastel shirts; and the canary waistcoat that he wore under his regulation school blazer were the objects of endless faculty ridicule. Ironically, the teacher who twitted him mercilessly about his Teddy Boy clothes and his interest in rock 'n' roll music was Cissy Smith, who turned out to be an uncle of John Lennon's.

On the other hand, when it came to that spacecraft that his mother had watched him drawing—the electric guitar—George was as diligent a student as any teacher could have wished for. Like Paul, he played the guitar as one possessed. He played until his fingers were so cracked and lacerated that blood dribbled onto the strings. The upshot of all this demonic guitar playing was that by the time he was fourteen, George was one of the finest guitarists in Liverpool.

His guitar virtuosity did not escape the notice of John Lennon, the founder of the proto-Beatles group, the Quarrymen. But owing to the difference in their ages—John was seventeen, George, fourteen—John was cool to the idea of George's joining. Eventually, however, John relented, but with one proviso—George first had to play for him a demanding guitar piece called "Raunchy," and perform it as expertly as the local guitar hotshot named Eddie Clayton. George gave John a mean "Raunchy," and an even meaner "Guitar Boogie Shuffle." George was an instant Quarryman.

For years John and Paul dominated the Beatles with their brilliant song writing, while George was content to play his guitar in the background, contributing little more than one or two songs to the early albums. But gradually as he gained in maturity and confidence, he began to come into his own as a songwriter. In 1968, the Beatles' *White Album* boasted four Harrison songs. All four of these songs, "Here Comes the Sun," "Within You, Without You," "While My Guitar Gently Weeps," and "Savory Truffle," have become rock 'n' roll classics. Had the Beatles survived intact into the 1970s, there is no question that George would have formed a song-writing triumvirate with Paul and John.

Ironically, George, who had snored through his classes at the Liverpool Institute, experienced an intellectual awakening of sorts in 1966, and became a late-blooming scholar in the field of Indian music and culture. While the other Beatles were off on psychedelic tangents and LSD trips, George was traveling to India; devouring books on Yoga, Hinduism, and Indian music; and studying the *sitar* with Ravi Shankar.

His interest in things Indian came about by pure chance. During the making of the Beatles' second movie, *Help!*, which had an Indian backdrop, and which featured Indian musicians, George got his first glimpse of such exotic instruments as the *sitar*, the *dillrube*, and the *tabla*. One afternoon, while he was lounging on the set, he idly picked up the *sitar* and tried to play it. Guitar virtuoso though he was, he was unable to coax anything even faintly melodious from this elaborate Indian guitar. Yet he was enchanted with it, exactly as he had been enchanted some twelve years earlier when he had heard Lonnie Donegan play the electric guitar.

Just as he had become obsessed with practicing the guitar, he developed a similar monomania for practicing the *sitar*. Day and night he would sit with the multi-stringed, giraffe-necked instrument tucked against his instep as he struggled to carry out the exercises set for him by his *sitar* guru, Ravi Shankar. By slow degrees, he began to be able to play simple *rāgas* (melodic patterns). At the same time, he started learning Indian musical notation so that he could incorporate the *sitar* and other Indian instruments into the Beatles' songs.

In 1966 the Beatles' album *Rubber Soul* featured a song called "Norwegian Wood," which George had interlaced with *rāgas* that he had learned to play on the *sitar*. It was the first time that a popular Western song had made use of Indian instruments. On its release, the album created a sensation, and helped touch off the "Hindumania" that was a feature of popular Western culture in the late 60s. Soon bands and groups throughout Europe and America were falling over themselves to work the exotic strains of the *sitar*, *dillrube*, and *tabla* into their compositions.

A highlight of the "Hindumania" of the late sixties, (of which the Beatles were the harbingers), was George's much publicized conversion to vegetarianism. Through his wife Patti, who had become interested in the teachings of the self-styled religious leader, Maharishi Mahesh Yogi, George and the Beatles were introduced to transcendental meditation and vegetarianism. To his credit, the Maharishi laid down as a condition for their joining his *ashram* that the Beatles must give up the eating of meat. So it was that George, Paul, and John first became vegetarians. Drummer Ringo Starr tried it for a while, but could never bring himself to give up that Liverpudlian delicacy—fish 'n' chips.

Dark Horse Lentil Soup

1 red chili
1 teaspoon cumin seeds
2 large onions, chopped
2 cloves garlic
1 cup lentils (one or more types
    of lentils can be used)
2 large tomatoes, chopped
2 green peppers, chopped
1 bay leaf
Salt and pepper to taste

Heat a small amount of oil in a frying pan. When oil is good and hot add the red chili and cumin seeds. When the seeds stop sputtering, brown the onions and garlic in seasoned oil. In a separate deep pan, wash the lentils in plenty of water. When clean, liberally cover with water. When the onions are browned, add them to the pan of lentils. Now add the tomatoes, peppers, bay leaf, salt, and pepper. Potatoes and carrots and small boiling onions may be added for a more substantial meal. Bring to a boil, cover and turn down to a very low heat. The soup is ready to serve in an hour and tastes even better the next day.

Serves four.

DICK GREGORY

In his two best-selling autobiographies *Nigger* and *Up From Nigger*, Dick Gregory's favorite metaphors are drawn from the track. Ever since he discovered that he could outrun and outwit bullies in the black ghetto of St. Louis, he has never stopped running—or polishing his celebrated wit. Born in St. Louis, Missouri, Gregory attended St. Louis's Sumner High School, where he was voted president of his high school graduating class. He was also—as the best distance miler in the State of Missouri—a rising track star, who was sufficiently fleet of foot to attend college on a track scholarship.

In 1968, he embarked on his most ambitious marathon when he entered the race for the U.S. Presidency. Unfortuantely, his election results were not all they might have been. No doubt he would have made a better showing had treasury agents not seized his campaign handbills, which had been printed in the form of dollar bills bearing a portrait of Gregory instead of George. (The T-men claimed they had been turning up in dollar-bill changing machines, prompting Gregory to remark: "It's a heck of a commentary on the technology, if a money-changing machine can't tell the difference between my face and George Washington's. I can't see how my face on a bill could confuse any human being or machine until the face of a black man appears on regular United States currency.") Not to be denied, he was proclaimed President-in-Exile by his supporters—an office which he held until August of 1974, when he relinquished it to his successor, Ex-President, Richard M. Nixon.

His humor always has had a social purpose. In the mid-1960's, he scored his first triumph as a comedian, satirizing race relations before frozen food executives from the deep South at the Chicago Playboy Club. It was the first time that a black comedian had dared to defy the convention that race-relations was a taboo subject for humor in big-time night clubs. His comedic courage was amply rewarded: Within a year he was playing to capacity crowds from Basin Street in Manhattan to the Hungry i in San Francisco. A protégé and friend of Dr. Martin Luther King, Gregory put his comedic talent in the service of the early civil rights movement. He is America's most conscience-stricken comedian. This is why, despite the barbed social commentary that he delivers to college-lecture- and nightclub-audiences, he is popular with crowds of all political colorations: beneath the japes and gibes, they sense the earnestness of a Gandhi in motley.

If Gregory bears more than a passing resemblance to Gandhi, it's because he absorbed many of Gandhi's ideas of *satyagraha*, purposeful fasting, and non-violent resistance from a deep student of Gandhi's methods—the Reverend Dr. Martin Luther King. (Gregory returned the favor by influencing Dr. King's son, Dexter Scott King, to become a vegetarian.) Gregory credits the civil rights movement with having actuated him to become a vegetarian: "Because of the civil rights movement, I decided I couldn't be thoroughly non-violent and participate in the destruction of animals for my dinner. I became a vegetarian strictly for moral reasons."[1]

Although he made his debut before the public as a comedian, he has since developed into something of a Renaissance man. He's become a talented author whose sheer output other authors might envy: two autobiographies (one of which, *Nigger*, has sold over a million copies), a book of Bible tales, over half a dozen books on history and politics, as well as a best-selling book on nutrition, *Dick Gregory's Natural Diet for Folks Who Eat: Cookin' with Mother Nature*. First published in 1974, *Dick Gregory's Natural Diet* is a primer of rawfood fruitarianism that has made countless converts in the black community. In the book, he looks back on a life of high achievement, and deems his physical rejuvenation and spiritual awakening through fasting and raw fruit diet to be his proudest accomplishment. Gregory believes that raw fruitarianism is "the highest form of vegetarianism because it comes closest to the body chemistry, which is 97 percent liquid against 3 percent solid; and fruit tends to have more liquid in it than anything else." Of course Gregory is careful to underscore that "By fruit, I mean anything that has a seed in it. So that a lot of what we call vegetables are actually fruit, like tomatoes, squash, eggplant, bell peppers—they're really fruit."[2] Writing at a time when it was considered cranky to be a vegetarian—much less a fasting, raw foodist—Gregory had the courage to champion a diet that is now being scientifically vindicated as a panacea against the degenerative diseases of heart disease, diabetes, high blood presssure, and cancer that are a particular scourge of the American black community. Although he doesn't preach rawfoodism and fruitarianism in his one-man stage show, *Dick Gregory Live*, which is running off Broadway this season, he does stress the importance of eating fruit and fasting. Asked why he doesn't exhort his audiences to swear off animal flesh and become instant fruitarians, he said the quickest way to turn people off is to start pontificating extreme views. Rather, he persuades them through his writings, and by dint of his personal example— his long fasts and his bunion-raising cross-country runs have been highly publicized. For the record he's fasted for 43 days on water, and he protested the Vietnam War by fasting for two years on fruit juice. During his two year fruit-juice fast, he got poignant letters from school children saying that they were praying for the war to end so that Gregory could eat solid food again, or, rather uncooked fruit: Gregory and his wife Lilian have raised their ten children as fruitarians; none has ever tasted—or has expressed any desire to taste—cooked food.

Raised as a Baptist, Gregory opines that Christ was a vegetarian: "As a spiritual person, he had to be. He had to have reached the conclusion that nothing with life in it should be killed under any circumstances."[3] Doubtless Gregory would agree with Rabbi Abraham Cook that the Messianic Age can be hastened by practicing a vegetarian diet. In the Messianic Age, says Kook, there will be no warfare, no carnivorism; no strife; love and peace will prevail. The last days (before the Messianic Age) will resemble the first, and as we know from Genesis the first days were fruitarian. "I have given you every herb-bearing seed, etc. and it shall be for you as food." Many modern day fruitarians take this to be a specific mandate to eat an almost exlcusively raw fruit diet.

Along with Dick Gregory, another pioneer of the modern fruitarian movement is T. C. Fry (a curious name for a rawfoodist). The author of *The Curse of Cooking*,[4] Fry believes that we are the symbiants to fruit-bearing vines and trees. In return for nourishing us with their fruit, we spread their seeds and assist in their propagation. By eating animal flesh, and cooked foods, we are violating the symbiotic compact, and we pay the price for it in abbreviated lifespans and diminished quality of life.

A few years ago, the comedian-turned-nutritionist came out with "Dick Gregory's Safe Slim Bahamian Diet"—a diet nostrum that is made from a vegetarian powdered food supplement of his own devising. Mixed with fruit juice, it supplies a nutritionally balanced meal. It has proved remarkbly effective in reducing body fat in the chronically obese as well as in people who are moderately corpulent. Obese once himself (Gregory at one time tipped the scales at 288 pounds), Gregory recently launched a national anti-obesity campaign, dubbing obesity America's number one nutrition-related problem. "America is the most obese nation in our world. We are 40 million tons overweight! Current estimates predict you lose at least one year of life for every ten pounds of excess body fat."

Mixed Salad*

Mix well: shredded cabbage, grated cabbage and chopped, minced or grated onions.
Garnish with pumpkin, sunflower or sesame seeds.
Top with one of the salad dressings.

Salad Dressing*

French Dressing:

Combine ½ cup olive oil, ¼ cup lemon juice, the juice of 1 tomato or ¼ cup lemon juice (freshly squeezed). Mix all ingredients thoroughly (use blender if available).

Banana Nut Roll*

Grind almonds, pecans or filberts in a blender or nut grinder. Peel and halve bananas. Roll each banana half in the nuts. And you have a nutty Chiquita Banana delight!

---

*These recipes from *Dick Gregory's Natural Diet: for Folks Who Eat: Cookin' with Mother Nature* (1974). They appear on pages 112, 119 and 141 respectively. Permission to reprint these recipes from Dick Gregory.

DAVID WALLECHINSKY

In January 1965, *Time* magazine did a cover story on the graduating class of Pacific Palisades High School. *Time* selected "Pali" (as it is affectionately called) because its students, among the world's most affluent, seemed destined to fulfill the wildest promises of the American dream. As *Time* put it, the students were "on the fringe of a golden era." In retrospect, *Time*'s expectations for the class of '65 seem a trifle overblown, but the cover story put Pali on the map, and guaranteed that its class of '65 would become one of the most talked-about in U.S. history.

David Wallechinsky was a member of Pali's class of '65, and his best-selling before-and-after account of thirty of its members, written from the perspective of ten years after graduation—*What Really Happened to the Class of '65?*—further ensured that both the class of '65 and David Wallechinsky would not be soon forgotten. Ironically, by virtue of his having written such bestsellers as *What Really Happened to the Class of '65?*, *The People's Almanac*, and *The Book of Lists*, David Wallechinsky, who was the class of '65's chronic underachiever, has become Pali's most celebrated and successful graduate. Still in his forties, he has over half-a-dozen books and one film documentary to his credit.

More than just a compiler of facts, as some critics have unfairly dubbed him, David is a literary innovator who has a gift for reinvigorating drab and pedestrian literary genres. For instance, who ever heard of a readable, entertaining almanac that one can curl up with for endless hours? Or for that matter, who ever heard of a high school yearbook that was of any but parochial interest? And what could be more boring than a book of lists? Yet David has taken the almanac in *The People's Almanac*, the high school yearbook in *What Really Happened to the Class of '65?*, and a collection of lists in *The Book of Lists*, and breathed new life into these arid, dry-as-dust literary forms. Few men since Diderot have done so much for the readable reference book as has David Wallechinsky.

As David has been a thoroughgoing vegetarian since 1969, it is not surprising to find the subject of vegetarianism cropping up from time to time in his books. For example, *The People's Almanac* devotes five pages to vegetarianism and biographical sketches of famous vegetarians. *The Book of Lists* contains a feature called "Famous Dinner Guests From All History," in which the contributors selected ten or more historical figures whom they would most like to have as guests for dinner. Himself a contributor, David picked ten famous vegetarians, with Pythagoras, the Buddha, Shelley, Tolstoy, and Shaw numbered among them. In *The Book of Lists #2*, English authoress and vegetarian Brigid Brophy makes great

play of choosing two vegetarians for her list of people "whose lives I would like to have lived in past incarnations"[2]—Thomas Tryon, an English dietician of the 17th century, and George Bernard Shaw.

Born on Feburary 5, 1948, David Wallechinsky is the son of Irving and Sylvia Wallace. The family name was originally "Wallechinsky," but an officious immigrations clerk at Ellis Island forced the name "Wallace" on David's grandfather, because to the clerk's ears "Wallechinsky" didn't sound American enough. In 1969 David resumed the ancestral surname, not so much to distinguish himself from his famous father as to dramatize his protest against the small-minded, rubber-stamp mentality of the bureaucrat who had stamped out his family name. On other hand, if David *had* chosen to change his name in order to distinguish himself from his famous father, it would have been altogether pardonable. Being the son of a famous man is never easy, and Irving Wallace is one of the most celebrated and successful authors in America. With the publication of his sexually explicit, mock-Kinsey, *Chapman Report* in 1960, Irving broke into bestsellerdom and has been there ever since. His other bestsellers include *The Prize, The Man, The Seven Minutes,* and *The R Document.* He was one of the first authors to be awarded a six-figure advance for a projected book (*The Man*) on the strength of an outline. His name appears on more than twenty-three books, and over 130 million copies of his books are now in print. David's mother, Sylvia, is also a successful novelist, having recently joined Irving in bestsellerdom with two books of her own—*The Fountains* and *The Empress.*

Although David is Pali's most renowned and successful graduate, the 1965 *Time* cover story completely overlooked him—which was perfectly proper, because academically David did not exactly cover himself with distinction. At school he was noted not for his good marks or his scintillating mind, but rather for being the shrewdest gin rummy and blackjack player on campus. David was prouder of his card game winnings, which were indecently high, than he was of his marks, which were fair-to-middling. Consequently, he didn't get to play blackjack at any of the Ivy League colleges that his best friends at school attended (in spite of his poor marks, David palled out with Pali's intellectuals). Instead, after a number of false starts at UCLA, he wound up at San Francisco State College, where he switched his major from English literature to film.

He had gone to San Francisco State hoping that the idyllic setting and the tranquil atmosphere might relieve his *weltschmertz* and soothe his free-floating angst. But not long after his arrival the campus was plunged into one of the worst student revolts of the late 1960s. Classes were suspended for months at a time, and for more than a year the campus was in a state of siege.

While other students were burning buildings, rioting, and hurling rocks at the police, David was off by himself, laughing. It is not that the riotous events on campus tickled his risibilities—in fact he was rather depressed by it all—but rather that he had finally found a tonic for his sagging spirits in the form of nitrous oxide (laughing gas). Nitrous oxide is such a powerful euphoric that not long after its discovery, people began taking it for the sense of well-being and euphoria that it promoted. Safe and inexpensive, it seemed the perfect way to inject a bit of levity into their cheerless lives and relieve *tedium vitae*. Here at last was the thing that man had been seeking since he started on the planet—a cheap, harmless way to get high. In becoming a laughing gas user himself, David was keeping excellent company. For as he points out in *The Book of Lists*, some of the great figures of the 19th and 20th centuries were users of laughing gas. Foremost among them were Thomas Wedgwood (English physicist), Samuel Taylor Coleridge (English poet), Peter Roget (author of *Roget's Thesaurus*), William James (philosopher), Theodore Dreiser (U.S. author), and Winston Churchill (English statesman).

Having majored in film at San Francisco State, David decided to combine his interest in cinema with his interest in laughing gas to make a documentary about one of his notorious laughing gas parties. At these parties David provided a five-foot-high tank of laughing gas around which guests would gather to improve their disposition. So improved did their disposition become, however, that invariably people started tearing off their clothes in a fit of giggles and the party degenerated into an orgy. Called *Gas*, David's film made no great stir when it was first shown in the U.S. But two years after its release it was rediscovered by critics abroad, and was selected as a U.S. entry to the 1971 Venice Film Festival.

At length David's enthusiasm for laughing gas began to pall on him. Like Paul McCartney and George Harrison, who had also had their psychedelic flings in the 60s, David became a student of the Maharishi Mahesh Yogi, and converted to vegetarianism in 1969. At first David became a vegetarian for health reasons, but after fifteen years of being "a devout vegetarian,"[3] as he describes himself, he has acquired moral and ethical scruples against eating meat as well. As he puts it: "I became a vegetarian fifteen years ago for health reasons, but since then the moral and ecological reasons have become more important to me. I don't believe in killing animals, humans, or insects (except mosquitos)."[4]

Actually vegetarianism runs in David's family. His sister Amy, with whom he co-authored the bestselling *The Book of Predictions*, and *The Intimate Sex Lives of Famous People*, is also a strict vegetarian. His father, Irving, with whom he has collaborated on *The People's Almanac* as well as its bestselling progenies *The Book of Lists*, and *The Intimate Sex Lives of Famous People*—was a vegetarian for thirteen years (1935 to 1948) before relapsing. On Thanksgiving afternoon of 1935 Irving closed the book that he had just finished reading, and resolved to become a vegetarian on the spot. As might be expected, a book that could move Irving Wallace to give up eating meat for thirteen years was no ordinary book. It was in fact Mahatma Gandhi's autobiography. That evening, with a Gandhian flourish, Irving declined a Thanksgiving dinner invitation from the family with whom he was visiting by pleading his hastily acquired vegetarian principles. For twelve years and two months (to be precise), Irving adhered to those principles. Then, prompted by one of his wife's food cravings during her pregnancy, he rushed out to a nearby delicatessen and bought her a corned-beef-on-rye. Overcome by the aroma (he had been much addicted to corned-beef sandwiches as a boy) he took a bite of her sandwich and slid back into meat-eating (exactly one month before the family's devout vegetarian was born—David Wallechinsky).

David now lives in Santa Monica, California with his wife, Flora Chavez Wallechinsky, and their two sons, whom they are raising as vegetarians.

Salad Sandwich

Cauliflower
Carrots
Zucchini
Yellow squash
Summer squash
Purple cabbage
Cucumber
Celery
Lettuce
Alfalfa Sprouts
Jicama (opt.)
Tomato (opt.)
Beets (opt.)
Radishes (opt.)
Avocado slices (opt.)
Whole-wheat hamburger buns
Mayonnaise (or eggless equivalent)

"This is a raw vegetable sandwich, simple to prepare, but quite tasty. All you do is grate the first seven ingredients into a large bowl, add chopped celery and mix it all together with your hands until the colors are well-blended. Then spread some mayonnaise on a toasted hamburger bun; add two or three large handfuls of veggies per sandwich; top with sprouts and lettuce; and pop on the top half of the bun. For variety and color I some-times add jicama, tomato, beet, radish, avocado slices, or anything else that is in season.

"This recipe is particularly important to me because I prepared it for my wife early in our courtship, thereby convincing her that I was a good catch."

D. W.

Chico's Sautéed Mushrooms

Good-sized mushrooms
    (three to four inches wide)
Pepper
Salt
Olive oil

"Let's talk about how you make real, honest-to-goodness mushrooms. You get good-sized mushrooms. I usually pick them three to four inches wide. Wash them, but don't dry the water off, and don't drain them. I cut the stems and put them stem-side up in a large pan. Sprinkle some pep-per over them, and then some salt, and put olive oil inside the caps of the mushrooms. I don't throw out the stems. I put them in the pan also. Put them in the broiler and let them cook about twenty minutes. When you take them out, let them cool off a little bit. Mmmm, you have a good meal."

D. W.

David comments: "This recipe was created by the late Frank "Chico" Bucaro, with whom I co-authored my first book, *Chico's Organic Gardening and Natural Living.* Chico thought that button mushrooms were ridiculous and firmly believed that mushrooms should not be picked until they had opened completely—the bigger the better."

Source: Frank "Chico" Bucaro and David Wallechinsky, *Chico's Organic Gardening and Natural Living* (New York and Philadelphia: Lippincott, 1972), p. 125. Copyright © 1972 by David Wallechinsky. Reprinted by permission of David Wallechinsky.

DENNIS WEAVER

As the game-legged, rube-comic Chester in "Gunsmoke" (the longest running adult western in television history), Dennis Weaver raised the job of acting as a sidekick to a high art. In the series, he played deputy to the strapping six-foot-six Matt Dillon (James Arness), marshall of the raucous and bellicose cattle town of Dodge City, Kansas. As a measure of Weaver's popularity (not to mention "Gunsmoke's") people all over the world (the Japanese are still rabid fans) used to amuse themselves by imitating Chester's shuffling gait, and mimicking his obsequious drawl, as he called, "Coming, Mr. Dillon!"

That Weaver was able to imbue the character of Chester with such astonishing credibility is, of course, a tribute to his talents as an actor. But so plausible were his performances, and so closely was he identified with the "Chester" role, that Weaver was in peril of being perpetually type-cast as a galumphing buffoon with a deputy's badge. As it was, people were astounded that off-screen Weaver's personality, tastes, and physical appearance could be so much at variance with Chester's. For, in truth, Weaver is everything that Chester was not. Where Chester was a block-head, Weaver is brainy and discerning; where Chester was clumsy, Weaver is still almost as fit and agile as the decathlon champion that he was in high school and college; where Chester was physically unprepossessing, Weaver is movie-star handsome; where Chester was inarticulate and spoke with a hillbilly brogue, Weaver is an eloquent speaker, who, one Sunday a month, gives a sermon to overflow audiences at the Self Realization Church's Temple of the Lake Shrine in Los Angeles. Finally, where Chester guzzled black coffee and ate meat, Weaver scorns coffee, and for almost thirty years has been a teetotaling vegetarian—a fact that used to stun his fans at the barbecues and dinner parties that were held in his honor. An actor who played a deputy marshall in the West's most notorious cattle town was expected to eat beef and gulp liquor like a cowboy.

Born on June 4, 1924, in Joplin, Missouri, he grew up during the depth of the Depression in a family of modest circumstances. He narrowly escaped the grinding poverty that saw him as a boy having to stand in bread lines to collect day-old bread for the family, and until his late teens, owning no more than a single change of clothes. But poverty was a goad to his ambition. By the time he finished high school he had become one of the Midwest's finest scholar-athletes. At the University of Oklahoma, where he was voted Most Versatile Man, he majored in Drama and was

225

a track and field athlete of national reputation. After graduation and a two-year hitch in the Navy, he married his college sweetheart, Gerry, by whom he had three sons. Shortly after the birth of their first son, Rick, in 1948, the family lit out for New York, where Weaver sought further training as an actor. Stage roles then, as now, were scarce and unremunerative. So he and Gerry toiled at odd jobs, while he studied at Actor's Studio along with such other unknown and aspiring thespians as Marlon Brando, Paul Newman, James Dean, Shelley Winters, Gene Hackman, and Cloris Leachman. At the urging of Shelley Winters, who had played Blanche Dubois to Weaver's Stanley Kowalski (the role that catapulted Brando to stardom) in *A Streetcar Named Desire,* Universal signed Weaver to a six-year contract. But because he sat a horse well and had a martial bearing, he was relegated to playing cowpunchers and catchpenny villains in celluloid horse operas. Feeling that his talent as an actor was being stifled, he won his release from his contract with Universal and supported himself as a free-lance player until he was offered the part of Chester in "Gunsmoke."

The 1950s were pivotal years in Weaver's life: in 1953 he landed the role of Chester in "Gunsmoke"; in 1956 he gave up smoking and drinking; in 1958 he became the first prominent stage and screen actor to embrace a vegetarian diet; and in 1959 he began to toy with the idea of quitting "Gunsmoke"—then the most popular series on TV.

After six years as Chester, Weaver felt that he was stagnating in the role, although acting jobs were scarce enough to make even the most gifted actors think better of chucking a series role that, however, unfulfilling, was financially rewarding. But acting is not a profession that prizes fidelity. The gold watch for fifty years of faithful, plodding service to the corporation is not among its emoluments. Indeed, the dogged devotion to playing a single role year after year can be stultifying. Rather, it is the actor who can disport himself in a variety of roles, leap nimbly from part to part, and defy typecasting, who becomes a consummate actor. So Weaver turned his back on the financial security that would have come with playing Chester for another twenty years, and took a balletic leap into the unknown. "It was the toughest damned decision I ever made in my life," he recalls, "but I had to break out of that mold or go berserk."[1]

Almost as if to confirm that his decision to leave had been a sound one, no sooner had he left "Gunsmoke" than he began to be cast in such highly acclaimed television movies as *The Great Man's Whiskers* (in which he played Lincoln) and *Duel* (in which he played a traveling salesman who tries to elude a runaway tractor-trailer rig that is bent on killing him). For one season he played the veterinarian father of a Chinese orphan in "Kentucky Jones," but according to Weaver the show was cancelled for lack of promotion by the network. He also starred in a series that ran for nearly three years. In "Gentle Ben," he played a game warden who kept a seven hundred pound black bear as a pet. This time, Weaver was sidekick to a bear instead of Marshall Dillon of "Gunsmoke." Of Ben, Weaver recalls, "Our bear was a vegetarian. There was a scene in which he was supposed to devour a hot dog, and he wouldn't have any part of it. In order to give the illusion that he was eating hot dogs, we had to make them out of a vegetarian product; as soon as we did, he gobbled them right up."[2] It was only when Weaver started playing Marshall Sam McCloud in the wildly popular "McCloud" series (which ran for eight years), that Weaver was able to shed once and for all his image as the perennial sidekick, and swagger forth as a tall-walking lawman with his own entourage of subordinates and galumphing deputies.

Avocado-Tomato Sandwich

Seven-grain bread (coarse bread)
Soy margarine
Strips of avocado
Sunflower seeds and/or sprouts (bean, or alfalfa)
Tomatoes, skinned, seeded and chopped
Thin slice of Mozzarella-style soy cheese (opt.)

Spread two slices of coarse, whole grain bread with soy margarine. On one slice, make a layer of avocado strips. Next, add a layer of sunflower seeds and/or bean sprouts. Then add a layer of chopped tomato; use a bit of mustard for added zest.

Dennis Weaver's daughter-in-law, Alice Ornstein Weaver, who works as his secretary and usually fixes his lunch, furnished the recipe. It's the sandwich that he used to have for lunch every day during the shooting of the "McCloud" series.

Crazy Mixed-Up Rice Skillet Dish

6 tablespoons melted soy margarine
2 cups celery, chopped in large pieces
2 cups green pepper, chopped
2 cups green onion, chopped
4 cups cooked brown rice
2 cups Crazy Mixed-Up Mixture (consisting of
    equal parts of whole almonds, pumpkin
    seeds, sunflower seeds, raisins, dried
    apricots, and dried apples)
Spike seasoning, or herbal seasoning to taste
2 cups tomatoes cut in eighths
½ lb. Cheddar cheese, cut in chunks, or ½ lb.
    cubed Cheddar-style soy cheese*
2 tablespoons vegetable stock

Toss cooked rice, celery, peppers, onion, Crazy-Mixed-Up mixture, and Spike. Melt the soy margarine in a large skillet and add to it the tossed vegetables and rice. Poke cheese or soy-cheese cubes into mixture and also on top. Do not cook after the soy margarine has melted. Add two tablespoons of vegetable stock and arrange tomatoes on top. Cover and steam for a few minutes only. Vegetables must not cook or they will lose color. Serve in the skillet.

D. W.

Serves four.

---

*I have added the option of soy cheese to enable strict vegetarians like myself (who take no dairy products) to enjoy this dish.

KILLER KOWALSKI

Legend has it that the greatest Olympic athlete of all time was Milo of Croton—a wrestler and disciple of Pythagoras—who flourished in the 6th century B.C. Legend also has it that Milo never lost a match, and that no opponent ever succeeded in bringing him to his knees. In the ancient Olympiads, which were held at three-year intervals, he was a victor five successive times (from 532 to 516 B.C.). He also won the senior wrestling event in the Pythian games, six times; in the Isthmian games, ten times; and in the Nemean games, nine times. His unequaled record of victories did much to promote the dietetic and metaphysical theories of Pythagoras (whom Milo gave credit for his triumphs).

Killer Kowalski is in the best tradition of Milo of Croton. Not only is Kowalski a wrestler of legendary prowess who has observed a Pythagorean diet for most of his career, but in keeping with Pythagoras's dictum that athletes should develop their minds, and philosophers their bodies—he has been a close student of theosophy for more than thirty years.

To look at his beetling brows, his menacing mien, and his hulking physique—he is six-feet-eight-inches tall and two hundred and fifty pounds—Kowalski is the last person whom one would ever accuse of being a vegetarian, much less a closet theosophist. For twenty-eight years on the professional wrestling circuit, Killer Kowalski was the arch-heel whom fans loved to hate. An unenviable role, one might think. But in the world of professional wrestling, a villain may enjoy a far more lucrative and durable career than a hero—as Kowalski's three decades in the ring attest. Heroes are a dime a dozen, but a heel like Kowalski, who can bring down a cascade of hisses and catcalls merely by stepping into the ring, has a rare and indispensable talent. After all, professional wrestling thrives on the tension given off when hero is pitted against villain. Every professional wrestling match is a species of morality play or seasonal duel that plays off good against evil, fall against spring, summer against winter— evoking the sacred rites held in the ancient Italian forests at Nemi in which the priests of Diana would fight for the annual kingship of the wood.

Of all the modern sports that have descended from the ancient Olympic games, professional wrestling is the most flamboyant and the least Olympian. The flamboyant tone was set back in the early 1950s by a peroxide-haired bully named Gorgeous George. Television was in its infancy, but even then programs lived or died by their ratings. For a time it seemed as if televised wrestling along with one of its anonymous practitioners, George Raymond Wagner, were heading for the skids. But then George Wagner hit upon the idea of camping it up for the cameras. He changed his name to Gorgeous George and resorted to such gimmicks as dying his coiffured locks golden, wearing sequined tights, and having his valet spray the ring with a flit gun filled with Chanel Number Five. After George's television ratings soared, every wrestler within camera range started to ham it up for the television audience. "Nature Boy" Buddy Rogers donned risqué outfits that warranted arrest for indecent exposure. Edouard Carpentier, "The Flying Frenchman," who was famous for his ring acrobatics, confounded his opponents with aerial somersaults and backward handsprings. Haystack Calhoun assiduously acted the hayseed and wrestled in bib overalls, as did his hillbilly cohort Man Mountain Dean. Not above a little showmanship himself, Killer Kowalski used to wear purple tights decorated with lightning bolts. There were many (and who can blame them) who thought that Kowalski's vegetarianism was, if not a gimmick, then at least a Gorgeous Georgian affectation.

But if there was anything phoney about Kowalski it was his ring villainy, not his vegetarianism. Outside the ropes he was the mildest of men—thoughtful, courteous, and articulate; but inside the ropes he was a . . . killer. Earlier in his career, Kowalski was called "Tarzan"—perhaps in humorous reference to his simian diet of fruits and vegetables—even though Lord Greystoke (Tarzan), as Edgar Rice Burroughs paints him, was no vegetarian. But on a fateful night in Montreal, Kowalski was tagged with the lethal sobriquet that has become his trademark.

It was a cool night in Montreal in the early fifties, and "Tarzan" Kowalski was giving the local fair-haired bruiser, Yukon Eric, a sound drubbing—much to the displeasure of the crowd, which had turned ugly the moment Kowalski set foot in the ring. Eric had Kowalski in a stranglehold. Suddenly Kowalski eluded Eric's grip by climbing to the topmost rope and leaping into the air. It was a brilliant escape, and a spectacular aerial maneuver, but on his way down, his shinbone accidentally struck Eric's cauliflower ear and lopped it off. The ear rolled crazily around the ring, while Kowalski and the referee tried to staunch the bleeding. The crowd, which had been howling for Kowalski's blood, was briefly silenced by the ghastly sight of real blood spurting from the hole where Eric's ear had been. As Kowalski and the referee were helping the hapless Eric out of the ring, the crowd roared "Killer! Killer!" at Kowalski, and the name stuck.

Now a naturalized American citizen, Kowalski was born Walter (Wladek) Kowalski to Polish immigrant parents on October 13, 1931, in Windsor, Ontario. His father was a factory worker in the Ford plant in Windsor. As soon as Walter was of age, he found a job in the same plant, as an electrician. There he might have stayed, had he not begun to make a name for himself in local wrestling matches at the Windsor YMCA. Word of his wrestling talent spread, and he was soon invited to participate in matches as far afield as Saint Louis. When he began to earn more money from wrestling than he was making in the Ford plant, he quit the assembly line to become a full-time wrestler.

Agile, astute, and above all, physically imposing, as soon as Kowalski turned pro he shot to the top of the professional rankings. With another slavic giant, Hans Hermann, he teamed to win the championship tag-team matches in the early fifties, and has been at the pinnacle of his sport ever since. In the book *Whatever Happened to Gorgeous George?* author Joseph Jares says of Kowalski: "one of the great villains, the tall, powerful Kowalski is a quiet, gentlemanly, religious man outside the ring. He has bloodied more heroes than practically any other heel alive."[1] There isn't a wrestler on the circuit whom Kowalski hasn't trounced, and he was as fearsome a grappler on the day he retired in 1978, as on the day he entered the "squared circle" in the early 1950s.

A year after his retirement, Kowalski founded a school for professional grapplers—the first of its kind—at the YMCA in Salem, Massachusetts (not far from his home). In addition to teaching his students his repertoire of seventy-nine holds, he also gives them nutritional advice. Not a few of his students have copied his vegetarian lifestyle as well as his villainous wrestling style, and have become popular villains on the wrestling circuit in their own right. Some of the most scoundrelly villains his school has turned out have actually been villainesses. Kowalski has bragged that his female graduates could beat not only most women, but could even defeat some male grapplers as well.

How did Kowalski come to be a vegetarian in the first place? Nothing about Kowalski is conventional, so it is not surprising that the reason for his conversion is as uncommon as everything else about him. Ever since his early teens, Kowalski has been intensely interested in spiritualism and theosophy. The more he delved into the subject, the more he was struck by how many of the great theosophists such as Annie Besant denounced meat-eating. But it was his reading of the spiritualist tome, *A Dweller on Two Planets* by Phylos the Thibetan, that really set Kowalski on the vegetarian path. So taken was he with Phylos's view that (as Kowalski phrases it), "no one who eats the flesh of animals can progress spiritually beyond the average,"[2] that Kowalski decided at the age of twenty-one to renounce meat, fish and fowl—much to the consternation of his manager, his physician, and his friends, who predicted a speedy demise to his wrestling career. On the contrary, as soon as he gave up meat-eating, Kowalski found that his strength and endurance, so far from diminishing, rapidly increased. As a result, he became one of the most fearsome grapplers since Milo of Croton.

Vegetarian Vegetable Borscht

1 cup carrots, grated
1 cup celery chopped
3 medium onions, chopped
2 cups beets, grated
6½ cups cold water
4 tablespoons vegetable oil
1 cup cabbage, shredded
1 cup mushrooms, sliced
2 cups tomato soup
1 tablespoon lemon juice
Salt and pepper to taste

In a heavy skillet place grated carrots, chopped celery, one chopped onion and grated beets. Add six-and-a-half cups cold water, and bring to a boil. After it has boiled for two minutes, lower heat and simmer for one-half hour. While this is simmering, sauté two chopped onions (in a saucepan) until they turn transparent; then add the sliced mushrooms and shredded cabbage. Sauté for five minutes more, and set aside.

When the soup has simmered for twenty minutes, add the sautéed vegetables to it. Cook for five minutes more, then add the two cups of tomato soup, and the lemon juice. Bring to a boil, then remove immediately from flame. Serve warm, or chilled (preferably chilled) with a dollop of yogurt, or soy-yogurt.

Serves four.

Peas and Sauerkraut

2 tablespoons soy margarine
1 cup yellow split peas or black-eyed peas
32 oz. sauerkraut, squeezed dry
½ cup grated carrots
1 stalk celery, chopped
1 medium onion, chopped
1 bay leaf
2 tablespoons parsley, chopped
Salt and pepper to taste

Boil four cups of water in a saucepan, and add to it the yellow split peas (or black-eyed peas). Keep water boiling until the peas are soft (about fifteen minutes).

While the peas are cooking, chop the onion and sauté it for a few minutes with soy margarine in a skillet. Then add the chopped celery, grated carrots, bay leaf, and chopped parsley. Cook gently until tender, then set aside.

Squeeze the water out of the sauerkraut. When the peas are soft, drain them in a colander or strainer, and mix them with the sauerkraut in a bowl. Then add the sauerkraut and peas to the skillet containing the sautéed vegetables, and cook until the sauerkraut is heated through. Serve with rice or mashed potatoes.

Serves four.

Cabbage Rolls

2 tablespoons vegetable oil
1½ cups long-grain rice
3 cups mushrooms, sliced
2 cups mushroom soup
2 cups tomato soup
1 large head of cabbage
Salt and pepper to taste

Cook rice according to directions on package. Sauté the mushrooms in vegetable oil for about five minutes. Then add one cup of mushroom soup to the mushrooms, and stir with a wooden spoon until soup and mushrooms are well-blended. As soon as the rice is done, mix it with the mushroom sauce, and season with salt and pepper. Set aside.

From a large head of cabbage, remove twelve leaves, taking care not to tear them. Fill a large skillet with enough water to cover two of the cabbage leaves, and bring to a boil. Blanch the cabbage leaves two-at-a-time, by immersing them in the boiling water for four to five minutes. Remove with slotted spoon, and let drain in a colander or sieve. When all twelve leaves have been blanched, drained, and cooled, take a knife and remove the hard stem from each leaf. Then flatten out each leaf, and line the left or right edge with a dollop of the mushroom-rice mixture. See to it that the edge is evenly coated; then roll up the leaves like a kind of green cigar. Place the rolls into an oven-proof baking dish, and set aside. Combine the two cups of tomato soup with the remaining cup of mushroom soup, and pour over the cabbage rolls. Cover the rolls with a cabbage leaf to prevent scorching. Bake in a 375° oven for forty-five minutes.

Serves four.

ISAAC BASHEVIS SINGER

Isaac Bashevis Singer has the singular distinction of being the second Nobel Prize winning author in history to be a vegetarian. The first of course was George Bernard Shaw, who won the Prize in 1925. By rights, Leo Tolstoy, who lived into the second decade of the 20th century should have been the first; Shaw, second; and Singer, third. But the Nobel Prize Committee erred—Tolstoy was passed over. Singer would have been the first to deplore the omission, for Tolstoy was one of his intellectual heroes. The mantle of Tolstoy's vegetarianism, however, did not descend to Singer in the same way that Shelley's descended to Shaw and Salt. Singer came to vegetarianism in his own inimitable way.

Born on July 14, 1904, in Radzymin, Poland, Singer had wanted to become a vegetarian as a child, but his father, who was an orthodox rabbi, would have none of it. He scolded Singer for wanting to be holier than Yaweh, who, with his appetite for animal sacrifices in the Old Testament, was obviously no vegetarian. Chastened, Singer put off his conversion to a more propitious time—some fifty years later.

The intervening fifty years were, however, not without their vegetarian interludes. At twenty-one he rewrote the Ten Commandments so as to include an eleventh—"Do not kill nor exploit the animal, don't eat its flesh, don't flail its hide, don't force it to do things against its nature."[1] Singer had almost become a vegetarian in 1924, while he was working for a Yiddish newspaper in Warsaw called *Literary Pages*. One of the editors for whom he worked, Melech Ravich, turned out to be an ardent vegetarian. Ravich believed that a new golden age was about to dawn in which Jews and gentiles would be united in brotherhood, and all men would be vegetarians. Although Singer was too pragmatic to subscribe to Ravich's utopian views, particularly in the face of creeping fascism and communism in Europe, he was deeply touched by Ravich's high-minded vegetarianism. There can be no doubt that Ravich's views played a part in Singer's eventual conversion.

What finally impelled Singer to fly in the face of his father's wishes and disavow meat-eating was, of all things, the death of his pet parakeet Matzi in 1962. On returning home from an engagement, he was grief-stricken to find his little Matzi sprawled lifeless on the floor (Singer allowed his birds to fly about his apartment uncaged). It suddenly dawned on Singer that this was how all animals looked after they were slaughtered for food, and by eating them he was an unwitting accomplice in their destruction. From then on, Singer's tepid vegetarianism (for he had always practiced it off and on) gave way to a fierce resolve. Friends who had found him

compliant at dinner parties in taking the tidbits of meat they offered him, were startled to find how stoutly he now refused meat, and his wife Alma (who is not a vegetarian) felt called upon to cook separate vegetarian meals.

Although Singer did not become a strict vegetarian until 1962, it is clear from his writings that he has always found the slaughter of animals repugnant. His earliest novel, written in 1935, *Satan in Goray*, contains vegetarian leitmotifs, as do many of his other novels and stories. When asked about this, Singer said that the vegetarian themes came out of his pen automatically, and that the eating of meat has always bothered him.

Judaism condones the slaughter of animals (as does Christianity) and this has shaken Singer's faith to its foundations. It is for this reason that even though he can trace his lineage to the great rabbinic sages of Eastern Europe, he has fallen away from the orthodoxy of his fathers. It troubles him that the prayer shawls and phylacteries should be made of animal skins, and that the sacred Torah itself should also be bound in hide. It distresses him that a just god could not merely condone, but also connive at and encourage the sacrifice of animals. "Sometimes," he says, "I feel like praying to a vegetarian god."[2] In one of his short stories, "The Slaughterer," he even has the ritual slaughterer Yoineh Meir, accuse God of being a slaughterer: "Father in heaven, Thou art a slaughterer . . . the whole world is a slaughterhouse!"[3]

Though slaughtermen function as symbols and agents of evil in Singer's fiction, Singer would be the first to protest that he bears them no personal grudge, and does not condemn them as individuals. In his opinion, the slaughtermen are no more culpable than the people who partake of animals as food. Nevertheless, despite his protests to the contrary, wherever slaughtermen appear in Singer's stories they are depicted as harbingers of doom and retribution (rather like the Eumenides of Greek tragedy).

To know how Singer really feels about ritual slaughter and slaughtermen, one should read his short story "Blood." There, the principle character, a wealthy Jewish woman named Risha, becomes by turns an adulteress, a slaughterer, a murderess, and by story's end—a werewolf. Risha's passage from slaughterer to werewolf appears to be a logical progression.

Similarly, in his novel *Satan in Goray* the principle character, Rechele, who is the daughter of a ritual slaughterer, becomes impregnated by Satan at the book's end. Prior to this dénouement, she also marries a ritual slaughterer. It is almost as though her being the daughter and the wife of a slaughterer had prepared her for her union with the archfiend. At the end of the book, when the town is given up to debauchery and Satan swaggers through the streets, there is an orgy of animal slaughter. The sudden abundance of animal flesh is like a sinister excrescence that symbolizes the spread of evil throughout the community. Likewise, in *The*

Family Moskat, another of Singer's novels, the slaughter of animals seems to be bound up with the failed marriages and the enfeebled health of the community.

In his memoir *A Little Boy in Search of God,* Singer wrote: "My view was then, as it is now, that this world is one huge slaughterhouse, one enormous hell."[4] In the 1930s Europe was beginning to seem more and more like the vast abattoir of his youthful imaginings. Techniques of mass slaughter that had been developed for use on animals were now turned against men and women of sensibility and refinement. In several of Singer's stories which are set in Germany and Poland in the pre-Holocaust period, he draws an analogy between the slaughter of animals and the mercilessly efficient slaughter of Jews and other minorities that took place in Nazi Germany and Stalinist Russia. In fact, Singer's own mother Bathsheba, and his younger brother Moishe, perished after the Russians had transported them in a cattle train to a forced labor camp. In Singer's fiction, as in life, the destinies of animals and humans are fatefully intertwined.

In 1935, Singer sensed that with the onset of Nazism, Warsaw was no longer a safe place in which to be a Yiddish writer. He decided to join his elder brother, the noted Yiddish novelist, I. J. Singer, who was living with his family in America.

Once arrived in New York, Singer stayed for a time with his brother and set about adjusting to the alien culture. For seven years Singer was so paralyzed by culture shock that he could not put pen to paper. Eventually, however, he gathered himself together and started to contribute stories, articles, and essays to the *Jewish Daily Forward.* After his brother's untimely death in 1944, Singer began to emerge from his brother's shadow (for at the time, his brother I. J. had been the more celebrated and successful of the two). Finally, in 1950, Singer won recognition with his dynastic novel *The Family Moskat,* which was set in the Warsaw of the shtetl. Three years later, Saul Bellow translated Singer's short story "Gimpel the Fool" for the *Partisan Review.* The story was an instant success, and Singer began his steady ascent to the seat on the literary Olympus that he occupies today.

Olympian though he may be, Singer is still a familiar figure in the humble cafeterias of Manhattan that have provided colorful backdrops for such stories as "The Cabalist of East Broadway" (whose hero, incidentally, is a vegetarian). Singer and his wife Alma became habitués of good, cheap restaurants back in the 1950s and 1960s when Alma worked as a saleslady at Lord and Taylor to help pay the rent. Since she was too tired to cook Singer's meals after a day spent on the sales floor, she and her husband took to eating in neighborhood cafeterias. Even though he now earns more than one hundred thousand dollars per year, and could afford to dine spaciously in New York's poshest eateries, he still favors the unpretentious restaurants that he used to frequent before he became rich and famous. When other diners ask him the inevitable question—"Are you a vegetarian for health reasons?" he quips that he isn't a vegetarian for his own health, but for the health of the animals. "I want the chickens to be healthy."[5]

Noodles with Mushrooms en Casserole

1½ lbs. fresh mushrooms, sliced
1 medium Spanish onion, chopped
¼ lb. butter or soya margarine
½ lb. noodles, cooked and drained
Vegesal instead of salt (as Mr. Singer eschews salt.)

Sauté the mushrooms and onions in the butter or margarine until soft. In a buttered, oven-proof casserole, alternate layers of noodles and mushrooms. Bake in a preheated 350° oven for thirty minutes, or until noodles on top are brown.

Serves four.

Singer and his wife Alma, who gave me these recipes, asked me to add as a footnote that Mr. Singer is a vegetarian primarily for ethical reasons: "I think that everything connected with vegetarianism is of the highest importance, because there will never be any peace in this world so long as we eat animals. This also applies to fish. I do not eat any fish. I became a vegetarian because all my life I had felt guilty and ashamed about the fact that I had eaten the flesh of an animal. I think that animals are just as much God's creatures as men are. And we have to respect them, and love them, not slaughter them."

Kasha with Onions

3 tablespoons vegetable oil
3 onions, chopped
1 cup buckwheat groats
2 cups boiling water
1 teaspoon sea salt, or "Vegesal"
1 large dollop butter or soya margarine per serving

Fry onion in oil until golden. Add buckwheat groats and sauté until the onions turn darker. Pour on the boiling water, and let simmer over low flame for about fifteen minutes. Serve with a large dollop of butter or soya margarine.

Serves four to six.

Kasha is one of Singer's favorite dishes. His wife, Alma, serves it without salt, but laced with plenty of butter, and with a glass of skim milk as a chaser. About Kasha, Mr. Singer waxes poetic: "I like mushroom casserole, and I like kasha—by kasha, I mean buckwheat. I like it if it is cooked plainly; and if my wife puts onions into it, I like it even better. And also, I'm a great lover of potatoes. If I have potatoes, and kasha, I feel that I have gotten everything."

MALCOLM MUGGERIDGE

Malcolm Muggeridge is the exact contemporary of the English novelist Evelyn Waugh, with whom, as a master of English prose, he has frequently been compared. Writing in *The New York Times,* Paul Johnson, former editor of *The New Statesman,* declared, "Next to the late Evelyn Waugh, he is, in my view the finest writer of English prose of his generation."[1] Muggeridge's three-volume autobiography *Chronicles of Wasted Time,* was hailed by the *London Times* as "One of the greatest biographies of our time."[2]

Long before it was fashionable for writers to appear in movies—before Norman Mailer appeared in *Ragtime,* novelist Jerzy Kosinski in *Reds,* and playwright Sam Shepard in *Country*—Muggeridge was making cameo appearances in English movies. In 1967, Jonathan Miller cast him as the Gryphon in Miller's production of *Alice In Wonderland.* Muggeridge also had juicy parts in two Peter Sellers movies—*I'm All Right Jack,* in which he played a television interviewer, and *Heavens Above,* based on Muggeridge's novel of the same title, in which he played a credulous Anglican clergyman.

Muggeridge is probably most familiar to Americans as the former book reviewer of *Esquire,* where, in the style of the great 19th-century essayists—Lamb, Hazlitt, and Macaulay—he would use the book review as a pretext for writing an illuminating essay on a subject tangential to the book itself. His post as book editor lasted from the early 60s into the early 70s—a period at *Esquire* when the magazine was at its peak of irreverence and iconoclasm. Under the circumstances, *Esquire* could not have found a more kindred spirit than Muggeridge, who has been flinging ink at Establishment icons ever since he was old enough to take up his pen.

Muggeridge reached his apotheosis as an anti-Establishment figure when, on January 1, 1953, he was installed as editor of the British humor magazine *Punch.* Launched in 1841, *Punch* had once prided itself on being daring and provocative. But in the 1940s and 50s its circulation had declined steadily, its satire grown enfeebled. In a word, *Punch* had lost its "punch!"

Desperate to halt the magazine's headlong slide, the owners cast about for an editor who could put life and bite back into poor old *Punch.* For the first time they broke with tradition, and went outside the *Punch* office to recruit Muggeridge, who was then deputy editor of the *Daily Telegraph.* Muggeridge's gifts for satire and invective were on routine display in the *Telegraph's* editorial pages. Of his appointment, the *New Yorker* commented: "Nothing in his career seems to have led up to his arrival at the

head of 'the table' on *Punch,* which is exactly why so many people feel that the appointment may be highly stimulating for all concerned."[3]

Right from the start, Muggeridge's effect on the bland and fusty humor magazine was galvanic. The very first issue featured a Muggeridge editorial that caricatured England's octogenarian prime minister, Sir Winston Churchill, as a power-ravaged old man, far gone in senility. As might be expected, the editorial brought down a storm of indignation from the British Establishment, and cost Muggeridge his friendship with Lord Randolph Churchill (Sir Winston's son). Lest anyone be under the delusion that Muggeridge thought any better of the man who had been appointed as Sir Winston's successor, Sir Anthony Eden, Muggeridge wrote: "Better a Churchill senile than an Eden in full possession of his faculties, such as they are."[4]

No figure was so sacrosanct, no institution so hallowed as to be able to escape Muggeridge's barbed humor. Some of his favorite targets included Sir Anthony Eden, the BBC, Field Marshall Montgomery, fellow journalists, politicians of every hue and stripe, and, of course, the Royal Family, about which he wrote a scathing article called "The Royal Soap Opera"—an act of lese-majesty for which he was pilloried in the British press.

Another of Muggeridge's innovations at *Punch* was to invite contributions from England's best writers—something that no previous *Punch* editor had done. Soon humorous and occasional pieces from such distinguished authors as Joyce Cary, Noel Coward, Lord Dunsany, J. B. Priestley, Dorothy Sayers, Hugh Kingsmill, Anthony Powell, and P. G. Wodehouse were gracing *Punch's* pages, and the magazine became as notable for its literary quality as for its lacerating satire.

Malcolm Muggeridge was born on March 24, 1903, in Croydon, Surrey, a suburb of London. His father H. T. Muggeridge was a socialist Member of Parliament from Romford, Sussex. He raised Malcolm to be, like himself, a free-thinking agnostic, and a libertarian socialist. But early on, Malcolm, with characteristic contrariety, rejected his father's agnosticism and socialism, and cast his lot with the most conservative of Anglicans. This is not to imply that Muggeridge was not fond of his father. On the contrary, he was, and remains the most filial of sons. Nor has he adopted the vengeful, boil-them-in-oil anti-socialism of many a regenerated Christian. For although he has disencumbered himself of his father's political beliefs, he hasn't scorned everything he learned from the Fabian socialists who used to gather at the Muggeridge household "to plot the overthrow of the capitalist system."[5] Many of these early Fabians like George Bernard Shaw, Edward Carpenter, and Henry Salt, were also ardent vegetarians. Even though Muggeridge was a mere stripling when he met them, he still vividly recalls that they provided him with his first glimpse of vegetarianism in action.

His next exposure to vegetarianism came when at age ten, exhibiting all the symptoms of tuberculosis, he was packed off to convalesce at a socialist commune called the "Colony," in the English Cotswolds. Modeled on the theories of Tolstoy, and also smacking faintly of the societies of the Essenes and Pythagoreans, the Colony banned meat as well as money, and encouraged nudism. Muggeridge stayed just long enough for his lung complaint to heal, then went home to his parents without having succumbed to either vegetarianism or nudism. But the image of two nubile female communards, named Elfie and Doddles, frisking about the grounds in the nude lingered in his memory. Perhaps a similar trace memory of the communards' vegetarianism may have contributed, however subliminally, to his decision to turn vegetarian in the mid-sixties.

His third major encounter with vegetarianism came after he had graduated from Cambridge, and had accepted a teaching post at Union Christian College in India. Unlike most British *sāhibs,* Muggeridge did not hold himself aloof from the Indians—quite the reverse. He corresponded with Gandhi, and made speeches urging the Indians to throw off the British yoke. With two Indian members of the teaching faculty—both strict vegetarian brāhmins—he formed a lifelong friendship. In no time they had converted him to sandals, Indian rigging made of homespun cotton (as prescribed by Gandhi), and vegetarianism. Although he persisted in his vegetarianism manfully, it eventually came to grief on the fiery dishes of Indian vegetarian cuisine, and did not survive his return to England at the end of his three-year teaching contract.

Back in England, he married Kitty Dobbs, a girl whom he had first met at Cambridge, and who was socially as well as socialistically well-connected. By wedding Kitty, Malcolm, much to his father's delight, had married into England's socialist aristocracy; for Kitty was the niece of Beatrice and Sidney Webb, who were England's principal theoreticians of socialism and who, in Beatrice's own words, "have become icons in the Soviet Union."[6]

However, it wasn't long before Muggeridge, one of England's most inveterate iconoclasts, had fallen out with the Webbs. The rift occurred over Muggeridge's book *Winter in Moscow* (1934), which was the first book by a Western reporter who looked at Russia through glasses that were not rose-tinted. It is an account of his progressive disillusionment with socialism and the barbarities of Stalinism which he witnessed during his tour as Moscow correspondent for the *Manchester Guardian.* The book caused a great stir in England, and influenced his friend George Orwell, whose novels *Animal Farm* and *1984* owe a great deal to Muggeridge's incisive reporting on conditions in a totalitarian police state.

After a year's stint as an editor of the *Calcutta Statesman,* and a brief passage as a columnist on Lord Beaverbrook's *Evening Standard,* Muggeridge wrote a scabrous biography of Samuel Butler, which effectively debunked the debunker and left Butler's reputation in tatters. He then completed a retrospective history of the 1930s, titled *The Thirties* (in England) and *The Sun Never Sets* (in America). In America, it was the first of his books to become a bestseller.

With the outbreak of the War in 1939, the least jingoistic man in England startled all his friends by being one of the first to join up. Entering the army as a lowly private, he emerged some six years later as a highly decorated and rather dashing major. "The galloping major" is actually how Evelyn Waugh described Muggeridge to novelist Anthony Powell, in a letter from this period.[7] Muggeridge served in British Intelligence (MI5), where two other *littérateurs* were his colleagues—Ian Fleming and Graham Greene.

Although in his autobiography he makes light of his espionage activities, Muggeridge was, in fact, a very effective secret agent. For his capture of a Nazi spy (who was turned into a British double agent), and for his gathering of covert information that led to the sinking of German warships, he was awarded the *Croix de Guerre* (with palm), the *Medaille de la Reconnaissance Française,* and was made a member of the Legion of Honor. But the war exploits in which he takes the greatest satisfaction took place, curiously enough, in Paris, near the War's end. In Paris, after the Liberation, he was assigned to process the cases of men and women who had been accused of collaborating with the enemy during the German occupation of France. Among the many innocent people whom he delivered from guillotine and gallows was novelist P. G. Wodehouse. Interned by the Germans in their sweep through southern France, Wodehouse was tricked into reading some of his stories over Radio Berlin. Were it not for Muggeridge's intercession, poor P. G. might have been hanged on the basis of charges which, according to Auberon Waugh writing in the London *Sunday Observer* (October 11, 1981), were trumped up by a high ranking British politician who suffered from the pangs of literary envy.[8]

After the war, Muggeridge set his hand to writing and narrating documentaries for British television that are regarded as masterpieces of the medium and are held to rival the best of his writing. His documentary on the dissolution of the British Raj, "Twilight of Empire," and his filmed interviews with Bertrand Russell, Lord Reith (founder of the BBC), and P. G. Wodehouse are landmarks of British broadcasting. "Something Beautiful for God," his documentary on Mother Teresa of Calcutta, gained her worldwide attention and was instrumental in her being awarded the Nobel Prize for Peace. About Muggeridge's documentary, Lord Kenneth "Civilization" Clark wrote: "it is the most beautiful and moving thing ever put on television."[9]

In the mid-sixties, horrified at the hot-house conditions in which animals were being raised on factory farms, Muggeridge became a vegetarian. He felt that he could not denounce factory farming and remain a meat-eater without sounding hypocritical. Now when he protests the intensive rearing of animals for food, he can silence questions about the morality of his own eating habits with the retort that he has been a vegetarian for more than twenty years.

Barn Brack
(A Handy Irish Recipe)

1 lb. flour (whole meal or white)
4 oz. butter or margarine
6 oz. sugar (brown or white)
10 oz. dried fruit (currants, raisins, sultanas)
1 teaspoon grated nutmeg
1 dessertspoon treacle
Small pinch cinnamon
½ pint sour milk
1 teaspoon salt
½ teaspoon bread soda

A well-greased 8-inch cake tin.

Sift the flour, spices, salt, and bread soda into a bowl. Rub in the butter. Mix in the sugar thoroughly. Add prepared fruit.

Warm the milk and treacle until thoroughly blended. Do not allow to boil. Cool slightly and add to the flour mixture. Mix to a smooth thick batter by stirring. *Do not beat.*

Turn the mixture into the prepared tin. If it is Halloween or another festivity, add a ring and any other trinkets (bachelor's button or thimble), making sure these are *well wrapped in grease-proof paper.* Push them into the center of the brack but not to the bottom.

Bake for fifty minutes in a "very moderate" oven—350° or gas mark three to four, choosing a central oven position.

Test to make sure the brack is properly done by gently pressing the top of it in the center. If it feels firm and shows no mark, it is fully cooked. If not, continue baking for a few more minutes and test again.

To give the brack a nice dark brown glaze, dissolve a teaspoon of sugar in a dessertspoon of hot water and brush over the top of the brack. Return the brack to the hot oven for a few minutes.

Cool the tin slightly. Turn out to cool completely on a wire tray. When cold, you can store the brack in an airtight tin or wrapped airtight in kitchen foil. Since it keeps well, you can bake it several days before required.

Kitty Muggeridge

Crunchy Brownies

4 oz. plain chocolate
A drop or two of almond or vanilla flavoring
4 oz. dried fruit (sultanas, currants, raisins)
2 oz. chopped almonds or walnuts
2 oz. wheatflakes

Slowly melt the chocolate in a basin over hot water. Place chopped nuts, dried fruit, and wheatflakes in a bowl.

When chocolate has melted, remove from heat and add flavoring. Pour chocolate into a bowl and combine with fruit, nuts, and wheatflakes.

Drop teaspoonfuls of the mixture into cake or sweet cases, and leave to set. Store in an airtight tin for future use.

Kitty Muggeridge

Makes 24 brownies.

BRIGID BROPHY

Time magazine called her "the acknowledged high priestess of the British intelligentsia."[1] At fifty-nine she is the author of fifteen works of fiction and non-fiction. Among them are her prize-winning first novel *Hackenfeller's Ape;* her psychobiographies of Mozart (*Mozart the Dramatist*), Aubrey Beardsley (*Black and White: A Portrait of Aubrey Beardsley*), Roland Firbank (*Prancing Novelist*); and her recent novel *Palace without Chairs.*

She is also a noted cultural gadfly whose pieces appear regularly in the *Spectator,* and the *New Statesman.* In 1965, in a controversial essay for the London *Sunday Times* ("The Rights of Animals"), she brought her stinging wit to bear on the hypocrisy of the animal-loving British public. Taking the occasion to proclaim herself a vegetarian and anti-vivisectionist, she issued a challenge: the British could demonstrate their much-vaunted lover for animals by ceasing to eat them. The article caused a furor, and for weeks it was the talk of London. It was the first time that a major English intellectual had come out of the closet and declared herself to be a vegetarian in the public prints. Brigid also wove vegetarian themes into many of her literary works. For example, in her weighty tome *Black Ship to Hell,* Brigid became the first author to analyze human carnivorism and man's relation to animals in Freudian terms. And in her recent novel *Palace without Chairs,* the book's heroine, the Queen of Evarchia, is a vegetarian. Even Bernard Shaw, who never hesitated to speak his mind on other subjects, lacked the nerve to discuss his vegetarianism in his essays and plays.

As a third generation Anglo-Hibernian, Brigid Brophy belongs to that curious British minority—the expatriate Irish writers—who, paradoxically enough, have penned some of the noblest works of English literature. These writers include: Jonathan Swift, Oliver Goldsmith, Richard Brinsley Sheridan, Thomas Moore, Oscar Wilde, George Bernard Shaw, and James Joyce. Her closest kinship however, is with Shaw, with whom she shares a sparkling wit, ardent anti-vivisectionist sympathies, and an ability to write works of criticism that are no less distinguished than her works of creative imagination. Coincidentally, both she and Shaw became vegetarians at the age of twenty-five.

Her twenty-fifth birthday year was an *annus mirabilis* if there ever was one. Not only did it witness the publication to critical raves of her first novel *Hackenfeller's Ape,* but it also saw her conversion to vegetarianism and her marriage to art historian Sir Michael Levey, who has succeeded Lord Kenneth ("Civilization") Clark as the director of England's National Gallery.

251

A brilliant art historian, Sir Michael's literary output is almost as prodigious as Brigid's. He has written more than a score of books on art and
art history, including *A History of Western Art, The Life and Death of
Mozart, The Case of Walter Pater,* and *Art and Architecture in Eighteenth
Century France.* Together with Charles Osborne, Sir Michael collaborated
with Brigid on the witty and irreverent reappraisal titled *Fifty Works of
Literature That We Could Do Without.*

At the time of their marriage, Sir Michael refused even to entertain the
thought of becoming a vegetarian. But at length, some eighteen years after
the birth of their daughter Kate, he changed his mind. This volte-face
came not at the prompting of Brigid (who scrupled to force her diet on
either her husband or her daughter), but at the insistence of their daughter
Kate. Herself having just been converted by vegetarian friends, and lack-
ing her mother's scruples about imposing her views on family members,
Kate made it plain to her father that with the exception of the family cat,
she wouldn't tolerate having another carnivore in the house. Sir Michael,
bowing to the inevitable, became a vegetarian—with the result that he
now plumes himself on being a vegetarian epicure, and does most of the
family cooking.

Now that Sir Michael and Kate are thoroughgoing vegetarians, Brigid
has gone them one better by becoming a vegan, which means that she
takes no food of animal origin—no eggs, no dairy products, no honey, etc.
Her veganism also extends to her wardrobe, which is innocent of furs,
feathers, and leathers. In fact, before buying a pair of shoes she makes a
point of picking them up and sniffing them to make doubly sure that they
are non-leather.

Brigid comes by her brilliance honestly—her mother was a headmistress
and Latin scholar; her father was a noted art collector and novelist. John
Brophy, her father, is perhaps best remembered for his life of Shakespeare
Man of Stratford, his twice-filmed war novel *Immortal Sergeant,* and his
thriller *The Day They Robbed The Bank of England,* which was also made
into a popular movie. From her father (who was an ardent shavian), Brigid
inherited her love for George Bernard Shaw, her gifts as a writer, and her
interest in Freudian psychoanalysis. Her parents met on the campus of
the University of Liverpool, and subsequently moved to London, where
Brigid was born on June 12, 1929.

Her mother's name "Charis," which means "Grace" in Greek, was
bestowed on her by Brigid's grandfather, an autodidact Greek scholar
who was such an incurable phil-Hellene that he christened all his children
with Greek names of his own devising. From her maternal grandfather
and her mother, Brigid inherited her love of Greek and Latin (in which
she excelled at the Saint Paul's School for Girls in London, and later as
a classical scholar at Oxford). In fact, one of Brigid's fondest girlhood
memories is of reading Plato's account of the last days of Socrates with

the high mistress (headmistress) at Saint Paul's, Ethel Strudwick. Miss Strudwick was the only mistress whose knowledge of Greek was up to Brigid's. In a delicious memoir called *Hi, Mistress* (1970), Brigid recalled how reading the account of Socrates' death in the *Phaedo* prompted the first emotional stirrings that would ripen into her passion for vegetarianism and anti-vivisectionism. Before tossing off the poisoned cup that would carry him into the next world, Socrates asked his friend Crito to sacrifice a cock in his honor to the god of healing, Aesculapius. While the high mistress's eyes "rheumed with tears,"[2] Brigid was revolted by the cavalier manner with which Socrates had condemned an innocent creature to share his fate: "Socrates remained orthodox in observance and died offering the sacrifice of a cock to Aesculapius. Already a non-agressor against animals, I conceived he had a right to sacrifice himself, but not a non-consenting beast."[3]

Having won a full Jubilee scholarship to study classics at Oxford, Brigid promptly acquired a reputation around the quad for being a brilliant but erratic student. In the best vegetarian tradition, inaugurated by Percy Bysshe Shelley in 1811, Brigid was sent down (expelled) from Oxford—not, as in Shelley's case, for circulating an atheistic pamphlet, but for the far less flagrant but no less unpardonable offense of being tipsy in chapel. Sacked from Oxford, she moved to London and took up her pen to create the brilliant literary career that would become the envy of her Oxford classmates.

Leek and Potato Pie

4 leeks
4 potatoes
Breadcrumbs

Boil the potatoes and then peel them. Slice the leeks, put them in a pan with vegetable oil, salt, and pepper, and heat them for a few minutes to soften them. Thinly slice three of the potatoes. Put the fourth potato and some of the softened leeks through a blender to make a purée. Put the rest of the softened leeks into an oven-proof dish. Pour the purée over them. Cover them with a layer of sliced potato. Cover that with breadcrumbs. Put the dish in the oven at gas mark seven (about 425°) for twenty to thirty minutes.

B. B.

Serves four.

Brigid Brophy Comments: "Although we share the conviction that eating one's kin is wrong, it is my husband (Sir Michael Levey, Director of the National Gallery, London, writer and art historian) who has the talent for cooking. He discovered it under the inspiration of that marvelous book *Gourmet Cooking for Vegetarians* (Andre Deutsch) by our friend and fellow writer Colin Spencer and now cooks adventurously, inventively and flexibly enough to accommodate my veganism. Vegans can eat both his leek and potato pie and his marrowfat pea soup, which is serious without being heavy and can serve either as a first course to a dinner or as a luncheon on its own."

Marrowfat Pea Soup

½ lb. dried marrowfat peas
Garlic
Lemon
Tabasco
Chili powder

Put the dried peas in a heat-proof bowl. Cover them with boiling water and let them stand for five minutes. Drain them and cover them with boiling water again, this time letting them stand in the water for an hour. Then drain them. Put them in a casserole with salt, pepper, several cloves of crushed garlic, and two-and-a-half pints of hot water. Put the casserole in the oven at gas mark four (350°) for an hour. Then drain off any water and mash the peas to a purée. Put the purée into a saucepan. Add salt, pepper, one crushed clove of garlic, the juice of a quarter of a lemon, a few drops of Tabasco, and a pinch of chili powder. Add one-and-a-half pints of cold water. Heat without bringing to a boil, stirring all the time, until the purée melts into soup of the consistency you like.

B. B.

Serves four.

ABOUT THE AUTHOR

Though born in Honolulu, Hawaii, Rynn Berry grew up in Coconut Grove, Florida and was educated at boarding schools. He attended the University of Pennsylvania, and Columbia, where he studied Literature, Archaeology, and Classics. While a graduate student at Columbia, he took courses in the history of gastronomy with Dr. Lorna Sass, author of *Dinner with Tom Jones*, et al. Widely traveled, he has lived in France, England, Italy, and India. Although he has had vegetarian tendencies from childhood, he has been a strict vegetarian since his teens. Feeling that it was essential to learn how to cook for himself in view of the exigencies of his diet, he studied privately with the noted Indian gourmet, Vithaldas Parek. Under his tutelage, Berry learned to make a range of vegetarian pulaos and curries. He had also been tutored in special techniques by Chinese and Japanese cooking teachers. In the years since, Berry has become an accomplished cook in his own right.

Berry was first prompted to consider becoming a vegetarian during a literature course on the Romantic poets, when he learned that Percy Bysshe Shelley was a deep-dyed vegetarian, and that even Lord Byron had flirted with it for a while. Later, when he found that such intellectual heroes of his as George Bernard Shaw, Malcolm Muggeridge, Isaac Bashevis Singer, and Leonardo were also vegetarians, there was nothing for it but to give it a try. So far from feeling ill-nourished or deprived, he found that he flourished on the diet. His health and outlook, which had never been anything to write home about, improved markedly.

Since he turned vegetarian, Berry has been an avid collector of vegetariana and vegetarian lore. He has also kept a sharp eye out for famous people who had become vegetarians. For as a fledgling vegetarian, it was reassuring to know that other people, particularly illustrious people, had been going through the same experience with no visible sign of deterioration.

Curiously enough, in the course of researching *Famous Vegetarians and Their Favorite Recipes*, Berry found that a number of well-known people who had announced publicly that they were vegetarians subsequently relapsed into meat-eating. To obviate this sort of thing happening to the notables in *Famous Vegetarians and Their Favorite Recipes*, Berry has been careful to select only those vegetarian notables whose vegetarianism is well-attested.

For his part, Berry has never once been tempted to backslide despite the pressure from peers, relatives, hostesses, and maitre d's, who have raised an eyebrow at his diet.

Through his writings and his personal example, Berry has made many happy vegetarian converts. He feels that so long as animals are being needlessly put to death to satisfy man's appetites, and so long as people are suffering in health because they are eating a toxic food, there is no higher calling than that of the vegetarian advocate, however quixotic it may seem.

Berry's first book, *The Vegetarians,* is a collection of interviews with famous vegetarians. It created a small sensation when it came out. It was the subject of an essay in *Time* magazine and was selected for recommended reading by *Bon Appetit.* It also inspired a feature article in the Wednesday food section of *The New York Times* and was praised by *Library Journal* as well as other journals throughout the US.

Famous Vegetarians and Their Favorite Recipes is in the nature of a sequel. Rynn Berry makes his home in Brooklyn, NY, and enjoys creative cooking (all recipes in FVTFR have been triple-tested), tennis, cycling, jogging, book-collecting and concert-going. He is also something of an amateur classicist.

Having studied classical philology for several years in a post-graduate program in ancient studies at Columbia, Berry formed the habit of translating Greek and Latin authors for pleasure—a hobby that stood him in good stead when it came to translating Leonardo da Vinci's recipes, which were written in Bartolomeo Platina's medieval Latin. It also enabled him to translate the relevant passages in Apicius, Plutarch, Porphyry, and Pliny that are cited in *Famous Vegetarians and Their Favorite Recipes.*

Mattar Panneer with Deep-Fried Tofu Cubes

1 lb. firm tofu
1 teaspoon black mustard seed
1 teaspoon cumin seed
4 cloves
1 inch stick cinnamon
1 medium white onion, chopped
1 cup fresh tomatoes, peeled
2 cloves garlic, minced
1 tablespoon ginger, chopped fine
1 teaspoon *garam masala*
1 teaspoon turmeric
2 green chili peppers, chopped
1 teaspoon salt
1 tablespoon fresh basil, chopped
4 cups fresh, shelled peas
1 teaspoon coriander powder

First, press the tofu by placing it under a cutting board with a five pound weight atop it. Press for one half hour, then cut it into half inch cubes. In a heavy skillet or fryer, deep-fry the tofu cubes until they are golden. Remove with slotted spoon and drain on paper towels.

While the tofu is being pressed, heat the hard spices—the mustard seed, the cumin seed, the cloves and the stick cinnamon until the mustard seed sputters and pops. Then add the chopped onions and fry until they turn transparent. As soon as the onions are ready, add the tomatoes and cook for about five minutes, then add the garlic, ginger, *garam masala,* turmeric, green chilies, salt and basil. Cook for three more minutes and add the deep-fried tofu cubes, and fresh peas. Simmer over a medium flame until the peas have absorbed the cooking liquids. A few minutes before serving, stir in a teaspoonful of coriander powder. Serve with long-grain American rice, or basmati rice.

Deep-Fried Tofu Balls
in Sweet and Sour Sauce

32 oz. tofu
3 tablespoons vegetable oil
½ cup finely chopped onion
½ cup chopped mushrooms
½ cup grated carrot
1 tablespoon fresh ginger, minced
1 clove garlic, minced
½ cup bread flour
1 tablespoon tamari

For the Sweet and Sour Sauce

1½ cups pineapple juice
1 tablespoon cornstarch
2 tablespoons cold water
1 tablespoon vinegar
3 tablespoons catsup
1 tablespoon tamari
1¼ cups pineapple chunks
Salt and pepper to taste

First, press the tofu by placing over the tofu cakes a cutting board weighted with a heavy skillet or such for half an hour, allowing the expelled water to drain onto a paper towel.

Next, sauté the chopped onion, the chopped mushrooms and the grated carrot in a heavy skillet. Add the garlic, tamari, and ginger with salt and pepper to taste. When the vegetables are soft, remove from flame and set aside.

After the tofu cakes have been pressed, mash the tofu and mix in the sautéed vegetables by hand. Add one-half cup of bread flour to the mixture and knead thoroughly. When the ingredients are well mixed, form the mashed tofu-cum-vegetables into little balls, each two inches in diameter, and roll them in flour until they are completely coated.

Fill a deep saucepan with enough vegetable oil for deep-frying. Heat the oil and deep-fry the tofu balls until they are golden brown. Remove from the oil and let drain on absorbent paper.

While the tofu balls are draining, bring to a boil one-and-a-half cups of pineapple juice. Mix one tablespoon of cornstarch in two tablespoons of cold water and add to the pineapple juice. Then add the vinegar and the tamari. Finally, add the pineapple chunks and cook over moderate heat for two minutes. Add the tofu balls and cook over low heat for five more minutes.

Transfer the tofu balls and the sweet and sour sauce to a serving dish, and serve with hot fluffy rice.

Palak Aloo

(Spinach and Potato Curry)

2 lbs. spinach
1 teaspoon black mustard seed
1 teaspoon fenugreek seed
1 inch stick cinnamon
1 teaspoon cumin seed
4 cloves
3 lbs. new potatoes
1 tablespoon chopped ginger
2 cloves garlic, minced
1 teaspoon turmeric
1 teaspoon *garam masala*
2 green chilies, chopped fine
Salt and pepper to taste

Wash and pick over the spinach, and set aside. In a heavy skillet, sauté the mustard seed, fenugreek seed, stick cinnamon, cumin seed and cloves until the mustard seed starts to sizzle and pop.

Next add three pounds of chopped and peeled new potatoes, and stir until they are well coated with spices. Then add the chopped ginger, minced garlic, turmeric, and *garam masala.* Cook unil the potatoes are tender.

While the potatoes are not quite tender, make a layer of spinach leaves over the potatoes, cramming in as many as possible before sealing the lid tightly. Cook for a few minutes until the layer of spinach leaves is wilted; then arrange another layer of spinach leaves over the wilted leaves until all the spinach leaves are wilted. When all of spinach leaves are wilted, mix the layer of spinach together with the potatoes until they are thoroughly mingled. Serve with hot fluffy rice.

Miso Coffee

1 teaspoon barley, red, or hatcho miso
1 teaspoon sweet white, or mellow white miso
1 cup hot water (almost boiling)
1 coffee mug

Combine the first three ingredients in a coffee mug and stir until the miso dissolves. Sip as you would coffee.

Serves one.

As a writer I've fallen prey to a few of the writerly vices—one of which is an addiction to coffee—of which I used to drink four or five cups a day strong enough to stand a spoon up in. In my fruitless search for a good coffee substitute, I've tried everything from dandelion root, to roast chickory, to an infusion of scorched brown rice, but none of them could adequately take the place of coffee—until I discovered miso. For aeons the Japanese have started their morning with a cup of miso soup. It wakes them up and propels them through the day. While researching my biographical profile for Bill Shurtleff, I came upon his recipe for "Instant Miso (Better 'N' Coffee) Soup" in *The Book of Miso*. I decided to give it a try. Darned if he wasn't right. My recipe for miso coffee is I think an improvement on Bill Shurtleff's because it calls for a mixture of light and dark misos. For those people who take cream in their coffee or tea, I would suggest mixing mellow white miso or sweet white miso with barley miso, brown rice miso, or hatcho miso. For those who take their coffee black, I would recommend drinking barley miso or hatcho miso straight. Barley miso and hatcho miso are the darkest of the misos. They have the robust flavor of a good bitter-sweet chocolate or a cup of steaming black coffee brewed from the choicest beans. But miso has something more—a certain *je ne sais quoi*—a subtle and elusive flavor that bewitches the palate, and of which one never tires. What's more miso is even more stimulating and energizing than coffee, but without coffee's caffeine kick that gives the nervous system a stimulating fillip but actually depletes it of energy and causes fatigue. Coffee has no food value, but miso is 15% protein, and is an excellent source of vitamin B-12. To other coffee addicts, I pass along this recipe for miso coffee in the hope that they too will find it to be the perfect coffee substitute.

ABOUT THE ILLUSTRATOR: GLORY BRIGHTFIELD

Glory Brightfield, who drew the portraits and the vegetable studies for *TFVCB*, in addition to being a talented illustrator, is also a master of Oriental brush painting, which she began studying in 1962. Her paintings have been widely exhibited in one-person and group shows in New York City, San Francisco, Berkeley, Honolulu, and Taiwan. With her husband, Rick Brightfield, she has collaborated on more than a dozen books for which she has provided handsome illustrations. When she is not illustrating books, she teaches Zen painting at her studio in New Paltz, New York.

NOTES ON THE TEXT

IMMORTALS

PYTHAGORAS
1. "A touch of nature makes the whole world kin," William Shakespeare, *Troilus and Cressida*, act 3, sc. 3, line 175.
2. "The largest precipitate of Pythagoreanism is to be found in Plato."; Moses Hadas and Morton Smith, *Heroes and Gods* (New York: Harper and Row, 1965), p. 44.

BUDDHA/None

MAHAVIRA/None

LAO TZU
1. D. Howard Smith, *Chinese Religions: From 1,000 B.C. to the Present Day* (New York: Holt, Rinehart and Winston, 1971), p. 111.
2. Holmes, Welch, *Taoism: The Parting of the Way* (Boston: Beacon Press, 1965), p. 19.
3. Jacques Gernet, *Ancient China: From the Beginnings to the Empire* (Berkeley: University of California Press, 1968), pp. 58–59.
4. Jacques Gernet, *Ancient China*, pp. 50–51.
5. Henri Maspero, *Taoism and Chinese Religion* (Amherst: University of Massachusetts Press, 1981), p. 30.
6. Welch, *Taoism: The Parting of the Way*, p. 2.
7. Dr. Michael Saso, *A Taoist Cookbook* (Rutland: Charles E. Tuttle, 1994), p. xviii.
8. Lao Tzu, *Tao Te Ching*, trans. by Victor Mair (New York: Bantam Books, 1990), p. 145.
9. Lao Tzu, *Tao Te Ching*, p. 145.
10. J. C. Cooper, *Chinese Alchemy, The Taoist Quest for Immortality* (New York: Sterling, 1990), p. 109.
11. Henry Maspero, *Taoism and Chinese Religion*, p. 33.
12. Henry Maspero, *Taoism and Chinese Religion*, p. 33.
13. Leon Jaroff, "The Man's Cancer," *Time*. April 1, 1996, p. 65.

PLATO (AND SOCRATES)
1. Diogenes Laertius, *Lives of the Eminent Philosophers* III, 4–5, "He learned gymnastics from Ariston the Argive wrestler and from him he took the name Plato on account of his splendid physique; others say it was because of his broad power of expression; or because his brow was broad. Still others claim that he wrestled in the Isthmian Games."
2. For a fuller discussion of Plato's travels during his *Wanderjahre*, see F.W. Woodbridge, *The Son of Apollo* (New York: Biblo and Tannen, 1971), pp. 17–20.
3. Theodor Gomperz, *The Greek Thinkers* (London: John Murray, 1969), Vol. 2, pp. 259–261.
4. G.R. Levy, *Plato in Sicily* (London: Faber and Faber, 1956), p. 42.
5. Later, after he had repaired his fortunes, Plato spent three times this amount 100 minae to purchase three books on Pythagoras that had been written by the Philosopher Philolaus, with whom Plato studied after the death of Socrates. (Diogenes Laertius, op cit., III, 5.)
6. Aristophanes, *Clouds*, (419–424) translation mine; the word that I've translated as "vegetarian diet" is *thumbroepideipnon*, which literally means "living on the herb savory" and has been translated by others as "living on spinach;" "living on herbs;" "living poorly;" etc.
7. Translation mine, italics mine.

JESUS

1. "The greatest challenge since Darwin's theory of evolution.": A. Powell Davies, *The Meaning of the Dead Sea Scrolls* (New York: New American Library, 1956), anonymous blurb on MDSS book jacket.
2. "Teacher of Righteousness": Edmund Wilson, *Israel and the Dead Sea Scrolls* (New York: Farrar, Straus & Giroux, 1980), p. 196.
3. "Purgations by sprinklings": Wilson, *Dead Sea Scrolls,* p. 204.
4. "The Essenes, also. . .": A. Dupont-Sommer, *The Jewish Sect of Quamran and the Essenes,* trans. R. D. Barnett (New York: The MacMillan Company, 1955), p. 117.
5. "The name borne...": Dr. Hugh Schonfield, *The Passover Plot* (New York: Bernard Geis Associates, 1965), p. 207.
6. "Epiphanius himself of...": Schonfield, *Passover Plot,* p. 207.
7. "Moreover, we learn...": A. Powell Davies, *The Meaning of the Dead Sea Scrolls* (New York: New American Library, 1956), p. 114.
8. "The express statement...": Robert Eisler, *The Messiah Jesus* (London: Methuen, 1931), p. 236.

PLUTARCH

1. "The *Moralia* celebrate...": Plutarch, *Makers of Rome,* trans. Ian Scott-Kilvert (Harmondsworth: Penguin, 1981), p. 11.
2. "The War-God Ares...": Michael Grant, *The Ancient Historians* (New York: Scribners, 1970), p. 312.
3. "But how can you ask...": Plutarch, "On the Eating of Flesh," I., in Plutarch's *Moralia.*
4. "Sulla the Carthaginian...": Plutarch, "Table Talk," VII, 6–7, 727 in Plutarch's *Moralia.*
5. "But the angling and the casting...": Plutarch, "Table Talk," VIII. 8, 730, in Plutarch's *Moralia.*

DA VINCI

1. "The gradual ascent...": Arnold Hauser, *The Social History of Art* (New York: Alfred Knopf, 1952), vol. 2, pp. 66–7.
2. "Zoroastro was a colorful figure...": Robert Payne, *Leonardo* (Garden City: Doubleday, 1978), p. 48.
3. "Elsewhere he justifies...": Roy McMullen, *Mona Lisa: the Picture and the Myth* (Boston: Houghton Mifflin, 1975), p. 107.
4. "Certain infidels...": Andrea Corsali, *Lettera allo,* Illmo. Sig. Duca Juliano de Medici, Venuta dell India del mese di Octobre Nel MDXVI, f. 4 recto; cited by Kenneth Clark, *Leonardo da Vinci* (Harmondsworth: Penguin, 1982), p. 19.
5. "As famous for having been a vegetarian...": K. R. Eisler, *Leonardo Da Vinci: Psychoanalytic Notes on the Enigma* (London: Hogarth Press, 1962), pp. 59–60.
6. "Leonardo was a vegetarian...": Barbara Gamarekian, "Leonardo Was A Vegetarian? Read on," *New York Times* (February 25, 1986).
7. "Had a 1487 edition of Platina...": Leonard N. Beck, "Praise is Due Bartolomeo Platina: A Note on the Librarian-Author of the First Cookbook," *Quarterly Journal of the Library of Congress* (July, 1975), pp. 238–253.

SHELLEY

1. "I will not...": Thomas Jefferson Hogg, *The Life of Percy Bysshe Shelley* (London: Edward Moxon, 1858), vol. 2, p. 415.
2. "Of low birth": Unattributed.
3. "The two cultures": David Landes, *Revolution in Time* (Cambridge: Belknap Press, 1983), p. 161.
4. "Man resembles no...": Percy Bysshe Shelley, *The Complete Works of Percy Bysshe Shel-*

ley, ed. Robert Ingpen and Walter E. Peck (New York: Charles Scribner's Sons, 1929), VI, p. 8.

5. "Man resembles no...": Shelley, *Complete Works,* VI, p. 13.

TOLSTOY

1. "Thanks, thanks for...": Aylmer Maude, *The Life of Tolstoy* (London: Oxford University Press, 1929), p. 217.
2. "And really from...": Maude, *Tolstoy,* p. 218.
3. "My congratulations. You wish to eat a carcass.": Ernest J. Simmons, *Leo Tolstoy* (Boston: Little, Brown, 1946), p. 458.
4. "He stretched out...": Simmons, *Leo Tolstoy,* p. 534.

BESANT

1. "Of all great..": Elizabeth Longford, *Eminent Victorian Women* (New York: Alfred Knopf, 1981), p. 129.
2. "A nation of coolies": Gertrude Marvin Williams, *The Passionate Pilgrim: A Life of Annie Besant* (New York: Coward-McCann, 1931), p. 296.
3. "Prince of parallelograms": This phrase is a pun (mine) on Lord Byron's ironic epithet for his mathematician wife, whom he called "the princess of parallelograms"; the quotation marks were for emphasis only.
4. "Proud as Lucifer": Longford, *Eminent Victorian Women,* p. 133.
5. "The greatest orator": Arthur H. Nethercot, *The First Five Lives of Annie Besant* (Chicago: University of Chicago Press, 1960), p. 225.
6. "Bradlaugh was always...": Nethercot, *Annie Besant,* p. 89.

GANDHI

1. "Behold the mighty...": Robert Payne, *The Life and Death of Mahatma Gandhi* (New York: E. P. Dutton & Co.), p. 38.
2. "The first hearty meal": M. K. Gandhi, *An Autobiography* (Ahmedabad: Navajivan Publishing House, 1945), p. 67.

SHAW

1. "One of the most brilliant...": Eric Blom, ed. *Grove's Dictionary of Music and Musicians* (London: MacMillan & Co., 1954), fifth edition, vol. VII, p. 743.
2. "One of the glories...": John Mason Brown, *Seeing Things* (New York: McGraw-Hill, 1946), p. 78.
3. "Effete vegetarian": Not a quotation; I used quotation marks here to suggest irony.
4. "The greatest world teacher...": Irving Wardle, "The Plays," in *The Genius of Shaw,* ed. Michael Holroyd (New York: Holt, Rinehart and Winston, 1979), p. 149.
5. "I was a cannibal...": Brigid Brophy, "The Way of No Flesh," in *The Genius of Shaw,* ed. Michael Holroyd, p. 100.
6. "Green-eyed millionairess.": Margot Peters, "As Lonely as God," in *The Genius of Shaw,* ed. Michael Holroyd, p. 193.

VISIONARIES

ALCOTT

1. "The Sage of Concord"—Odell Shepard, *Pedlar's Progress* (Boston: Little, Brown, 1937), pp. 487, 490.
2. "Emerson's Master"—Shepard, *Pedlar's Progress,* p. 490.
3. "Those fierce and formidable..."—Shepard, *Pedlar's Progress,* p. 51.
4. "He has the manners...": Shepard, *Pedlar's Progress,* p. 53.
5. "The true university of these days is a collection of books."—Thomas Carlyle, *Thomas Carlyle: Selected Writings* (Harmondsworth: Penguin Books, 1980), p. 242.

6. "After-dinner member"—Shepard, *Pedlar's Progress*, p. 441.
7. "For the best of the feast..."—Shepard, *Pedlar's Progress*, p. 441.
8. "But Mr. Emerson..."—Shepard, *Pedlar's Progress*, p. 441.
9. "Slovenly greatness"—Shepard, *Pedlar's Progress*, p. 480.
10. "Wherever Alcott went..."—Shepard, *Pedlar's Progress*, pp. 310–11.

GRAHAM
1. "Graham arose and lectured..."—James Parton, *The Life of Horace Greeley* (New York: Mason Brothers, 1855), p. 150.
2. "So taken was Bronson..."—Madelon Bedell, *The Alcotts: Biography of a Family* (New York: Clarkson Potter, 1980), p. 121.
3. "Put back the bran!"—Ronald M. Deutsch, *The New Nuts Among the Berries* (Palo Alto: Bull Press, 1977), p. 30.
4. "The saccharine disease"—T. L. Cleave, *Diabetes, Coronary Thrombosis, and the Saccharine Diseases* (Bristol: 1969), passim.
5. "For its salutary effect"—Gerald Carson, *The Cornflake Crusade* (New York: Rinehart & Co., 1957), p. 46.
6. "The ripe sound berry..."—John Harvey Kellogg, *Natural Food of Man* (Battle Creek, 1925).
7. "Vampires"—Bedell, *The Alcotts*, p. 121.
8. "Shroud"—Carson, *Cornflake Crusade*, p. 48.

KELLOGG
1. "Our medicine should be..."—Rynn Berry, *The Vegetarians* (Brookline: Autumn Press, 1979), p. 128.
2. "Kellogg scar"—Gerald Carson, *The Cornflake Crusade*, p. 95.
3. "Would play a large..."—furnished by William Shurtleff, from his work-in-progress on the pioneers of soyfoods in America.

SALT
1. "Don't you think that animals were sent us as food?" Henry Salt, *Seventy Years Among Savages* (London: George Allen and Unwin, 1921), p. 63.
2. "What is Eton Coming to?"—Stephen Winsten, *Salt and His Circle* (London: Hutchinson & Co., 1950), p. 153.
3. "A vegetarian was of course..."—Salt, *Seventy Years Among Savages*, p. 63.
4. "Cannibals in cap and gown"—Salt, *Seventy Years Among Savages*, p. 64.
5. "Like Shelley I am a..."—Archibald Henderson, *George Bernard Shaw: Man of the Century* (New York: Appleton-Century—Crofts, 1965), p. 216.
6. "I have no doubt..."—George Hendrick, *Henry Salt: Humanitarian, Reformer and Man of Letters* (Urbana: University of Illinois Press, 1977), p. 95.
7. "It was Mr. Salt's book..."—Mohandas Gandhi, *The Collected Works of Mahatma Gandhi* (Ahmedabad: Navajivan Press, 1971), XLVIII, 326.

WYNNE-TYSON
1. "Nevertheless, the ménage à trois seems..."—Sheridan Morley, *A Talent to Amuse* (New York: Doubleday, 1969), pp. 66–7.
2. "We may observe..."—Esme Wynne-Tyson, *The Philosophy of Compassion* (London: Centaur Press, 1962), p. 264.

SWAMI PRABHUPADA/None

SHURTLEFF
1. "I would be happy..."—Diana Waggoner, "With His Book on Tofu William Shurtleff Hopes to Bring Soy to the World," *People Weekly* (October 13, 1980), p. 58.

2. "Providence likes to be tempted." George Bernard Shaw, *Misalliance* (New York: Brentano's, 1914), p. 26.

LAPPÉ

1. "The Great American Steak Religion"—Frances Moore Lappé, *Diet For a Small Planet* (New York: Ballantine Books, 1982), p. 94.
2. "Why Food?" (Lappe, op. cit., 1982), p. 18.

CONTEMPORARIES

McCARTNEY

1. "The preachers cut up..."—Jim Miller, ed., *The Illustrated History of Rock and Roll* (New York: Random House, 1980), p. 22.
2. "He played it in the..."—Philip Norman, *Shout* (New York: Simon and Schuster, 1981), p. 41.
3. "That was it!...": Dalma Heyn, "The Alarmingly Normal McCartneys," *McCalls,* August, 1984, p. 94.

HARRISON

1. "They are all trying to..."—Hunter Davies, *The Beatles: The Authorized Biography* (New York: McGraw-Hill, 1968), p. 42.

GREGORY

1. Rynn Berry, *The New Vegetarians* (New York: Pythagorean Publishers, 1993), pp. 154–155.
2. Rynn Berry, *The New Vegetarians*, p. 160.
3. Rynn Berry, *The Satya Interview: A Word with Dick Gregory*, Satya, Vol. 2, Issue 10, April, 1996, pp. 11, 23.
4. T. C. Fry, *The Curse of Cooking* (Health Excellence Systems, 1991).

WALLECHINSKY

1. "On the fringe..."—Michael Medved and David Wallechinsky, *What Really Happened to the Class of '65?* (New York: Random House, 1976), p. 5.
2. "Whose lives I would like..."—David Wallechinsky, et al., *The Book of Lists #2* (New York: Bantam Books, 1981), pp. 405-6.
3. "A devout vegetarian"—personal correspondence, David Wallechinsky to Rynn Berry, August 5, 1981.
4. "I became a vegetarian..."—personal correspondence, David Wallechinsky to Rynn Berry, August 5, 1981.

WEAVER

1. "It was the toughest..."—Tom Burke, "Include Me Out!" *TV Guide* (June 30, 1973), p. 36.
2. "Our bear was a vegetarian..."—Rynn Berry, *The Vegetarians* (Brookline, Mass.: Autumn Press, 1979), p. 63.

KOWALSKI

1. "One of the..."—Joseph Frank Jares, *Whatever Happened to Gorgeous George?* (Englewood Cliffs: Prentice-Hall, 1974), p. 153.
2. "No one who..."—personal correspondence, Killer Kowalski to Rynn Berry, February 6, 1981.

SINGER

1. "Do not kill..."—Paul Kresh, *Isaac Bashevis Singer: The Magician of West 86th Street* (New

York: The Dial Press, 1979), p. 103.

2. "Sometimes I feel like..."—Rynn Berry, *The Vegetarians*, p. 72.

3. "Father in heaven..."Isaac Bashevis Singer, "The Slaughterer," *The Collected Stories of Isaac Bashevis Singer* (New York: Farrar, Straus & Giroux, 1983), p. 215.

4. "My view was..."—Isaac Bashevis Singer, *A Little Boy in Search of God: Mysticism in a Personal Light* (Garden City, New York: Doubleday & Co., 1976), p. 49.

5. "I want the chickens to be healthy..."—Joseph Roddy, "Tales of the Ghetto with a Universal Message Bring Isaac Bashevis Singer to the Nobel Award in Stockholm," *People Weekly* (December 11, 1978), p. 56.

MUGGERIDGE

1. "Next to the late..."—*The New York Times* (September 30, 1973).

2. "One of the greatest..."—Malcolm Muggeridge, *Chronicles of Wasted Time: The Green Stick* (New York: William Morrow & Co., 1973), anonymous blurb on CWTGS book jacket.

3. "Nothing in his..."—Mollie Panter-Downes, "Letter from London," *The New Yorker* (January 31, 1953), p. 43.

4. "Better a Churchill..."—Malcolm Muggeridge, *Tread Softly for You Tread on My Jokes* (London: Collins, 1966), p. 150.

5. "Plot the overthrow..."—Malcolm Muggeridge, *Chronicles of Wasted Time: The Green Stick* (New York: William Morrow & Co., 1973), p. 46.

6. "Have become icons..."—Malcolm Muggeridge, *Chronicles of Wasted Time: The Green Stick*, p. 206.

7. "The galloping major"—Evelyn Waugh, *The Letters of Evelyn Waugh*, ed. Mark Amory (New York: Ticknor and Fields, 1980), p. 498.

8. "Were trumped up by a..."—*The Observer* (October 11, 1981).

9. "It is the most..."—Ian Hunter, *Malcolm Muggeridge: A Life* (Nashville: Thomas Nelson, 1980), p. 234.

BROPHY

1. "The acknowledged high priestess..."—Fred Hauptfuhrer, "Brigid Brophy and Michael Levey: Why Wed at All?" *People Weekly* (November 4, 1974), p. 37.

2. "Rheumed with tears..." Brigid Brophy, "Hi Mistress," *Vogue* (February 15, 1970), p. 92.

3. "Socrates remained orthodox..."—Brigid Brophy, "Hi Mistress," *Vogue* (February 15, 1970), p. 92.

REFERENCE NOTES

RECIPES

JESUS

Jesus—"Barley and Lentils"—Molly Lyons Bar-David and Yom-Tov Lewinski, "Food: The Biblical Period," *Encyclopedia Judaica*, 1971 ed., VI, p. 1416. "Cereals such as wheat and barley were cultivated crops. Stew made of lentils or beans was common and was eaten after being softened by cooking."

SINGER

Singer—"Noodles with Mushroom en Casserole"—footnote for "I think that..."—Interview with Alma and Isaac Bashevis Singer, Miami Beach, December, 1979.
Singer—"Kasha with Butter and Onions"—footnote for "I like mushrooms..."—Interview with Alma and Isaac Bashevis Singer, Miami Beach, December 1979.

BROPHY

Brophy—"Leek and Potato Pie"—footnote for "Although we share..."—personal correspondence, Brigid Brophy to Rynn Berry, February 24, 1981.